Across New Worlds

Nineteenth-Century Women Travellers and their Writings

Shirley Foster

Lecturer in English Literature,
University of Sheffield

HARVESTER
WHEATSHEAF

New York   London   Toronto   Sydney   Tokyo   Singapore

First published 1990 by
Harvester Wheatsheaf
66 Wood Lane End, Hemel Hempstead
Hertfordshire HP2 4RG
A division of
Simon & Schuster International Group

Typeset by Witwell Ltd,
Southport

Printed and bound in Great Britain by
BPCC Wheatons Ltd, Exeter

British Library Cataloguing in Publication Data

Foster, Shirley
Across new worlds: nineteenth century women travellers and
their writings.
1. Travellers, Women History
I. Title
910.8804
ISBN 0–7108–1138–1
ISBN 0–7450–1001–6

---

1 2 3 4 5   94 93 92 91 90

Across
New Worlds

Contents

Preface

The recent proliferation of books on female travellers has made clear the vast scope of this topic, and suggests how much more material is still to be investigated. A work such as the present one can merely hope to touch on some of this material, and to look at some of those indefatigable women who between the early years of the nineteenth century and the beginning of the twentieth century took themselves all over the world in search of new and ever-varied foreign experience. Some of those discussed are relatively well known, made familiar by the fast-growing numbers of reprints of their works; others, like so many of their literary sisters, have slipped out of sight, and must be reinstated within this fascinating band. Since the women chosen for treatment are representative, they range from those who were tourists following in others' footsteps to those who, with greater intrepitude, penetrated remote areas of the globe and who may be thought of more as explorers. The study also includes some who, because of their extended stays in the countries they visited, could be considered temporary residents rather than travellers in the strict sense, but whose records make a valuable contribution to the genre of travel literature.

Many of the women journeyed to more than one of the regions examined and make interesting cross-references between them. Apart from the world-voyagers such as Mrs F. D. Bridges, Ida Pfeiffer and Lady Brassey, there were others kept perpetually on the move by their restless desire to widen their horizons: Isabella Bird, never well unless she was abroad; Marianne North, painting and collecting botanical specimens throughout southern Europe, the Americas and the Far East; and lifelong travellers like Frances Trollope, Fanny Kemble, Lady Emmeline Stuart-Wortley and Anna Jameson, particularly interesting here because they visited – and compared – both Italy and North America. With all of them, their eagerness to discover the new and exciting underlay their undertakings and their openness to the foreign. Their responses were of course partly directed by their social position and nationality. All were white, middle or upper class, and with the means to travel. Almost all were British, the most notable exception being the Frenchwoman Alexandra David-Neel (whose later dates make her a chronological exception, too) but without whom no study of women travellers to Tibet would be valid. Inevitably, then, their viewpoints are to some degree coloured by the inherent colonialism of much Victorian social and political thought. But more importantly, they see and react as women, and it is with this aspect of their activities and writings that this study is especially concerned.

The extent of available material has also necessitated some geographical selection. Three main areas have been chosen, each representative of a certain kind of environment attracting a particular class of traveller. Italy, a country notably fascinating to early nineteenth-century visitors inspired by Romantic literature and art, drew the less adventurous women who desired the fulfilment of long-standing dreams rather than the physical and mental challenges of the totally new. North America (which includes here the United States and Canada) attracted both those who wanted to investigate a new republic in its relative infancy and those who wished to escape the centres of civilisation and encounter the natural wilderness. The East, much of which was opened to foreigners only in the latter part of the nineteenth century, lured those who sought the completely alien and remote: Japan symbolised the exoticism of the Orient, and while not topographically inaccessible, called for re-evaluation of basic assumptions and beliefs; Tibet was a land for the real adventurers who were prepared for incredible physical and mental hardship in their search for the unknown.

As individual travellers, each with her own aspirations and goals, the women did not see themselves as a group. Marianne North, for instance, was not amused when at a party an acquaintance enthusiastically brought together her, Isabella Bird and Constance Gordon-Cumming as 'three globe-trotteresses all at once!' [1] But they were often personally connected – Kemble and Jameson were friends, and Trollope's friendship with Frances Wright took her initially to America – and they read and acknowledged each other's work. Textual influences are hard to pinpoint, but characteristics in common suggest the existence of a distinctively female genre of travel writing. In the following study, how the women re-enacted their foreign experiences is as important as what they did and saw; it therefore pays considerable attention to narrative and stylistic features of their accounts, hoping to show the travellers' appeal and significance as female interpreters of 'abroad'. In doing this, it approaches closer to trends in American academic treatment of women travellers (which interprets the texts from a literary and linguistic angle) than to the work of British scholars (which tends to take a more historical point of view), though it must be noted that the study of colonial discourse is beginning to emerge strongly in British academic circles as well.

I should like to acknowledge financial assistance from the British School at Rome and also many useful exchanges with Italian women academics, with whom I participated in a conference on nineteenth-

century female travellers held in Florence in December 1986. Friends at
the Libreria Delle Donne in the same city, who organised the conference,
were most helpful, too. At home, discussion with other members of
'Northern Network' to whom I offered some of my ideas in July 1988
gave me further encouragement; I am particularly indebted to Sara Mills,
whose research on the discourse of travel literature (listed in the
Bibliography) has proved invaluable. Dr Gordon Daniels of Sheffield
University lent me his books and his time to help me with the section on
Japan, and various other friends and colleagues, too numerous to list, have
offered advice and suggestions. I should like to express my thanks to Janet
Allen and the staff of the Portico Library, Manchester, for advice and
help with the project as a whole and the illustrations in particular. I am
also grateful to the University of Sheffield for a contribution made to me
from the Research Fund. And of course my chief inspiration has been
provided by the ladies themselves.

1

Women travellers and their writings

In 1889, Lillias Campbell Davidson, pointing out that Continental travel for women is now 'too common to excite remark', adds triumphantly, 'among the many and valuable advantages which have come to the sex from the more rational treatment they experience in these days at the hands of the world, none is more excellent than this.' Newly emancipated women may, she admits, misuse some of 'the privileges too long withheld from them, in the first bewilderment of feeling a new power in their hands', but of all the valued liberations,

> none, perhaps, is less open to abuse, and surely none is more excellent in itself and in its results, than the power which has become the right of every woman who has the means to achieve it – of becoming in her own unescorted and independent person, a lady traveller.[1]

Her enthusiastic observations would not have been inappropriate several decades earlier. Women travellers were already a familiar phenomenon before Victoria had come to the throne, and by the time Davidson was writing it was a question of where rather than whether the ladies would go. Indeed, forty years before this, Elizabeth Rigby, herself having been to Germany, Switzerland and twice to Russia (she continued her travels after her marriage in 1849 to Charles Eastlake, painter, art historian and, later, President of the Royal Academy, the couple indefatigably combing Europe for purchases for the National Gallery), claims that the well-worn routes no longer satisfy the eager appetites of the lady traveller. Women, she argues, now start from Trieste, not Dover; they want to see not Rome, but Constantinople, Jerusalem and Cairo before they die; and for them,

> Rides on horseback have now given way to rides on camel-back, dromedary-back, pick-a-back, or any back that can be had; gondolas have yielded to caiques . . . couriers to dragomens; convents have merged in harems; the Pyramids have extinguished Vesuvius, and St Sophia has cut out St Peter's.

Her own solution to her mock fear that soon there will be no more places for aspiring ladies to explore – there is in fact, she suggests, 'a great deal of lady's work still on hand' in Africa, Asia, the Pacific and Central America[2] – was to be more than adequately actualised in her own

THE DISCOMFORTS OF SEA TRAVEL
from *Lispings from Low Latitudes; or, extracts from the Journal of the Hon. Impulsia
Gushington,* (Anon. undated)

lifetime. Less than twenty years later, Frances Power Cobbe was
confirming the sprightly geographical mobility of the single woman:

> The 'old maid' of 1861 is an exceedingly cheery personage, running about
> untrammelled by husband and children; now visiting at her relatives'
> country houses, now off to a favourite *pension* on Lake Geneva, now scaling
> Vesuvius or the Pyramids.[3]

By the end of the century there were few parts of the globe that remained
unvisited by women determined to extend their horizons, and many took
pride in boasting that they were the first female visitors in particular
areas.

As a result of their undertakings, nineteenth-century Englishwomen
acquired a reputation for their intrepitude and energy as travellers, noted
by their own countrymen and foreigners alike. Sydney, Lady Morgan,
novelist and society wit, herself no stay-at-home, expresses her admiration for three English sisters travelling together all over Europe

LADIES AND THEIR LUGGAGE
from *Lispings from Low Latitudes; or, extracts from the Journal of the Hon. Impulsia Gushington*, (Anon. undated)

protected only by a large Newfoundland dog, whom she meets in Milan in the early 1820s.[4] Mary Shelley, her own early experience having accustomed her to a wandering European life, amusingly records the astonishment of a French lady for the English female mania for travel:

> how women, who can command the comforts of an ordinary English house, could leave the same, and by *diligence* and *voiturier*, harassed and fatigued, should find pleasure in exposing themselves to a thousand annoyances and privations, surprised her beyond measure.[5]

Rigby suggests that it is the peculiarly domestic nature of an Englishwoman's life which makes her excel 'all others in the art of travelling'; since 'the four cardinal virtues of travelling – activity, punctuality, courage, and independence' have already been developed and exercised at home, they enable her to achieve so much abroad[6] – a nice application of contemporary sexual ideology.

These energetic and admirable women were of course assisted by the ever-widening opportunities which became available to them throughout the century, the result both of improved communications and modes of transportation, and of the gradual loosening of restrictions on their movements which made it easier for them to broaden their activities. It must also be noted that they were all from the upper or middle classes, hence had the means, lesser or greater, to travel. But in the same way that professionally – as writers, educationalists and doctors – they found it hard to gain recognition, so as travellers they often encountered if not outright hostility at least patronising ridicule. Fanny Kemble quotes a satirical article in a French review of the 1820s, picturing the English female traveller of that period:

> Coal-scuttle poke bonnets, short and scanty skirts, huge splay feet arrayed in indescribable shoes and boots, short-waisted, tight-fitting spencers, colours which not only swore at each other but caused all beholders to swear at them, – these were the outward and visible signs of the British fair of that day.[7]

The eccentric lady traveller, like the old maid and the scribbling bluestocking, took her place in society's collection of caricatures. There may have been some truth in the exaggerations. With somewhat regrettable disloyalty to her own sex, Kemble herself laughs at the way English female tourists are immediately recognisable, as she observes four veiled women on board a ship at Marseilles in the 1840s, 'who began stumping up and down the deck, each on her own hook, betraying in the very hang of their multitudinous shawls, the English creature'.[8] As the century progressed and perhaps because of the sheer numbers such oddities ceased to draw so much attention to themselves, but there was continuing reluctance to consider female travellers on the same terms as their more 'serious' male counterparts. This is demonstrated by the difficulty women explorers experienced in gaining official acceptance by the Royal Geographical Society. Not until 1892 were some of the most notable, including Isabella Bird, Kate Marsden and May French Sheldon, admitted as Fellows; and this was a concession which the following year a Special General Meeting, endorsing Curzon's now famous opinion that the 'genus of professional female globetrotters . . . is one of the horrors of the latter end of the nineteenth century',[9] rescinded by refusing to allow the election of any more women Fellows. It took another twenty years for this resolution to be overthrown, and only in January 1913 were women officially granted Fellowship privileges, an extraordinarily belated triumph for them.

Equally indicative of masculine prejudice towards women travellers, though less directly punitive, are some of the contemporary commentaries on them. Here, gender-based dismissal is masked as patronising admiration. William Carey's introduction to Annie Taylor's diary of her extraordinary journey into the interior of Tibet, which he edited and had published, is a good instance of this. He presents her undertaking as an oddity, 'quaintly pathetic in its simplicity and . . . richly amusing in its unpreparedness', and reduces her to 'a plucky and resourceful woman . . . an unsophisticated pilgrim' who furnishes him with material for condescending humour: 'what a comical little bundle it must have been for the merry stars to wink at!' he remarks blithely of her endurance of many nights out in the open in sub-zero temperatures, adding coolly, 'There is something whimsical in the thought of this weak woman leading in her tiny expedition to accomplish so great an object'.[10] The last comment also reveals Carey's need to place Taylor and her achievement in the appropriate feminine context. For him, her diary is properly modest and understated, yet allows detection of her 'natural' timidity and fearfulness – 'how much [of her apprehensiveness] . . . that is not mentioned can yet plainly be read in the quivering of the lines and the frequent sunny expressions of hope and trust!' [11] (It seems not to have occurred to him that lack of adequate writing facilities may have accounted for some of the quivering.)

Another example of late nineteenth-century male opinion occurs in W. H. Davenport Adams's popular biographical study of selected 'celebrated' women travellers. Adams is more ambivalent, though as inherently patriarchal as Carey. On the one hand, he admires those female adventurers who most approximate to masculine ideals. Enthusiastically praising Ida Pfeiffer, the intrepid Viennese world-voyager, he points to her sexually uncharacteristic daring and perseverance, arguing that her exploits in Borneo prove her 'a woman of scarcely less heroic temper than the boldest adventurers of the other sex'.[12] Similarly, Bird 'carried in her bosom a man's heart' (p. 433), and in the Rocky Mountains showed that she possessed the 'high' (and masculine) virtues of 'endurance, courage, promptitude, decision, the capacity for quiet and accurate observation, the ready adaptability to circumstances' (pp. 436–7). At the same time, Adams is anxious to confirm the essential femininity of his subjects. So, despite the 'masculine attire' (p. 229) she wore in Tahiti, Pfeiffer was not, he assures us, at all mannish. His evaluation of the travellers' written accounts depends equally on gender-biased assumptions. Lady Brassey's record of her world voyage is enhanced by its lack of affectation or conscious superiority, and 'we feel that we are in the company of a woman with a woman's heart – of a woman with broad sympathies and a happy nature' (p. 347). Conversely, Adams, while admiring Mrs Trollope's energetic and sharp observations, deprecates the fact that 'she is often vulgar' and that her lively but coarse style contains a 'somewhat masculine' humour (p. 386). As these remarks indicate, he found it hard to deal with women who broke out of current ideological moulds.

Most female travellers of the period were not particularly concerned about public recognition or prestige. Few were overt sexual iconoclasts,

though some of the more unconventional figures such as Harriet
Martineau, Anna Jameson and Frances Cobbe incorporated their radical
views into their travel writings. Indeed, although their success was seen
as a victory for women's rights, the first RGS female Fellows had not
actually agitated for their acceptance and they themselves, like most of
the travellers, clung tenaciously to a properly ladylike image. Nevertheless, in undertaking their foreign journeys these women were, albeit
unconsciously, asserting certain positions with regard to their status and
abilities – their right to do what men had done for centuries, their
capacity to meet challenges while still maintaining their female integrity,
and their claim to be regarded as individuals, choosing and expanding the
channels of their lives. Not many were as openly rebellious as Barbara
Bodichon, whose early unorthodoxy was encouraged by her free-
thinking and liberal family (her grandfather had supported Wilberforce's
anti-slave trade campaign, and her father, a Unitarian and a radical MP,
not only allowed her as a young woman to make an unchaperoned
Continental tour with a friend but also gave his daughters their own
incomes when they came of age). Frustrated by the restraints of polite
society, she describes herself as 'one of the cracked people of the world',
never happy 'with English genteel family life' and always longing 'to be
off on some wild adventure';[13] 'it is quite natural', she writes, 'that my
life abroad and out of doors should make me more enterprising for boar-
hunts or painting-excursions, than for long sojourns in stifling rooms with
miserable people'.[14] All of them, however, shared her excitement about
travel, eagerly tasting its novelty and relishing the freedom from the
duties and mundane drudgery of daily existence which it gave them.

    The concept of escape is of particular significance here. To a greater or
lesser extent, the women voyagers saw their journeying as a release, an
opportunity to experience solipsistic enjoyment and to enrich themselves
spiritually and mentally; like Eve, they demanded the liberty to roam
and, moreover, without the need for male approval. As we have seen, the
prevalence of female travel meant that this activity was not necessarily
linked to bold radicalism, and it should not be regarded exclusively as a
challenge to a dominant ideology of female powerlessness. But such
desire still smacked too much of self-pleasing and irresponsibility, and so
certain strategies were employed to 'cover' it, regarding both the
journeys and the published accounts. Chief of these is the insistence on
'proper' purpose, a way of validating the respectability and usefulness of
the activity, especially where this could be related to current notions of
womanhood. Some women set off from a sense of family duty. Catherine
Traill and Susanna Moodie, for instance, early settlers in Canada,
encountered the harshness of the New World wilderness as long-
suffering wives, loyally supportive of their husbands' undertakings.

Though they were initially reluctant pioneers, they not only learned to adapt to their new surroundings but actually came to enjoy 'roughing it in the bush' (the title of Moodie's first book about her experiences). But they were wary of admitting too much to this enjoyment, and their accounts are full of pious reminders that they are essentially doing what God and family are asking of them. Jameson and Kemble also crossed the Atlantic from duty rather than from inclination. Jameson, having made the mistake of marrying a lawyer, Robert Jameson, who practised abroad for much of his career leaving his wife to discover that she preferred the company of her own friends in England and on the Continent, nevertheless felt obliged to join him in Upper Canada where he was Attorney General when he called her in 1835. Miserable at the prospect, and unhappy when she got there, immured in a freezing Toronto and neglected by Robert whom she quickly decided was wholly uncongenial, she still thrilled at the chance of seeing more of the New World; it was 'safe' for her to relish her subsequent exciting adventures in the wilderness since she had first proved herself an irreproachably dutiful wife. Kemble, likewise, making her first trip to America as an obedient daughter, accompanying her father on an acting tour planned as a last desperate attempt to save the Kembles' Covent Garden theatre from bankruptcy, began her travels purely in a state of moral obligation (she claims to have been homesick even before getting off the boat). She too, however, became an eager tourist before long, though her subsequent unhappy marriage to a Philadelphian plantation owner somewhat soured her enthusiasm for trans-Atlantic delights.

Kemble's circumstances reveal another common motivation for travel – the need to alleviate financial distress. Often admitted to very discreetly, if at all, the recovery of family fortunes sent many women abroad, especially to Europe, since it had long been recognised that living here was much cheaper than in England. For many travellers to Italy this was their prime purpose, though once there they were able to indulge in the less mundane pleasures of foreign residence. A few hoped to obtain the same benefit in America, the most notable being Frances Trollope who, with three young children and an impoverished French artist in tow, aimed at recouping some of the losses which her unbusiness-like husband had incurred at home by setting up a fancy-goods bazaar in Cincinnati. Interestingly, she omits all reference to this intention in her account of her American experience, merely describing her other main motive, her plan to join and assist her friend, Frances Wright, in the latter's Utopian settlement in Nashoba, Tennessee.

More easily admissible was the search for health. With these travellers there is often a link between physical weakness and geographical mobility, not in itself extraordinary, since certain locations or circumstances were obviously curative – a long sea-voyage, well-accredited spas, healthful mountain resorts or warm tropical climates, for example. Illness is also a highly respectable if somewhat gloomy motive for travel, as in the case of Sarah Maury, a mid-century visitor to America who, somewhat undermined, as she delicately puts it, by bearing eleven children in twelve years, and nearing insanity after nursing nine of them through whooping-cough in one winter, acts on her husband's (guilt-ridden?) advice that 'I should try the experiment of a passage across the Atlantic'.[15] The significant factor, however, is not that such journeys were undertaken but that their physical and psychological results were often quite surprising, a point which will be discussed further below.

Other respectable purposes which could cover a more suspect wish for self-pleasing encompass some kind of idealistic zeal, usually connected with the idea of woman as a specially civilising influence, and particularly associated with those travellers who went into more remote areas. Sometimes there is an actual religious or social ideology behind the journeying. Missionaries like Annie Taylor, who endured incredible hardships in order to take the Gospel into Tibet, or Kate Marsden, who crossed Siberia in midwinter to find a cure for leprosy and to help the lepers themselves, travelled ostensibly in a spirit of service and self-sacrifice, even though an underlying urge for self-fulfilment or self-testing may have fuelled their relentless pursuit of the furthest horizons. Frances Wright, who went to America early in the century, left England with an equally visionary aim, though hers was secular. Fired with enthusiasm for the new social and political ideas which were emanating from the reborn Democracy, she wished to assist the development of such principles by setting up an Utopian community in the backwoods of Tennessee. In the eyes of at least one of her admirers, Mary Shelley (herself closely allied to a socially idealistic group of people), Wright represented the epitome of noble purpose:

> a woman, young rich & independant [sic] quits the civilization of England for a life of hardship in the forests of America that by so doing she may contribute to the happiness of her species . . . Such a tale cannot fail to inspire the deepest interest & the most ardent admiration. You do honour to our species & what perhaps is dearer to me, to the feminine part of it.[16]

Wright's frequent returns to the States, involving travelling widely to lecture on her reformist theories, even after the failure of her Nashoba settlement, are however further evidence that motives of self-gratification may underlie the most honourable humanitarian ones.

Propagandist or philanthropic purpose is related to the desire for 'improvement', so dear to the Victorians. This could mean both self-betterment through increased knowledge and experience and the enlightenment of others through communication of this knowledge. This motivation impelled those women who explored foreign countries ostensibly in order to collect 'facts' – sociological, botanical, medical or, less frequently, political. The reaction of the Royal Geographical Society to female globe-trotters shows how difficult it was for women to be taken seriously in such purposes; it also shows how this more academic or intellectual activity was often considered unfeminine or beyond the female sphere. At the same time such avowed motivation could provide a useful protection against charges of self-pleasing, and certainly does not always match with subsequent exploits. Jameson, for example, announced that she was going into the Canadian interior to study the condition of Indian women, but her primary urge was to get into the wilderness and escape from the prison that Toronto had become to her. Mary Kingsley needed some kind of ulterior motive to make her escape into the West African jungle seem socially useful. Finally free after the almost simultaneous deaths of both parents when she was nearly thirty, she was able to realise her dreams of travel, stimulated by her father's overseas expeditions and scientific and medical interests. Her trip had been meditated for years, and both the light-hearted explanation given at the beginning of her *Travels in West Africa* (1897) (it was undertaken on a kind of whimsical impulse) and the more serious ones offered later (she went to study tribal religions and customs in order to complete her father's anthropological work and also to collect rare fish for the British Museum) are incomplete and misleading reasons for what she seems to have regarded on the one hand as an opportunity for personal spiritual expansion and on the other as a deliberate courting of danger and death. Bird undertook her later travels ostensibly to establish hospitals for women and children in eastern and central Asia and to support missionary work there but, as a recent writer has commented, her endless passion for exploration and her triumphant delight in overcoming danger and discomfort signify 'an unabashed pleasure in an entirely selfish achievement'.[17]

Evident purpose was necessary not only because of contemporary distrust of self-indulgence but also because as women became able to travel more widely and more independently they had to adopt a position of gender ambiguity, taking on the 'masculine' virtues of strength, initiative and decisiveness while retaining the less aggressive qualities considered appropriate to their own sex. As we shall see, the same ambiguity is to be found in their written accounts. This is why so many lay stress on their femininity, even while engaging in the most daring and hazardous pursuits – Kingsley writing letters to the press, stressing her passion for babies and cooking, or Bird indignantly meeting charges of immodest appearance by insisting that her riding dress was totally

womanly. The insistence may have been partly designed to counter the
impression that such divergence from normal female behaviour was
direct feminist protest, since to many beholders that was what it
appeared. It may also indicate the travellers' covert awareness that in
trying to escape the confines of their own culture and its expectations of
them they were defying some of their society's most cherished ideals.

As subsequent discussion will show, many other factors impelled
women to seek the foreign and remote: the anticipated fulfilment of long-
cherished dreams, often awakened in childhood; the desire to enter a
fairy-tale or legendary world, glamorised by the romantic imagination;
the lure of the unknown and the 'uncivilised', with their accompanying
challenges; the search for a new selfhood, released from the narrow
parameters of home life. But these were less easily articulated than the
more obvious motivations, often merely hinted at or becoming evident
only indirectly. Thus the psychological significance of travel for women
reveals itself in sometimes surprising ways.

In physical terms the most striking evidence of spiritual revival and
widened horizons is the manner in which frailty or invalidism at home
were replaced by extraordinary endurance and strength abroad,
especially in wilder or more primitive regions where travel was hardly an
obvious means of bodily restoration. Rigby's somewhat chilling warning
to fellow women travellers that 'the enjoyment of foreign travel all
depends on being strong'[18] seems to have been ignored by most of them,
even the more delicate. Bad food, wretched accommodation and awful
weather were the objects of much complaint but were rarely regarded as
serious hindrances, and most of the women cheerfully coped with
conditions which they would have found intolerable at home. The
novelist Elizabeth Sewell, for instance, gives an amusingly laconic
account of a evening expedition in the Rhône valley when, though
soaking wet after a day's walking and riding, she decides to see more of
the area:

> Unfortunately, I had no other dress with me, and part of the one I wore
> being already as wet as it could be, I thought it was no use to trouble myself
> about a little rain more or less; but, as the weather was clearing, I put on
> another pair of boots and galoshes, and set off . . . to walk up to the
> glacier.[19]

Though she explains that her Continental tour was arranged for her by
friends concerned about her health, she shows no sign of being hampered
by bodily weakness. Martineau, another indefatigable traveller, remained
sprightly and seemingly untireable throughout her strenuous visit to the
New World, though she avowedly went there to recuperate from the
effects of literary overwork. Catherine Symonds's picture of her sister,

Marianne North, a world traveller who sought out plants to collect and paint, provides another instance of female stoutness:

> She could apparently sit all day painting in a mangrove swamp, and not catch fever. She could live without food, without sleep, and still come home . . . ready to enjoy to the full the flattering reception which London is always ready to give to any one who has earned its respect by being interesting in any way.[20]

The splendours of the 'new images, new ideas, and new emotions' [21] which travel offers to its passionate disciples outweighed the more mundane inconveniences, as Mrs F. D. Bridges, another world-voyager, notes:

> Recalling the unavoidable fatigues, frequent fever-fits, and occasional perils of our journey, I am tempted to offer to 'ladies about to travel' the advice of an eminent satirist of the period with regard to matrimony – 'Don't'. To all, however, who rightly feel that the weariness of the way is amply compensated for by the delight of realising long-cherished visions, of mentally annexing vast territories which before were only a geographical expression . . . [I] would say – go round the world.[22]

The transformation from invalidism to vigorous strength effected by the excitement of travel was often only temporary: once away from the stimulus of foreign novelty, the traveller frequently reverted to her previous state of physical debility. Kingsley remained astonishingly healthy in the West African jungle, but on return to England, no longer challenged at every step, she became prey to a host of minor ailments. Bird offers the most extreme example of this phenomenon. As an adolescent she underwent an operation to remove a tumour on her spine and suffered from back trouble for the rest of her life, but this never prevented her from undertaking some of the most intrepid female expeditions of the century. The symptoms never actually disappeared – she frequently remarks that her back is so painful she has to dismount and rest, or walk instead – but she never allowed them to hinder her progress. Yet on her return to Britain she reverted to a kind of genteel invalidism; without a satisfying outlet for her energies, she could express her frustration only by capitulating to suffering once more. Her obituary in the *Edinburgh Medical Journal* notes this paradox, albeit with no attempt to comprehend its psychological significance: Bird presents 'many characteristics of a physical type which can hardly be considered as common. . . . The Invalid at Home and the Samson Abroad do not form a very usual combination, yet in the case of the famous traveller these two ran in tandem for many years'. She must have had some unusual reserves of strength, the article continues, and yet

> there is much to be wondered at in the physical history of Mrs Bishop.

When she took to the stage as pioneer and traveller, she laughed at fatigue,
she was indifferent to the terrors of danger . . . but, stepping from the
boards into the wings of life, she immediately became the invalid, the
timorous, delicate, gentle-voiced woman that we associate with the Mrs
Bishop of Edinburgh.[23]

The writer, one suspects, prefers the latter kind of womanhood, but for
Bird, as for many of these women travellers, bodily rejuvenation abroad
was of prime importance, related less to outward conditions than to state
of mind; weakness, an indulgence and possible source of power at home,
had no role to play in a life of movement and adventure, in which the
newly expanded psyche had to express itself in physical terms.

If the women could ignore the body's shortcomings, they paid careful
attention to other practical difficulties connected with their journeys,
especially when they travelled as 'unprotected females'. The question of
dress, as has already been indicated, could be problematic: precipitous
ascents or scrambling in hilly areas were particularly awkward for the
wearers of long skirts and tight boots, as Matilda Houston, trying to
climb up a steep landing-place in Texas, or Mrs Dalkeith Holmes,
ploughing through the mud beside her horse in a storm-wrecked region of
the Alps, discovered. One remedy was to do as Bird did and invent a
travelling-dress to suit the conditions; her adoption of trousers (concealed
beneath an appropriately feminine-looking skirt) enabled her to ride
comfortably astride her horse.[24] Other horsewomen, less bold or less
ingenious, found that the absence of a side-saddle made equestrian travel
virtually impossible in their usual costume. If they chose to ride in their
normal style, however, they had to be prepared for the mockery of
astonished local people – Holmes's husband is asked by an Alpine hostler
'if I did not belong to a peculiar race called Amazons, always attired
thus'.[25] Only the real 'explorers' could feel truly free to dress as they
pleased: in Tibet, for example, native dress was almost obligatory for the
traveller, certainly for practicality, often for disguise.

Those women who travelled alone could anticipate greater hazards
than these. Jameson, recognising 'that a woman of very delicate and
fastidious habits must learn to endure some very disagreeable things, or
she had best stay at home',[26] herself escaped most *desagréments* in America,
finding on several occasions a respectable settler who was 'a fit guide and
protector for a lone woman',[27] but others were less fortunate. When
Kemble and her maid were journeying together to Italy in the 1840s they
found it worthwhile to pay for a third place in the diligence, just to be
safe from 'the proximity of some travelling Frenchmen'.[28] The young
Mary Shelley, finally leaving Italy in 1823 lonely and depressed after the
death of Shelley and three of her children, and with only her little son for
company, describes how she was actually exposed to such unwelcome

proximity while travelling through France at night in a public coach: at
Lyons, 'such a wretch . . . had the impudence to say something to me – *I
did not say* a word . . . but there are certain situations that one never
foresees as possible, & so one is perfectly unprepared'.[29] Jameson, in
Europe for the first time at the age of twenty-seven and proud of her lack
of 'weak timidity', loses her assurance when on her own in Naples and
confesses herself scared by the numerous beggars, loungers and 'ruffian
lazzaroni' who make her feel 'so stunned, so astonished, so pushed, so
frightened, that I lose my presence of mind and am glad to run home like
a frightened bird'.[30] Selina Martin, a much more innately nervous
traveller in Italy, experienced a series of *desagréments* on her unaccompanied journey to visit her sister in Rome in 1819; these included being
frequently interrogated by fierce officials, having to search for a party of
other tourists to whom she could attach herself and riding in a public
coach alone with three foreign men. North vividly describes 'the only
unpleasant adventure that ever met my wanderings in any land' which
befell her at Safed, though she is retrospectively more amused than
perturbed by the experience – 'the ludicrous part of the affair was so
much greater than the disagreeable that I would now have hardly have
missed it'.[31] Threatened by three rough men who suddenly appeared and
tried to grab hold of her while she was sketching alone in an old fortress,
she reacted with admirable aplomb:

> that was too much for a freeborn British woman to put up with, so I picked
> up a great stone, nearly as big as my head, and told him [one of the three] in
> good English to 'be off'. I did not swear, that would have been unladylike,
> but the words were effective, for all three men ran off as hard as they
> could.[32]

Neither North's situation nor her method of dealing with it were
probably in Davidson's mind when she expressed her conviction that a
woman traveller is in no danger from the unwelcome attentions of the
opposite sex if she conducts herself with suitable decorum. It is also true
that on the whole evidence seems to confirm her assertion that

> the greater independence of women, which permits even young girls, in
> these days, to travel about entirely alone, unattended even by a maid, has
> very rarely inconvenient consequences. (p. 63)

Many women, for instance, stress how much safer they feel on their own
in America than in England, as we shall see. But the risk was there, not
always to be avoided merely by a sublime belief in female invulnerability.
    There were other disadvantages to being a lady traveller in the
nineteenth century. Trollope, for instance, looks somewhat resentfully at
the greater liberty of male travellers, unhampered by the ties of house
and children:

> They can come, and they can go, with so much greater facility . . . such little, or such no preparation suffices to bring them out, and to take them home, that they need rarely feel that painful emotion arising from the consciousness that what they look upon with interest can hardly by possibility be looked upon again. They may come again if they will.[33]

Shelley, longing to explore further into the heart of Italy, also voices envy of masculine privilege, in this case of freedom of movement: if she were a man, it would be easy for her to wander off into the remoter regions, she remarks wistfully.[34] Mary Duncan, a pious-minded explorer of mid-century America, points wryly to the difficulties a woman traveller encounters if she wishes to investigate institutions, such as prisons, not customarily visited by ladies:

> My means of observation were limited. It is not easy for a female to penetrate such places alone, nor easy, amid the busy and obliging multitude, to meet with gentlemen who do less than marvel at your taste in sight-seeing, if you hint at a wish to visit such scenes.[35]

At the same time there were certainly considerable benefits to be enjoyed by women tourists, as many of them are quick to point out. For one thing, despite Duncan's disheartening experience, they were often able to gain access to spheres of foreign life from which men were excluded or discouraged. Most obvious, of course, is the harem, and many female travel accounts give fascinating details about this much speculated-on feature of Middle Eastern culture which would have otherwise remained relatively unknown. As Houston pertinently observes, lack of informed knowledge about the kinds of existences women lead can give quite the wrong impression about a country, a defect which only women themselves can remedy.[36] Martineau recognises her own personal advantage in this respect: as a woman visitor to America who has spent some time in private family homes,

> I am sure, I have seen much more of domestic life than could possibly have been exhibited to any gentleman travelling through the country. The nursery, the boudoir, the kitchen, are all excellent schools in which to learn the morals and manners of a people.[37]

Martineau's insight is reiterated some sixty years later by Alice Bacon, an American visitor to Japan. Offering as her reason for writing yet more on a well-worn subject the fact that one half of the country – its female population – has been virtually ignored by previous commentators, she asserts,

> Only life in the home itself can show what a Japanese home may be; and only by intimate association – such as no foreign man can ever hope to gain – with the Japanese ladies themselves can much be learned of the thoughts and daily lives of the best Japanese women.[38]

Having had this privilege herself, she feels qualified to pass on her knowledge to others.

Another aspect of female travel which, despite some demurs to the contrary, is widely noted as having positive advantages is the chance for women to organise their own doings. Many preferred to be without male escort or guidance, probably anticipating the kind of irritation suffered by Jameson on her trip to Europe with the family to whom she was governess – her employer is so unadventurous that she scornfully dismisses him as 'a complete wet blanket'.[39] Sewell not only coped without masculine support but actually relished its absence. Travelling in Europe in 1858 with a female friend, she stoutly asserts that she would rather have her lady companion than a gentleman, because the former manages so well, with a minimum of fuss. Together they deal with lost luggage, missed connections and unpleasant encounters with drunken Germans, carried along by the self-confident image they present – 'I like being so independent. People wonder at us a little, but they all think we know what we are about'.[40] Freedom from hampering social contact was a particularly valued state for these women, to the extent that they desired to ingest their new experiences undistracted by the pedantic prosings of scholar-guides or the idle chatter of other tourists, regrettably often members of their own sex who, among other misdemeanors, whispered and giggled in churches. Many concur with Davidson's view that a lady's maid is usually a hindrance rather than a help on a foreign trip and that the female traveller does better without one. Sewell's maid's grumbles about the discomforts and strangeness of life abroad became tedious; and North's maid soon proved a nuisance, her mindless loquaciousness a constant source of irritation – 'I advise no women travellers with average brains and energy to cumber themselves with a maid in foreign countries, however much she may be considered a treasure at home',[41] comments her employer crisply.

In any case, women on their own could always exploit their situations. In Sicily, when a local villager told North she would be safer if she had a proper man to look after her, she immediately took up his offer of carriage and guidance; she also observes that she usually got a better cabin on boats because she was unaccompanied.[42] Sewell too was quite prepared to make use of their being 'two unprotected females' in order to gain admission to a Prussian fortress without a ticket.[43] The assumption that female determination would get its own way, and that to dispense with male company could be positively advantageous, was not always borne out in actuality. Some travellers, especially the more nervous ones, did not find the prospect of having to fend for themselves encouraging. But the nineteenth-century women who chose to travel alone give few hints of regretting their decision and seized every benefit that their treasured freedom offered them.

For most of the women, the experience of travel was not in itself enough. Though there must be many who ventured abroad without leaving any record of their adventures, the voluminous body of nineteenth-century female travel literature suggests a predominant urge to encapsulate the enterprises in the written word. Since their texts are our chief – and in many cases only – means of knowing about their authors today, consideration of the writings themselves must form an essential part of any study of these fascinating figures. Of particular interest here are why the women chose to write about their exploits, how they themselves regarded their literary efforts and whether a specifically female version of this genre can be posited.

As several recent critics have pointed out, by the beginning of the century certain conventions of travel writing had been established, powerful textual constraints which determined the reconstruction of the foreign experience. The language of this literature has been termed 'colonial' or 'imperialist' discourse and many of its characteristics – the use of a predominantly 'objective' style, careful documentation and the 'othering' of the foreign country by emphasising details which will assign it an inferior or alien status – may be considered intrinsic elements in a masculine linguistic tradition. Women who committed themselves to this genre – which is not as fluid and 'open' as is sometimes suggested – therefore found themselves caught in a series of paradoxes or tensions. In the same way that they had to adopt various behavioural strategies in order to avoid being charged with overthrowing feminine propriety, so they had to meet various conditions determining the literary re-enactment of their travels. In order to authenticate their accounts and to guarantee the accuracy of their commentary they had frequently to take on a masculine voice, and at such points there is no discernible distinction between male and female writing. As we shall see, they frequently appeal to earlier authorities, they include technical data often avowedly gleaned from male sources and consciously or unconsciously they base many of their interpretations on the assumption of their own personal and national superiority as white, British, middle-class observers.

At the same time, these women were subject to another set of literary conventions, predicated upon their sex. Throughout the nineteenth century, women writers were defined according to a canon of 'female literature', with its prescriptions of appropriate subject matter and style – topics of romance and home and family life, emphasis on feeling and sentiment, and delicacy and emotionalism of expression. Thus the traveller who employed a masculine voice (and the very act of writing 'factual' material symbolised entry into male discourse) ran the risk of being regarded as unwomanly and presumptuous. On the other hand, to speak consciously as a woman was possibly to devalue her own creation, undermining its authority and indicating its inferiority. The contradictions inherent in the literary undertaking make it impossible to isolate any one overriding impulse of articulation. It is clear that many women found the 'feminine' elements of travel writing appealing, especially its confessional nature which permits self-exploration under cover of response to an external reality, and constructs a subjective identity within an objective context. It is equally clear that many of them were knowingly conforming to current criteria of literary femininity in order to make their works acceptable. While implementing this strategy they could obliquely overthrow the gender-oriented constraints upon them, even if all were not as bold as those more iconoclastic writers who deconstruct or openly challenge the authoritarianism of male discourse within whose parameters they are working.

Various approaches are employed in order to guarantee the writer's womanliness. Details of 'unseemly' behaviour are omitted or played down, and the sexual attractiveness of foreign men is hardly ever admitted to. A suitably private and domestic orientation is suggested by the journal or letter forms which are frequently employed, even though they may be merely formal devices. Houston's *Hesperos* (1850), for instance, is addressed to a 'friend' in Liverpool to whom the author has purportedly promised to 'commence a "journal" for your edification',[44] and many letters were probably never sent at all.

Most importantly, the women travel writers have to substitute self-effacement or self-mockery for more aggressive or positive assertiveness in order to demonstrate a true femininity. In the first place, they prove their modesty by claiming that they never intended to expose their writings to the common gaze. Mary, Baroness D'Anethan, the wife of a Belgian diplomat, prefaces her 'leaves from the Diary' of her fourteen years in Japan with the declaration that 'These records were written with absolutely no thought of publicity' but were printed at her husband's request,[45] and her avowed reluctance is echoed by many others. The strategy of putting the responsibility upon importunate family or acquaintances is widespread. Martineau explains that she has written a successor to *Society in America* (1837) only because 'I have . . . been strongly solicited to communicate more of my personal narrative';[46] Lady Emmeline Stuart-Wortley, a mid-century traveller to the Americas, avers that friends 'to whose better judgment I am bound to defer' (why, one wonders?) have pressed her to print the letters written during her tour;[47] Isabella Trotter, also in the United States in the 1850s, asserts that her letters to her daughter back home 'were written without any intention of going beyond yourself and our own family circle; but some

friends have persuaded me to publish them'.[48] Bird takes care to convey
the similar impression that nothing as unwomanly as self-advertisement
was in her mind when she undertook her foreign trips: though 'at the time
of my visits to the States I had no intention of recording my "experiences" in print', she says 'I was requested by numerous friends to give an
account of my travels';[49] the observations made on her second tour of
America, also recorded privately 'without the remotest idea of publication', were avowedly offered to a wider audience at the request of the
editor of Leisure Hour, where as articles they were so favourably received
'that I venture to present them to the public in a separate form, as a
record of a very interesting travelling experience'.[50]

Beneath all this self-effacement there is probably some genuine
uneasiness about the public revelation of private feelings and experiences.
But there is also certainly some element of lip-service to the notion of
'appropriate' femaleness. We cannot always believe denials of literary
aspiration, even where the records reputedly began life as journals or
diaries with no wide audience in mind. Jameson's preface to her Winter
Studies and Summer Rambles (1838), for example, explains that these are
'fragments' of a journal, written to please a friend but never intended to
be exposed to the world 'in its present crude and desultory form',[51] but it
is clear from a contemporaneous letter to her mother that she had always
considered publication:

> I have had such adventures and seen such strange things as never yet were
> rehearsed in prose or verse, and, for the good of the public, thinking it a shame
> to keep these wonders only to make my own hair stand on end, I am just
> going to make a book and print it forthwith.[52]

Many of these works are framed by apologia in the form of a preface
which appeals for leniency towards any subsequent deficiencies, in
contrast to the the prefaces appended to the works of most male travellers
which positively burst with confident self-assertion. Predominant here is
acknowledgement of the writer's presumption in daring to tread on what
is noted as well-worn ground. This is especially true in the case of
travellers to Italy who see no hope of offering anything new to their
readers. Jameson mocks her own young-ladyish effusions in her Diary of an
Ennuyée (1826) 'in which is to be recorded and preserved all the striking,
profound, and original observations – the classical reminiscences – the
thread-bare raptures – the poetical effusions – in short, all the never-
sufficiently-to-be-exhausted topics of sentiment and enthusiasm, which
must necessarily suggest themselves while posting from Paris to Naples'.[53]
Without such irony, Selina Martin, another early nineteenth-century
Italian tourist, begins her account by confessing that 'In consenting to the
publication of this volume, I am well aware that the world is overstocked

with Diaries and Tours in Italy'.[54] Her self-deprecation is echoed by
Maria Graham, a seasoned traveller who visited Rome and its hinterland
in 1819:

> When there are so many travellers in Italy, and when so many travellers
> have published tours, picturesque and classical . . . it may appear presump-
> tuous in one not capable of adding anything to what is already known on any
> of these points, to write at all upon that country.[55]

Even voyagers to less tourist-ridden Japan produce the same covering
apologia. One of the earliest English female visitors, Anna D'[?Almedia],
who spent a few months there in 1863 before the country was officially
opened to foreign tourists, prefaces her reminiscences with a coy
disclaimer of any more serious purpose than light amusement:

> no one need expect to find in these pages the results of scientific research, or
> tedious disquisitions on the ethnology and early history of the country. My
> little work, which has no such ambitious aim, professes only to represent
> Japan and its people as they exist at the present moment.[56]

Mary Fraser, wife of the British minister in Tokyo, begins her rendition
of three years' diplomatic residence in the same country with the
declaration that 'this work is in no way a handbook or a history, but
merely a humble and faithful effort to transcribe what I have seen and
learnt'.[57] With similar self-belittlement, her contemporary, Bacon, finds
it necessary 'for a new author to give some excuse for her boldness in
offering to the public another volume upon a subject so well written upon
as Japan'; in a field so well-covered by male commentators, she sighs
'what unexplored corner can a woman hope to enter?'.[58] After Marie
Stopes – later to gain notoriety from her birth-control campaigning – had
visited Japan in 1907 in order to study fossils and coal-mines there, she
produced a book out of her journal of daily impressions; her Preface
skilfully turns modesty into positive self-vindication:

> Several of those who have read it [the journal] have asked me to publish it in
> book form, and although I vowed that I would not add to the already
> excessive number of books written on Japan, I have decided to publish this
> just because it was *not* written with a view to publication. It is this which
> gives it any claim to attention, and guarantees its veracity.[59]

However, despite making no attempt to disguise the fact that her journey
was for 'purely scientific purposes', she finds it necessary to explain that
her book is not a technical text but merely 'a record of some of the human
experiences through which a scientist goes in search of facts lying beyond
everyday human experiences',[60] a statement which both validates her
analytical undertakings and gives assurance of her natural womanhood.

As well as initially contextualising their works in apology, the women travellers confess throughout to 'faults' such as scrappiness, unstructured narrative, the substitution of trivia or domestic gossip for 'serious' or intellectual material, second-hand information and prominent self-absorption. Jameson refers disparagingly to 'the impertinent leaven of egotism' [61] which obtrudes in her *Winter Studies and Summer Rambles*, and Kemble calls her *Journal* (1835) 'a purely egotistical record . . . a mere mass of trivial egotism'.[62] They also disclaim any scientific or political expertise, a position succinctly represented by the title of a work of 1878, by a Mrs Gill: *Six Months in Ascension: An Unscientific Account of a Scientific Expedition*. These faults are often attributed to female mental deficiencies. Moodie, for instance, passes off her sprightly and informative *Life in the Clearings* (1853) as a mere collection of 'general impressions', which though it may amuse conveys little useful fact, and must be excused for its unstructured and gossipy format, the result of 'infirmities' peculiar to her sex:

> Women make good use of their eyes and ears, and paint scenes that amuse or strike the fancy with tolerable accuracy; but it requires the strong-thinking heart of man to anticipate events, and trace certain results from particular causes. Women are out of their element when they attempt to speculate upon these abstruse matters – and are apt to incline too strongly to their own opinions – and jump at conclusions which are either false or unsatisfactory.[63]

It may be difficult to detect any disingenuousness in this, a perfect example not only of crushing self-devaluation but also of hierarchical gender-thinking – masculine objective rationality is admirable, feminine impressionistic observation is attractive but inferior. But there is certainly a distinct element of pseudo self-abasement in other apologies for a 'womanly' style. Morgan, for example, innocently excuses herself for the feeling which overlays 'the impartiality of veracious narrative' in her book on Italy:

> From pages like the present, the bias of affections and the influence of sentiment should be excluded. I trust, however, that in a woman's work, sex may plead its privilege; and that if the heart will occasionally make itself a party in the *concern*, its intrusions may be pardoned, as long as the facts detailed are backed, beyond the possibility of dispute, by the authority of contemporary testimonies.[64]

Trollope, too, hardly notable for her deference to contemporary opinion, takes up a similar subversive position of mock-humility about her responses:

> I am very often, when greatly struck by some new spectacle, fearful of

expressing what it makes me feel . . . affectation, hyperbole, exaggeration, are accusations that seem perpetually staring me in the face.[65]

In her earlier *Domestic Manners* (1832), however, after admitting to her womanish superficiality and inability to reason, she adds, 'there are points of national peculiarity of which women may judge as ably as men, – all that constitutes the external of society may fairly be entrusted to us'.[66]

All such apologia fails to disguise the strong attractiveness of writing about travel experiences. Though publication was sometimes sought as a means of income – the Countess of Blessington and Trollope are good examples of this[67] – there were deeper impulses at work. Recreation of the foreign reminded of an 'alternative' existence; it was a mode of self-definition, confirming the sense of new identity; it allowed both self-exploration and challenge to convention within the context of 'objective' literature. It also offered a way of establishing a specifically female species of the genre.

In fact the special strengths of female travel literature were often recognised by the practitioners themselves. One of the earliest and most extensive discussions of this topic is Rigby's *Quarterly Review* article on 'Lady Travellers' (1845). Significantly, Rigby seizes on many of the self-confessed faults and turns them into virtues. She begins immediately by taking for granted the 'peculiar powers inherent in ladies' eyes',[68] and trenchantly compares the exercise of these powers as exhibited in men's and women's travel books,

> the gentleman's either dull and matter-of-fact, or off-hand and superficial, with heavy disquisition where we look for a light touch, or a foolish pun where we expect a reverential sentiment . . . the lady's – all ease, animation, vivacity, with the tact to dwell upon what you most want to know, and the sense to pass over what she does not know herself. (p. 99)

Women's capacities, she argues, lie in their superior knowledge of human nature and domestic affairs, and these areas, often viewed as limited or narrow, are precisely those of the greatest interest in travel literature. Moreover, she praises the apparent stylistic flaws of such writing:

> one of her [the female travel writer's] greatest charms, as a describer of foreign scenes and manners, more even than the closeness and liveliness of her mode of observation, is that very *purposelessness* resulting from the more desultory nature of her education . . . a woman, accustomed by habit, if not created by nature, to diffuse her mind more equally on all that is presented, and less troubled with preconceived ideas as to what is most important to observe, goes picking up materials much more indiscriminately, and where, as in travelling, little things are of great significance, frequently much more to the purpose. (pp. 99–100)

Quite aware of the female strategy of apology ('it is a remarkable fact that ladies never publish their tours to please themselves' [p. 100], she comments suavely), she demonstrates convincingly that women travel writers are pre-eminent for their personally engaged, lucid, closely detailed and truthful commentaries. In such works, too, she argues, the personality of the author herself is often 'the highest attraction' (p. 137). Her article wins the approval of Margaret Fuller, the American feminist and herself a recorder of personal foreign experiences, who makes a similar defence of the genre. Women travel writers, she claims, may have less cultural knowledge and a narrower scope than men, but they excel in 'observation of particulars and lively expression . . . tact and quickness', and the reader's pleasure consists in journeying with them as charming and amusing companions.[69] For both these critics, sexual differentiation becomes a literary strength.

If protest and apology obliquely suggest strategic acceptance of current conventions, rather than 'natural' female discourse, it is nevertheless possible to recognise a distinctive and overtly feminine voice in the women's texts, ways of seeing and recreating foreign experience which are clearly gender-related. First, there is the treatment of topics not generally explored in any depth in male travel writing. These include the appearance, costume and manners of women; details of domestic life such as household management and culinary habits; behaviour towards children; marriage customs and female status; the importance of 'space' in the physical environment. All these often suggest a covert means of challenging the male norm and of establishing a new female-oriented genre. On a more psychological level, the literary re-enactment can be seen as an act of self-expression, combining the urge to articulate and communicate with a desire to examine the self in an unfamiliar context. This is a more unconscious mode of articulation – there may be no evidently confessional element – which expresses otherwise inadmissible feelings through response to landscape and sudden shifts in stylistic register. Such writing may be therapeutic, a voyage of self-discovery in which the traveller may be forced to re-adjust her attitudes towards herself and her sex in general, and experience a liberation both disturbing and invigorating. In other ways, too, a feminine viewpoint may be in evidence. The woman writer often represents foreigners sympathetically, as individuals with whom she tries to identify rather than as symbols of an alien 'otherness'. In her concern with relationships, rather than with larger political or social issues, she blurs the demarcation between 'them' and 'us' and may be less assertive than her male equivalent in her establishment of a subject position. As we shall see, these are not constant elements in the women's texts, but they are present to some extent in all of them, forming a sense of a generic and gendered discourse.

The presence of such a discourse, together with the distinctive group

whose experiences had created it, rapidly gained contemporary recognition and by the last decades of the century, as has already been shown,
female travellers and their accounts were well established in the nation's
cultural and social consciousness. It was this that made Davidson's guide
so necessary and pertinent, with its 'suggestions to women of all means
and conditions' (p. 7) and its sensible practical advice. Furthermore, the
vision with which she concludes her book was not only to be more than
realised in the next century, but is justified by the endeavours of those
energetic and forward-looking women with whom this study deals;
wishing to help 'those members of my own sex to whom the world of
travel is still a wide and unexplored region', Davidson has high hopes of
encouraging many 'to join the path of travellers by land or sea' (p. 256).
The nineteenth-century lady traveller certainly proved herself a worthy
subject of such aspirations.

2

Italy:
the land of dreams

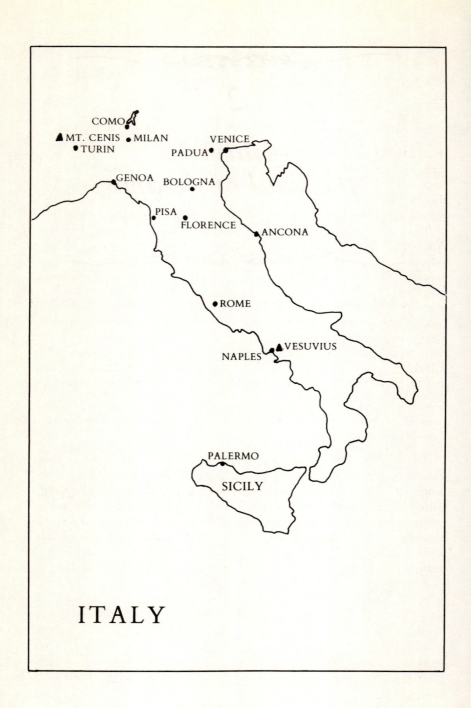

COMO

MT. CENIS MILAN

TURIN

VENICE

PADUA

GENOA BOLOGNA

PISA

FLORENCE

ANCONA

ROME

VESUVIUS

NAPLES

PALERMO

SICILY

ITALY

'Italy to be now seen for the first time, after a life passed in longings to look at her',[1] exclaimed Mrs Trollope, barely able to contain her excitement as she and her fellow travellers approached the Savoy Alps on their way to Turin. Her fever of anticipation is echoed by Mary Shelley, for whom, returning to Rome in middle age in an almost reverential spirit of 'pious pilgrimage' and recalling visions of youthful happiness before so much tragedy overtook her, 'the name of Italy has magic in its very syllables . . . every [Italian] name we hear satisfies some desire and awakens some cherished association'.[2] Such passionate excitement and heightened expectation are the keynotes of the response to Italy made by nineteenth-century women travellers, for whom the country had a very special significance. France and Germany attracted them and aroused their artistic and social interest; Italy spoke to their emotions and claimed their involvement in a much more deeply personal way, epitomised in Elizabeth Sewell's regretful closing lines as she describes leaving Como and turning towards Germany to complete the rest of her foreign trip:

> At another time the tour would have been pleasant in anticipation . . . but we had no heart then to look forward to it, for who has ever without a pang said farewell to Italy?[3]

Italy was 'a land to dream of',[4] a touchstone for everything magical and visionary, not just for women travellers alone. By the beginning of the nineteenth century, its romantic image was deeply enshrined in England's cultural consciousness and it had become mythologised as a place of enchantment and spiritual transformation, where solipsistic desire for pleasure could be indulged and where dreams could be actualised. The source of its constant allure was two-fold. A steady flow of English visitors, increasing dramatically as the century progressed, retailed on their return first-hand information about its glories for the benefit of prospective travellers. In 1820 there were thirteen new travel books on Italy and in the 1840s they continued to appear at the rate of four a year; numbers fell off after this, but despite the exhaustive treatment accorded it the country was still a constant source of inspiration for writers, whose works prompted successive generations of tourists. The literary part played in the creation of Italy's attractiveness points to the other main source of its magnetism – the aesthetic. The interest in things Italian among the English, probably partly awakened by Gibbon's writings and Sir Joshua Reynolds's art, was enlarged and intensified by the Romantic poetry of Byron, Keats and Shelley, with its sensuous appreciation of the Italian scenery, its passion for the Mediterranean spirit of freedom and its nostalgic dwelling on the bygone splendours of a past-haunted land. At the same time, the eighteenth-century Italian landscape painting of Claude, Poussin and Salvator Rosa captured visually the country's romantic and emotional appeal. Such works not only drew the traveller to Italy but also rendered the country, earlier encountered vicariously through literature and art, 'known' even before arrival. Hence response to it was two-directional: experience confirmed and enhanced the preconceptions of the aesthetic imagination; but the preconceptions themselves coloured, even determined, observation and experience, so that fantasy and reality merged in an ever-shifting relationship.

The women's sense of the magical quality of Italy is thus representative of a general contemporary response. They saw their visits not only as an opportunity to encounter directly the sights and artefacts already familiar to them, but also as a link or continuity with a personal past; their delight of recognition, as actuality confirmed or transcended its artistic representation, is combined with the joy of realising youthful aspirations, of living an experience which in many cases had become an almost obsessive ambition. For them, as for their age as a whole, Italy was a place where memory and vision coalesced, where 'the outward eye' saw for the first time scenes and objects that had 'been familiar through life to the imagination',[5] and where the soul encountered 'the reality of what for so many years has haunted you, and which you have so often been tempted to believe was a trick of your imagination'.[6] Italy took on another and deeper symbolic meaning for these women, however. Standing for the fulfilment of desire and the possibility of spiritual expansion beyond the confines of normal life, it promised release from the prosaic conditions of domesticity and enjoyment of an alternative reality which both permitted and encouraged self-gratification. The women centred their dreams not on territorial exploration or entry into the wholly unknown, but on encounter with a brilliant, sensual world appealing to the feelings and quite remote from England and English female experience. Here they could be in touch with their more passionate selfhood, often suppressed at home, and discover a new relationship between themselves and their environment.

For this reason, despite their avowed awareness of the weight of literary tradition behind them which, as we shall see, gives a certain derivative quality to some of their writing, their texts still reverberate with expressions of wonder and joyousness as 'day-dream . . . become[s]

reality' and 'girlish visions'[7] are translated into actuality, often more
splendidly than was thought possible. Their enthusiasm was called up by
the initial impact which the Italian scenery made on them – the clear
skies, the luxuriant growth, the brilliant colours – especially when they
approached the country via the Alpine passes and caught their first
glances of the sunlit landscape from the barren and snowy mountain
heights. Scenic beauty continued to attract them, particularly the views
around the Italian lakes or the Tuscan hills. But the main sources of their
excited responses were the buildings and artefacts, glorified by expectation and historical association, which dominated their visits. These
ranged from the impressive gateways through which the city of Rome
was entered and the panorama of architectural treasures which everywhere greeted them to individual structures of striking visual beauty. The
most memorable feature of Shelley's first visit to Milan, for instance, was
her sight of Milan cathedral in the moonlight, with its 'multitudinous and
snow-white pinnacles', as she passed 'now beneath the black shadow of
the building, then emerging into the clear white light – and looking up to
see the marble spires point glittering to the sky' (*Rambles*, I, p. 113).

   The novelist and society figure, Sydney, Lady Morgan, travelling to
Italy with a literally prosaic motive (she had been commissioned to write
a book on the country, after the success of her earlier one on France),
similarly expresses her excitement as she enters a region to her 'unknown
and unexplored' but already part of her life through imaginative
depiction. There is a near sexual intensity, for example, in her description
of her emotions in the Uffizi gallery in Florence, as she tries to assimilate
all its treasures – 'a rush of recollections, a fulness of hope, that almost
amounts to a physical sensation . . . the breath shortens, as imagination
hurries from object to object, and knows not where to pause, or what to
enjoy'. Here, like all the travellers, she comes 'influenced by associations
imbued with early love' deriving from childhood dreams and fancies, and
finds that 'expectation becomes too eager for enjoyment'[8] as sights
already familiar to the inner eye are confronted directly. The Countess of
Blessington, too, greedily devours the scenes which are 'such as the mind
pictures to itself of Italy, before one has seen this beautiful land'.[9] Even
the sturdily pragmatic Trollope finds the experience of attempting to
come to terms with all those sights 'upon which the heart and fancy have
fixed themselves long before leaving our own firesides' (II, p. 23) almost
too intense; as with Morgan, her fevered anticipations are aroused in
Florence, a place 'that has been during long years the object of hopes and
fears, of wishing and despair' (I, p. 95).

   Fanny Kemble's highly emotional response to her first sight of Italy –
'the intense longing of many years fulfilled'[10] – was the culmination of
romantic aspirations in part awakened by her early acquaintance with the

anonymously published *Diary of an Ennuyée* (1826) whose author, Anna Jameson, was to become a life-long friend. This is a curious semi-fictional, semi-autobiographical work, in which the authorial persona, a distraught and self-pitying female tourist, journeys through Italy agonising over her sufferings, eventually supposedly dying from the anguish of some deep but unspecified grief.[11] The book exploits current popular fictionalised accounts of Italian travel such as Byron's *Childe Harold* (1812–18) and Madame de Stael's *Corinne* (1807), in which the broken-hearted wanderer in Europe seeks a reflection of his or her spiritual malaise in the surrounding environment. The latter was especially important for Jameson, as for many women tourists, since alongside its pain-ridden love story it contains extensive female travel commentary, the eponymous heroine conducting her admirer round Rome, Naples and Venice and instructing him on their beauties. The *Diary* also partly dramatises Jameson's experience of going to Italy as a governess in 1821, having just broken off her engagement; her individual voice is detectable in it, expressing her own emotional attraction to Italy. The work fired the young Kemble, already filled 'with a wild desire for an existence of lonely independence', with 'such a passionate longing to go to Italy, that my brain was literally filled with chimerical projects of settling in the south of Europe, and there leading a solitary life of literary labour'.[12] The scholarly ideals diminished, but the country itself retained its allure and when, about six years later, in America on an acting tour with her father, she re-read Jameson's work, all her former enthusiasm revived – 'that book is most enchanting to me, – merely to read the names of the places in which one's imagination goes sunning itself for ever, is delightful'.[13] She was in fact to wait another decade before her adolescent yearnings were finally realised when in 1845, emotionally battered by the upheavals of a broken marriage and separation from her two children, she visited her married sister Adelaide in Rome. Her eager expectations were, however, as acute as ever: arriving in the city after a long and wearisome journey and knowing that she must be at the gates because of 'all the descriptions of travellers that I had read', she experiences on seeing 'a huge shadowy cupola' rising up before her, 'a perfect tumult of doubt, fear and hope' and knows that 'I was in Rome, and it was the very Rome of my imagination'.[14]

Like Morgan, too, Kemble suffered 'nervous trepidation' of anticipation when she went to see the artefacts which she had imaged to herself for so long; preparing to view the Apollo in the Vatican, she declares herself 'absolutely sick with excitement', a combination of hope of satisfaction and fear lest she be disappointed, which blurs into extreme physicality of response when she actually confronts the sculpture:

I could believe the legend of the girl who died for love of it; for myself, my eyes swam in tears and my knees knocked together, and I could hardly draw my breath while I stood before it.[15]

As day-dreams of anticipation were realised in Italy, the experience itself came to seem visionary or dream-like. This sense of the 'other-worldly' is, as we shall see, heightened in certain key environments, but it also represents the travellers' response to the country as a whole. Thus, in the book which Kemble found so compelling, Jameson speaks passionately of Italy as a place where enthusiasm – that personal, inner quality which beautifies all that we see – comes into play, making cities such as Rome 'affect the imagination like a dream'.[16] Blessington, in one of her flights of poetical utterance, draws on a similar image as she describes the way in which, in Italy

> the imagination soars into regions of its own; and the memory, as if touched by the wand of an enchanter, opens its long-hoarded stores, and enjoys them anew on the spots identified with the scenes and facts it treasured. (III, p. 283)

The landscape evokes the same metaphor: Shelley compares the ecstasies she feels while looking at the mountains around Lake Como to dreams from heaven, while Sewell sees the magnificence of the Friuli mountains as a 'vision',[17] 'a lavish beauty which I had dreamt of and never thought to see realised'.[18] All the writers, in using the analogies of dream or vision, are seeking to express their awareness of another level of apprehension from the normal, rational one – the strange, the unbounded, the magical world of the spirit.

Personal though these impressions are, they are also representative of a wider response to Italy, which, as has already been noted, formed part of the age's cultural consciousness, and was constantly revitalised by direct contact. This contact intensified as the century progressed and the women who joined the ranks of visitors could hardly be called adventurers or explorers, since in both the areas of and the motives for their travel they were largely conforming to well-established patterns. During the Victorian era the popularity of Italy as a tourist attraction grew enormously, especially after new trans-Alpine routes were opened up in mid-century. Later, extended railway construction (the Mount Cenis tunnel was opened in 1871, making it possible to go from London to Rome by train) further eased the journey, and facilities in all major towns and cities developed to accommodate the burgeoning numbers of visitors. Tourism in Italy was of course not a new phenomenon, since in the seventeenth and eighteenth centuries the Grand Tour had been a well-established feature of British upper-class cultural education. It was essentially a province of male experience and apart from a few

exceptions, Lady Mary Wortley Montagu and Hester Lynch Piozzi being
among the most notable, women did not share the chance to sample its
riches. In 1800, however, Mariana Starke published her *Letters from Italy*
(re-issued by Murray as *Travels on the Continent* in 1820), and from then on
the notion of Continental travel as an unexceptionable and, for those
fortunate enough to indulge in it, a highly desirable female activity was
widely accepted. As Elizabeth Eastlake, herself a traveller to Italy in the
1850s, remarks in her article of 1845, 'modern Europe . . . has been
tolerably tutored into the anticipation of every English want; and the
daintiest woman may now traverse the greater part of it without a rough
road, a sour dish, or a doubtful bed'[19] – a statement which, despite its
undoubted excess of optimism, certainly points to the ubiquity of female
tourists at this time. Indeed, by the last decades of the century they had
increased so much that they had begun to outnumber male tourists.
Though the women themselves may have viewed their undertaking as
personally challenging or momentous, as representatives of their age they
were becoming increasingly familiar figures whose presence in Europe
occasioned no surprise. Moreover, they were becoming more independent as travellers. Shelley admires three unaccompanied Scottish ladies
who have been all over Europe and who are her companions on her
journey from Milan back to Geneva, Morgan comments on the three
adventurous English sisters she meets in Milan and Selina Martin chuckles
about an eccentric young woman of her acquaintance 'who being seized
with the universal mania of seeing foreign countries did not wait for
guide or conductor, but with a truly independant [sic] spirit sallied forth
alone, and arrived at Rome about a year ago'.[20] Even if solitary or
unescorted female travel was still considered something of an oddity, it
was becoming less and less exceptional.

By the beginning of the nineteenth century a 'set' itinerary had been
established, covering most of the major Italian cities including Pisa,
Florence, Rome, Naples, Bologna, Verona, Venice and Milan. The
pattern of most tours was to spend the autumn in Florence, go to Rome
for Christmas and New Year, travel south to Naples for the rest of the
winter and return to Rome for Holy Week and Easter, probably taking in
Venice on the way home. There was also an ever-growing number of
guidebooks available for consultation; as well as the frequent re-issues of
Starke's, these included John Chatwode Eustace's *Classical Tour through
Italy* (1st edition 1813) and Murray's series of guides to Italy, the earliest
his *Handbook for Travellers to North Italy* (1842), written by Sir Francis
Palgrave, with others on Central and Southern Italy, and Rome following. The women travellers therefore rarely had the opportunity to be
inventive about where to go and what to see. Some were not wholly
content with the straitjacket thus imposed on them. Frances Cobbe, for

instance, a very inquiring-minded traveller who sought out aspects of
Italian life beyond the normal tourist's investigations, is wittily scathing
about the average English traveller's approach to Italian cultural experience:

> The purely *intellectual* process of hunting up a page in a book, and verifying
> what the writer says with the objects before our eyes, is about the most
> ingenious ever devised for nullifying all *aesthetic* sentiments on the occasion.
> Hurry-scurry is bad enough, but Hurry-Murray decidedly worse.[21]

She also tells an amusing story of an Italian sacristan who is convinced
that the little red volume (Murray) which English female tourists are
always consulting in the churches they visit is a prayer-book (p. 426). But
though pre-conceived familiarity with Italy and its treasures certainly, to
a considerable extent, dictated both the matter and the manner of
sightseeing, exposure to the land of their dreams could still open new
worlds for these women, as will be seen.

The motives which took nineteenth-century women to Italy were
often ostensibly as conventional as the journeys themselves. Many of the
travellers – misguidedly, as it frequently turned out – followed a
traditional pattern by going in search of health. Starke herself, in her
Preface to the 1802 edition of her *Travels to Italy*, hints delicately that her
enjoyment of the sights has been deflected by the constant nursing of sick
relatives, partly for whose sake she has made the tour. Shelley, accompanying her son and two of his university friends on their summer vacation
study trip to the shores of Lake Como, gives as one of her reasons for
travel the desire to regain former strength and vigour, confident that
'renewed health will be the result of frequent changes of place' (I, p. 158).
The newly married Brownings fled to Italy not only to escape the
tyranny of Elizabeth's father and to find romantic fulfilment, but also in
the hope that the kinder environment would physically regenerate
Elizabeth. Sewell gratefully accepted the generous offer of friends to take
her abroad with them on a recuperative trip when she was completely
broken down by poor health and overwork.

Many other women, carrying the monetary burdens often created by
their menfolk, followed another traditional pattern in departing to the
Continent for financial reasons. Getting there was costly but, as they
discovered, Italian living expenses were comfortingly small. The novelist
Lady Charlotte Campbell (later Bury), widowed and with seven children
to support, took her family to France and Switzerland in 1814 and to Italy
in 1817 because she could not afford to stay in England; as her daughter,
Beaujolois, smugly observes, comforts were possible in Florence that they
could never have enjoyed at home.[22] Trollope, whose first trip abroad had
been partly an economy measure, went to Italy because of the financial

problems caused by her late husband's airy incompetence in money matters. Though she never lost her sense of travel as a novel and exciting experience, she was always aware of the basically income-generating purpose of her foreign excursions and expected to make money from the books she subsequently produced. She decided to settle eventually in Florence partly because of its cheapness, a factor also influencing other expatriate women settlers in the city, including Isa Blagden, a friend of the Brownings, and Cobbe. For many women, especially the younger ones, the presence of relatives already established in Italy was another respectable excuse for a visit. We have seen how Kemble's long-awaited trip was made possible because of her sister's residence in Rome, and others made family a reason for going. Selina Martin, a clergyman's daughter, joined her sister and brother-in-law in Rome in 1819 and travelled in Italy with them for three years, while a later commentator, Mrs Gretton, spent much of her youth with her merchant uncle and his family in Ancona, one of the less tourist-ridden regions of Italy. Unfortunately for the former, the pleasures of foreign experience were cut short by the sudden deaths of her niece and her brother-in-law; not surprisingly, she comes to the conclusion that it may well be better to stay in England after all.

By far the most common motive for going to Italy, however, was to encounter all the artistic and environmental delights of this treasure-house, even if it meant retracing the cultural itinerary of generations of previous travellers. For many of them much of the enjoyment depended on being able to share the experience – Jameson comments wistfully that she wishes she had a companion with whom to exchange ideas and enthusiasms about the Roman galleries[23] – and the majority journeyed in the company of others. In addition, of course, this meant that they were cushioned from the hazards and annoyances threatening the completely solitary female traveller. Morgan went to Italy with her husband on the invitation of her publisher, Colburn, in order to research for a joint work on that country (interestingly, Colburn had specified that she should write on 'morals and manners' while he should take on the more masculine subjects of laws, government institutions and so on:[24] the published result was, however, distinctly her book, since her observations make up the bulk of the three volumes while his data is confined to Appendices). She had already gained the reputation of being something of a social and political rebel, and, according to her biographer, relished the prospect of 'a dash of the heroic'[25] in the undertaking. Nevertheless she had her spouse to turn to in the more difficult or disheartening moments of the journey, as well as to provide intellectual companionship. Blessington's husband featured rather more prominently in her travels. A generous, somewhat vacuous aristocrat, the Earl of Blessington indulged

FLORENCE IN THE 1860s
from *Sketches and Stories of Life in Italy*, by an Italian Countess (London, undated)

his wife's every whim on their Continental tour of 1822–8, which included extended periods of residence in Naples, Rome and Florence. For the first section of their journey the party took with them so much paraphernalia of vehicles, luggage and servants that the entourage was nicknamed 'the Blessington Circus'; much of this was discarded on leaving France, but her specially fitted-out double-springed carriage, containing among other luxuries a writing-desk at which she could pen her foreign impressions (just one instance of his prodigality) was retained. Despite her mention of the inconveniences 'experienced in a rambling life on the Continent' (I, p. 150), there was clearly no question of hardship here: if necessary, furnishings in lodgings were changed to meet her high standards (on one occasion, she even had the room whitewashed and the beds in it removed before consenting to take it), and during their three years' residence in Naples the Earl installed her in a magnificent palace wholly adapted to their British notion of domestic comfort, including Neapolitan servants dressed as far as possible like London footmen.

Mrs Dalkeith Holmes, making a rather more notable European round-trip tour in the early 1840s from Liverpool to Florence on horseback, was,

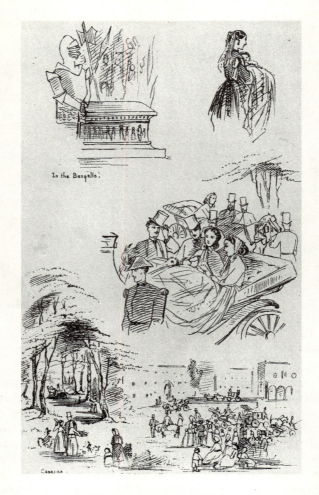

In the Bargello.

Caserne

SKETCHES OF LIFE IN FLORENCE
from *Beaten Tracks or Pen and Pencil Sketches in Italy*, by the
authoress of 'A Voyage en Zigzag' (London, 1866)

like Morgan, clearly a woman of some resourcefulness, but she too was
helped over difficulties by an obliging husband. The couple in fact seem
to have come to a very satisfactory mode of procedure whereby she dealt
with recalcitrant innkeepers and deficient accommodation while he
looked for adequate stabling for the horses. Decisions and responsibilities
were thus equally divided, though on one instance she wryly records

being required to abandon a prospective night's lodging at her husband's insistence, due to his overweening irritation at un-British incompetence. Eastlake, wife of the well-known art critic, Sir Charles Eastlake, and herself to become something of an art authority in her own right, also first went to Italy with her spouse, in this case to collect paintings for the National Gallery, a joint expedition repeated almost every year of their married life; while rapidly developing aesthetic tastes and judgement of her own, she clearly relied considerably on his guidance and support.

Widowed or unmarried women also frequently relied on travelling companions. Trollope enjoyed having her son, Thomas, and other friends with her when she went to Italy in 1840 – indeed she always took at least some of her family on her trips abroad – while Shelley, having happily spent the summer sharing the fresh enthusiasm of the younger members of her party, felt apprehensive and abandoned when they returned to England, leaving her alone in Milan waiting for her passport to arrive. Her misgivings about solitary travel are echoed by Kemble, travelling only with her maid who could hardly be expected to take any initiatives; she in fact warns 'future ladies errant' [26] of the possible hazards for women on their own, including unpleasant company in public coaches, doubtful inns and being overcharged, though it is noteworthy that she frequently describes the joys of walking alone and visiting beauty spots without the intrusive presence of a guide.

The underlying impulse for all these modes and patterns of travel in Italy is, whatever the ostensible purpose, the desire for pleasure associated, as we have seen, with emotional release and fulfilment. It is important to note the readiness with which the women admit to the self-gratification which is at the root of their journeyings. The admission is made easier for them than for many of their more adventurous sisters, since they did not have to justify any unorthodoxy or iconoclasm in their proceedings; but it does nevertheless challenge the more puritanical elements of Victorian moral ideology. They are often quite open about their expectations and achievement of enjoyment. The consciousness of the self-gratifying pleasures of travel is well encapsulated in the title of Blessington's book *The Idler in Italy*, which images the female tourist as the relaxed wanderer, sampling the delights of the foreign environment with no more profound purpose than amusement, a state described more pompously in her definition of travel as 'the true secret of multiplying enjoyment, by furnishing a succession of new objects' (I, p. 311). This emphasis on the excitement and novelty of continual change, remote from mundane daily affairs, resonates in the vibrancy of the writers' accounts. For many of them, indeed, it is as if an eager, passionate personality, submerged or constrained at home, can now rise to the surface and express itself. Trollope speaks enthusiastically for 'the

pleasure of having our minds awakened to fresh impressions and new
trains of thought' (I, p. 33) as she energetically makes her way from one
well-known sight to another. For Elizabeth Barrett Browning, always
sensitively attuned to the joys of Italy, Florentine life seen from her
window at the Casa Guidi seemed the epitome of carefree existence in
which she herself could participate, even if only vicariously, its 'innocent
gaiety . . . shining away every thought of Northern cares and taxes, such
as make people grave in England'.[27] Shelley speaks even more eagerly for
the rewards of travel to a country rich in sensual and emotional
allurements and offering sybaritic delights:

> When we visit Italy we become what the Italians were censured for being –
> enjoyers of the beauties of nature, the elegance of art, the delights of
> climate, the recollections of the past, and the pleasures of society, without a
> thought beyond. (I, p. xvi)

Even Sewell, devout Churchwoman and firm upholder of the orth-
odoxies of female duty and self-abnegation, found herself seduced by the
relaxed Italian atmosphere which seemed to negate creeds of useful
activity, though she clearly felt half guilty at making such an admission;
starting to adapt to the Italian pace of life, to 'move slowly, and bask in
the sun, and take the world easily' like the locals, she comments
cautiously on her growing sense of sympathy with such a *modus vivendi*:

> The indolent look of the Italians gives one the idea that it must take a great
> deal to induce them to exert themselves; and indeed I can feel with them to
> a certain extent. The soft air is exceedingly pleasant, but it does not inspire
> the least wish to work. On the contrary, one cannot help believing that it
> must be very pleasant to sit out of doors under the vineyards and do nothing
> all day, though I dare say experience would make one change one's mind.[28]

Having at last reached her beloved Italy, Kemble too was irresistibly
drawn by the sensuousness of the environment,

> . . . for the first time in my life, almost comprehending the delight of listless
> inactivity . . . Yes, I think I actually could be content to sit on that
> fountain's edge, and do nothing but listen and look for a whole summer's
> afternoon.

Yet while receptive to the 'Italian enjoyment of sheer being', she shared
the same suspicion as Sewell that such solipsistic and indulgent idleness
should be resisted; equally inclining towards her more 'respectable' active
impulses, she pronounces somewhat sententiously, 'there is something to
be done from morning till night, and to find out what, is the appointed
work of the onward-tending soul'.[29]

Despite the sneaking feeling that there was something vaguely
immoral about the kind of self-indulgence offered by the Italian environ-

ment, these women were willing to open themselves to it, whether it were the sensuality of climate, the richness of artistic encounter or merely the fun of riding in a rickety old barouche on a bumpy road, just because it made a refreshing change from the routine of everyday life. In stressing their feelings of pleasurable release and spiritual renewal they frequently employ the motif of rebirth or transformation. Jameson, speaking as her self-pitying and depressive persona, describes how she is gradually restored to health and to new selfhood by the 'continual activity, continual novelty' (III, p. 197) of Italian travel, 'enabl[ing] me to look upon the glorious scenes with which I am surrounded . . . with the eye of the painter and the feelings of the poet' (IV, p. 224); only Italy, with its 'reviving sunshine' and blue skies, can restore 'the languid frame, and the sick heart' (IV, p. 157). The sentiment is echoed by Eastlake, who recommends the reviving influence of Florence 'when the heart has suffered great affliction',[30] and proved by Kemble who, as the title of her work *A Year of Consolation* indicates, found in Italy a source of comfort for her sadness, her stay there recalled as a 'blessed time'.[31] Shelley, too, having first seen Italy as if through the eyes of a saint newly in Paradise 'after dreary old age and the sickening pass of death' (I, p. 60), was confident that, like a chrysalis, 'my mind will, amidst novel and various scenes, renew the outworn and tattered garments in which it has long been clothed, and array itself in a vesture all gay in fresh and glossy hues' (I, p. 2); she rejoiced to find that she had been able to shake off her 'weariness of soul' (I, p. 7) and to be awakened to 'such ecstasy as . . . [I had thought] dead to me for ever' (I, p. 94). Sewell, another traveller who returned to the country of her dreams after an absence of several years, recognised afresh how Italy made her forget 'practical life . . . with its cares, and anxieties, and disappointments',[32] and felt newly in touch with the spiritual realities of existence. This transformation, associated with sunshine and freedom, was viewed as a means of self-development and Cobbe speaks for all of them when she declares that in Italy 'we feel that we have left behind the atmosphere of black frosts, moral and physical, and may expand ourselves happily in a much milder medium' (p. 1).

This sense of new or restored selfhood, awakened by experience which was at once strange and familiar, was at its most intense in Venice, their response to which can be seen as paradigmatic of how Italy affected these women, both physically and psychically. The city itself, so unlike anything encountered elsewhere in Europe, came to represent for them the essence of all they sought in Italian travel – realisation of dreams, escape from prosaic conditions, expansion of emotional selfhood. It was both reality and symbol, like Italy as a whole, only here the two perfectly coalesced: as a physical environment it was mysterious and remote from the normal world, thus embodying all the expectations of 'difference'

which, as we have seen, lay at the heart of all these female tourists'
journeyings; as an imaginative construct, known through art and literature, it signified a dream or visionary world uniting the historical past
and personal desire. Moreover, more than any other Italian city, Venice
offered to women release from the everyday, an opportunity to forget the
sphere of duties and responsibilities and to abandon themselves to pure
sensation. The common mode of sightseeing – the gondola voyage –
became the image of a new medium in which they could literally float
free, opening themselves to experience with a willing passivity expressing spiritual receptiveness, not suppression of personality.

So Morgan, gliding in silence down the Grand Canal 'in the temporary
suspension of thought and care', gave herself up to 'existence for
existence's sake' (III, p. 385) while Blessington, conscious that being in
Venice 'is wholly different . . . from what I have experienced in other
parts of Italy' (III, p. 197), similarly abandoned herself to the state of
contemplation induced by the absolute calmness, her cares forgotten as
she drifted along the canals, steeping herself in the past. Eastlake, too,
experienced in her gondola rides a kind of 'Elysian floating life on an
element not existing elsewhere' (I, p. 294). Sewell, coming by water to
'Venice [which] had been uppermost in all our thoughts, as the place we
most longed to see' and delighted that their original plans to arrive by rail
had been changed, immediately found a whole new set of responses called
into play by 'the exceeding dreaminess and beauty of the scene . . . the
quietness of the great city, the strangeness of finding myself at last in
Venice'; this night journey by gondola, whose unreality was unbroken by
any familiar landmarks, is for her 'a voyage of discovery' revealing to her
the 'luxury in the mere feeling of existence'.[33]

To enter Venice was to enter a new state of being for Trollope also, as
she indulged in the 'lazy luxury' (II, p. 71) of water travel whose
attraction consisted of

> avoiding every species of research and abandoning myself in delicious
> idleness to the gentle movement of our gondola . . . without any other end
> or object than the enjoyment of that waking dream of beauty which, go in
> what direction we will, can never fail. (II, p. 133)

Her nagging concern with practicalities, however, made her more
consciously uneasy than the other women about the sybaritic allure of this
'strangely beautiful' (II, p. 96) place which was 'in no way connected
with our ordinary mode of living' (II, p. 96). She confesses herself slightly
uncomfortable here, ultimately relieved to depart from the disorienting
experience, unlike others who left the city with deep regret. Her
misgivings perhaps articulate her awareness that Venice represents a
threat to the protective privacy of the female inner world; to be in touch

VENICE IN THE 1860s
from *Sketches and Stories of Life in Italy*, by an Italian Countess (London, undated)

with such deep and normally unacknowledged feelings is disturbing as well as seductive.

The element of subversion, moral and psychological, which lies beneath Venice's appeal was implicitly recognised by almost all these women. Their sojourns here often changed the nature of their preconceptions, not only about art and the exercise of the imagination but also about themselves. As women, they could find the experience particularly disturbing, undermining the stability of the familiar, and thus both desired and feared because it brought the individual into direct contact with the suppressed world of the subconscious. Almost universally, Venice is defined as a fantasy, a compellingly enchanted environment which unsettles as well as attracts. Morgan calls its landscape 'magic' because here the distinction between fancy and actuality is blurred in a both discomforting and satisfying way:

> memory, no longer deadened by external impressions, sends forth from her 'secret cells' a thousand fanciful recollections . . . then the dream of many a youthful vigil is realized; and scenes long gloated over in poetic or romantic pages, gradually form and incorporate, and take their local habitation among real existences – objects of delight to the dazzled eye, as once to the bewildered imagination. (III, p. 362)

For Jameson, the city possessed the same kind of transporting witchery; it is 'the proper region of the fantastic' (III, p. 253), a place for imaginative indulgence, not for daily living:

> I feel, while I gaze round me, as if I had seen Venice in my dreams – as if it were itself the vision of a dream . . . All is yet enchantment: all is novel, extraordinary, affecting. (III, p. 251)

Trollope images the intoxicating excitement which Venice produced in her (a personal impression, she stresses, not the result of reading others' poetic accounts) in similar terms:

> a piquant novelty, an untasted pleasure, that can only be described by comparing it with what we may presume might be the effect of magic, if some great enchanter took possession of us, and carried us through a world of unknown and imagined loveliness, taking care to show us nothing that we had ever seen before. (II, p. 69)

Both Shelley and Eastlake turn to metaphors of bewitchment to describe the effect Venice has on them. For Shelley 'there is something so different in Venice from any other place in the world, that you leave at once all accustomed habits and everyday sights to enter enchanted ground' (II, p. 82); it is somewhere 'where you may dream away your life, quite forgetful of the rubs, thorns, and hard knocks of more bustling cities' (II, p. 101). For Eastlake the city casts a 'wondrous spell over the imagination . . . I find the witchery of Venice surpassing all I had heard or expected' (I, p. 293); it is 'a thing never to be believed in till seen, a dream strangely made up of the pictures one has known, yet different from all a painter ever did, and which, like a dream, one expects will depart' (I, p. 294). Sewell too was disoriented by the feeling of being 'suddenly transported into one of those magic scenes of which in my childish days I used to read in the tales of fairy land'.[34] Spells and the transformation of the personality are both treacherous and yet irresistible; the Venetian experience encapsulated for these nineteenth-century women the dichotomy between the allure of personal gratification and carefree existence, and awareness of the sterner creeds dictated by contemporary moral and social ideologies.

The psychic and spiritual revitalisation which travel to Italy produced was often accompanied by an improvement in physiological well-being; the discovery of hitherto repressed emotional responses was paralleled by discovery of hidden sources of bodily strength. Those women who journeyed across Europe to Italy had far fewer physical hazards to encounter than the more adventurous female explorers (though, as we shall see, the Alpine crossing could be treacherous, and many regions of the country were still relatively inaccessible and liable to bandit attacks), and the most dramatic changes from feebleness or chronic ill-health at home to rugged endurance abroad occurred among those who ventured into wilder parts of the world. Yet even the milder experiences of the Italian tourists had a beneficial effect on their bodily conditions, an indication that their sickness or feelings of debility were often psychological in origin. So, despite her claim of 'indifferent health', Holmes unhesitatingly struggled through a series of adversities, including a perilous journey across the Simplon Pass, ravaged by recent floods, an adventure she describes in some detail and with evident self-congratulatory enjoyment. Forced to take an alternative route from the usual one, she and her husband had to dismount and to climb on all fours up a narrow path only two feet wide, during which, irritated by the encumbrance, she removed her soaked riding-skirt with relief and continued, lighter in weight if less respectable. Further on, all signs of a bridge having vanished, she had to cross a swollen torrent on a pine-trunk flung across it, at last arriving at their destination, a scarecrow in 'tattered boots and muddy habit',[35] but apparently none the worse for the experience and able to laugh at her momentary fears of imminent annihilation. She was not deterred either by a bad cold on the chest, caught after a dangerous passage across Mount Cenis through snow and ice and exacerbated by damp and draughty accommodation. As with Morgan, whose admission that the fatigue of her Italian journey 'was *killing*'[36] in no way prevented her feeling that the whole undertaking was

one of her most enjoyable ventures, the pleasures of the experience far
outweighed the momentary hardships.

A new sense of bodily vigour inspired a refusal to accede to the notion
of female weakness and a readiness to ignore discomfort. Trollope, now
in her sixties, forgot her weariness in the exhilaration of change; herself
an early riser, she was scornful of the feebler tourists who stayed in bed
late and missed all the best sights and declared herself 'hardly fatigued' (I,
p. 317) by getting up at six o'clock in order to visit a distant convent after
a late ball the night before. Emily Birchall, touring Italy on her
honeymoon in 1873 with a husband twenty-four years her senior, would
bounce off on her own whenever he was temporarily indisposed; proudly
recounting that she was almost the only passenger not seasick on the
crossing from Naples to Sicily, she describes a splendid day in Taormina
which included getting up at five to see the sunrise, climbing up to the
ancient citadel of Mola in the very hottest part of the day ('I afterwards
found that it is customary to make [the ascent] only either very early in
the morning, or else in the evening', she adds complacently), and enjoying
a lively sociable evening with other hotel guests, among whom are a
woman and her three daughters who, much to Birchall's admiration, 'are
making a most spirited sort of tour, without courier, servant or attendant
of any kind'. Two days later, Birchall took another 'very exertive walk,
scrambling up a small mountain, and then down again by a most
precipitous descent clinging on to trees, and twigs, and prickly cactus-
leaves'.[37] Shelley, her passion for new experience making her oblivious to
the harassments and fatigues, the 'thousand annoyances and privations' (I,
p. 160) suffered by someone who could not afford to travel in luxury, is
another of these women who were prepared to ignore or endure – and
even seemed to flourish on – the kinds of discomforts and physical
challenges they would never have expected at home. Indeed, despite their
ubiquitous complaints (made by all travellers to Italy) of filthy and
freezing rooms, flea-ridden mattresses, watery liquid which passed for
tea, inedible meat of suspicious origin and ancient carriages which shook
them to pieces on appalling roads, their grievances and sufferings were
quickly forgotten in their determination ۰to squeeze every ounce of
enjoyment from their travels.

One of the most marked instances of this physical transformation and
unexpected resilience, a symbol of the power of desire and will to bring
inner energies into play, is the readiness with which the ladies climbed up
to the crater of Vesuvius, a feat which, however unspectacular it seems
now, represented a kind of self-testing for them. Morgan clambered to
the top, and though a little disgruntled at encountering there a merry
party of English acquaintances instead of the anticipated 'new and . . .
strong sensation . . . of meeting Nature, all solitary and sublime, in the

awful process of one of her profoundest mysteries' (III, pp. 167–8), could
not but admire her compatriots'

> energy of character that belongs alone to British women, seemingly
> superior to fatigue, reckless alike of the sun that sullied their bloom, and the
> lava that burnt their chaussure, and excoriated their feet. (III, p. 168)

Martin, having achieved the same goal – which for her involved being
pulled up the gritty incline by leather straps and making the descent by
sliding rather than stepping – somewhat disingenuously expresses her
astonishment at 'my own strength and resolution, for had any one told me
three years ago, when I believed myself but a step from the grave, that I
should live and regain strength to endure fatigue which often overcomes
even stout young men, I could not have believed it' (p. 89). Blessington,
having temporarily abandoned her luxurious carriage, was so proud of
her own successful climb that she devotes several paragraphs of her
narrative to a comic description of a very fat Englishman, sweating and
exhausted, struggling to reach the summit in order to say that he had been
there (II, pp. 374–6). Catherine Taylor, a long-stay tourist of the late
1830s and generally nervous about physical hazards, also gives a vigorous
account of her ascent, made in her case in an odd chair-like conveyance,
in which, despite her claim never 'in my life to have been so entirely
overcome with terror' (II, p. 95), her palpitations clearly contributed to
her general sense of excitement.

Jameson climbed Vesuvius on her 1821 Italian visit, and her account in
her *Diary of an Ennuyée* shows her forgetting all her maudlin self-pity as
she is swept up in the magnificence of the flaming crater, conscious of the
possible dangers but quite unperturbed by them:

> I had . . . no fear: in fact I was infinitely too much interested to have been
> alive to danger, had it really existed. (IV, p. 149)

Even when she just missed being hit by a huge falling stone, she refused to
turn back – 'I have shuddered since when I have thought of that moment;
but at the time, I saw the danger without the slightest sensation of terror'
(IV, pp. 151–2), she avers – and was quite provoked when the party
decided to descend without reaching the top. In a letter to her family
describing this adventure (which incidentally confirms the autobiogra-
phical source of much of the *Diary*), she is even more openly boastful
about her achievement:

> I was exposed at one moment to imminent danger from an immense red-hot
> stone which came bounding down the mountain, and saved myself by an
> exertion of presence of mind, which (though I say it that should not say it)
> was hardly to be expected from a woman at such a moment.[38]

Birchall, making the ascent fifty years later, claimed the same exemption

VESUVIUS
from Julia Kavanagh *A Summer and Winter in the Two Sicilies*,
2 vols. (London, 1858)

from stereotypical femininity. Determined to go up on her own two feet,
she stoutly resisted the importunate chair-bearers with their cries of ' "it
is too far for a lady – La signora would be much better in a chair; ladies
never walk all the way" ' (pp. 55–6). At last, she adds acidly, 'we shook
ourselves free of these wretches and were on our way' (p. 56). Proving
her capabilities, and overwhelmed by the beauty and magnificence of the
scene, she was unconcerned by the intense ground heat which threatened
to burn through the soles of her boots and was thrilled by the precipitous
descent which could have been fatal 'had not the nature of the ground
removed all possibility of danger, for no one could fall down, since one
sinks in, "up to one's knees," at every step' (p. 57).

These triumphal celebrations of female strength show how much the women were resolved to respond to the actual experience, not merely to enact accepted patterns of behaviour. Since, unlike at home, physical debility was for the nineteenth-century lady traveller neither an attraction nor an asset, energy and resilience became essential elements of the foreign tour. At the same time the apprehension – as well as the actual experience – of danger and difficulty could seem positively alluring, another chance to enter a sphere beyond orthodox social and sexual parameters.

As has already been indicated, many perils encountered on the way were no worse than bad accommodation and inedible food or the mockery of natives at what seemed the extraordinary behaviour or dress of the travelling Englishwoman. Some women, however, came closer to experiencing real danger. Starke, in Italy in the 1790s during the French invasions of Nice and Rome, saw revolutionary disturbances at first hand and had to escape from Nice disguised as a servant. Other women travellers were similarly caught up in the social and political unrest which was endemic in Italy for much of the nineteenth century. After the treaties of Vienna (1815) Austria came to be the predominant power in Italy, but the Napleonic regime had introduced the idea of Italian unity into the country and from the 1820s onwards the Risorgimento worked towards this end. Resistance to the Austrians, fuelled by the temporary triumphs of the Italian cause in the revolution of 1848, climaxed in the new liberation movement led by Garibaldi and his legendary 'thousand' which finally achieved the establishment of Victor Emmanuel as king of Italy, presiding over a new Italian government, in February 1860. British residents and travellers in the country in this period not only often enthusiastically supported the revolutionary activity (many sent material for or even made the red shirts for which Garibaldi's band became so famous) but were likely to be involved in it, sometimes too closely for comfort. Travellers in Venice in 1866, too, were in danger of being caught up in the war between Austria and a joint Prussian–Italian force, and further troubles in Rome at this time also posed threats. Trollope faced the possibility of being taken prisoner at Modena in 1842 because of disturbances there; and almost all mid-century visitors make some anxious reference to the troubled political situation and its possible effect on them, including the revived hazards of road travel in southern Italy due to the activities of the Risorgimento. There were other potential perils facing the Italian visitor. Alpine crossings, particularly the notorious Mount Cenis route, could be treacherous in bad weather; shipwrecks were not uncommon off the west coast of Italy; and even boat travel on the lakes could be endangered by sudden storms.

More significant than the perils themselves is the fact that the prospect of encountering such adventures added considerable spice to the women's undertakings. Their anticipations about travel in Italy seemed to have included the inbuilt assumption, often based on their reading of imaginative literature such as the novels of Ann Radcliffe (to which they refer quite frequently), that there would be dangers; part of the projected glamour of the trip thus depended on a fine balance between fear of and longing for a hazardous reality wholly different from the security of their normal lives. Though the threat of brigands was virtually over by the 1830s, the thought that such romantically villainous figures might still be encountered in lonelier regions was rather thrilling; the possibility represented the exotic element of foreign experience, enhanced by the knowledge that anticipated excitement could easily become real disaster. So Graham, having actually come across such personages and claiming to be presenting a truthful rather than a romantic picture of them, stresses their picturesque wildness in order to heighten her own and her readers' sense of drama. For Taylor, travelling through the desolate and unsafe country near Radicofani, the possibility of attack from these outlaws added an extra dimension to the journey by 'awak[ing] all one's recollections of Italian romance' (I, p. 90); the apprehension, it should be noted, has a literary source, hence is divorced from real fear.

Sewell, too, thinking of the stories which frightened her as a child, took a certain pleasure in reflecting that the gloomy Alpine pass hotel in which she was staying en route to Cortina d'Ampezzo was the perfect setting for robbers. She clearly found the possibility of meeting brigands quite inspiriting, as, on a later visit to Italy, she comments merrily on her party's elaborate strategies for dealing with the hold-ups which might occur on the land route from Rome to Florence:

> I can't help being amused at the calm way in which we talk over the possibilities of being robbed, – it has become rather a pleasant excitement than not.

The attack – which anyway, travelling in three carriages, they all felt 'quite bold' enough to confront – failed to materialize, but Sewell confesses herself 'rather pleasantly excited' on hearing that a few hours later a carriage travelling the same way was actually stopped by bandits:

> It made me feel that I had not been frightened for nothing; and my sympathies were the less called forth as, I believe, the passengers were all men, and no one seemed to have suffered particularly or lost much, though doubtless it was very unpleasant at the time.[39]

On another occasion she responded to potential danger with equal coolness: stuck on a boat in the middle of the Ticino river during a fierce nocturnal storm, with unfriendly Austrian troops stationed on the opposite side, she could philosophise that 'it was all very odd, and I thought of home, and wondered whether my friends would guess where to look for me if they wanted to find me'.[40]

Part of the excitement depended on the build-up of tension followed by its comic release when fearful apprehensions turned out to be groundless. Both Kemble and Holmes write with amusement of such experiences. Kemble almost revels in her account of travelling on her own to Italy through very desolate mountain regions in a carriage driven by an alarming-looking one-eyed peasant whom she was sure intended to murder her or deliver her into the hands of brigands; but after the only 'attack' she encountered was from a merry company of locals coming to clear away the snow she felt bold enough to strike up conversation with the driver and discovered a pleasant companion beneath his fierce exterior. Similarly, Holmes describes meeting in the mountains on the way to Florence 'an ill-dressed suspicious looking party [of men]' (II, p. 267) carrying guns and sticks, and comments with retrospective irony, 'and as one must needs be imaginative in the Appennines, we began to think that robbers we had heard of were indeed abroad' (II, p. 267); she too, however, was disabused of her horrid fantasy when the 'banditti' turned quietly down a side path and a small girl informed her that they were sportsmen.

The incipient perils of the Alpine crossing into Italy provided another source of pleasurable fearfulness. Although Napoleon had built splendid roads across the Simplon and Mount Cenis passes, the route continued to be physically treacherous in winter and certainly very uncomfortable. But, coloured by the Romantic imagination which endowed mountainous regions with a ghastly glamour, it could prove an oddly enjoyable experience. Morgan, crossing Mount Cenis with her teeth clenched and her hands tightly clasped, allowed her imagination to become totally absorbed 'in the sublime horror that surrounded me',[41] the sublimity rather than the terror clearly predominant in her response, while Eastlake also thrilled at the awefulness of such 'scenes of savage dreariness' (II, p. 9). Trollope, making the same crossing, shows how fear can be converted 'into an emotion of the most delightful kind, produced by a mixture of real sublimity, fanciful mystery, excited curiosity, and passive atmospheric exhilaration' (I, p. 14); despite her own enjoyment of the 'strange magnificence of the scene' (II, p. 395), though, she does issue a warning to 'all *ladies* whose will and pleasure induces them to cross the Alps, not to attempt performing this in the middle of winter' because it is likely to 'convert what might be very agreeable into what is most exceedingly the reverse' (II, p. 390). She found a similar kind of excitement on her horseback trip to the monastery at Camaldoli, near Florence, which she and her friend Fanny were apparently the first women to visit. Here, her

feelings of apprehension aroused by the rough and precipitous track, the
gloom and desolation of the storm-ridden region and the sinister-visaged
guides looking as if they came out of a painting by Salvator Rosa, are
transmuted by her Gothic–Romantic imagination, making 'a picture that
it will take a good while to forget' (I, p. 233). Shelley declares herself
quite disappointed that the summer season denies her exposure to snowy
Alpine horrors on the Simplon Pass; and even when chillingly reminded
of past events by the momentary threat of shipwreck on the way to
Chiavenna, voices the pleasure of having 'a little apprehension of danger,
just enough to make the heart beat' (I, p. 50). The taste of risk, albeit
often more theoretic than actual, was clearly one of the attractions of
travel for women tourists in Italy. Perhaps if they had had to encounter
genuine perils, as did the more pioneering-spirited women, they would
have been less enthusiastic about the experience and more prosaic in their
recall. But nevertheless such travel still represented for them an
encounter with the unknown, a chance to walk the tightrope between
caution and foolhardiness which they could never have done at home and
which thus opened up possibilities of self-exploration and self-testing,
with its accompanying sense of physical and spiritual renewal.

The personal transformation effected by the novelty and enrichment of
Italian travel did not wholly vanquish the difficulty which many women
felt when they sought to formulate their experiences in artistic terms. To
some extent this was because, as has already been shown, they recognised
only too well that whatever their journeys represented to them personally, their literary recall could only be rehearsal of a well-worn topic.
Acknowledgement of this problem prefaces nearly every woman's work.
Taylor, for example, promptly apologises to her readers that 'the present
work may seem an unnecessary, if not a presumptuous undertaking', since
undoubtedly many will ask, ' "Can anything new be said of Italy?" ' (I,
p. iii). Trollope, not known for self-deprecation, opens her book with a
similar apology to her fictive correspondent:

> How, my dear friend, can I hope to make letters from Italy interesting to
> you? how dare I venture to attempt it after the rich multitude of descriptive
> travellers who have gone before me? (I, p. 1)

The writers are particularly conscious that detailed accounts of artistic
items are both superfluous and unilluminating, if only because such
discussion has become the province of the professionals and there is no
longer room for uninformed judgement. Morgan speaks for many in this
respect: pointing to the abundance of catalogues listing works of Italian
art and architecture, she tells her readers that since she lacks the
specialised knowledge to compete with them she will not risk boring both
herself and her audience with the attempt:

THE ESCAPE FROM THE TORRENTS
from *Sketches and Stories of Life in Italy*, by an Italian Countess (London, undated)

The vanity would be unpardonable, and the bad taste obvious, which should tempt a traveller of the present day to enter on all the details of that stupendous collection [in the Uffizi] on which volumes have been written, to be found in every library in England. (II, p. 173)

These disarmingly apologetic confessions of inadequacy, a constant feature of women's travel writing, may be regarded less as genuine modesty than as a female strategy which permits the travellers to express their own opinions and impressions, protected by the avowed declarations of ignorance or incompetence. It is a diplomatic move, in view of the genuinely formidable amount of travel literature on Italy by then extant, much of it detailed and learned. Moreover, while their tactical humility operates to forestall their critics, the women in fact offer pertinent reasons for writing about their experiences, thus asserting their right to add to an already substantial body of material. One of their most common justifications is that they are describing and commenting on areas – geographical, social, or political – which have not been treated before or which have not been subjected to their particular kind of personalised and female vision. So Graham claims that in dealing with the Roman Campagna she is discussing a region virtually unknown to most travellers to Italy, who merely follow the well-worn paths straight to the city. The same claim is made by Gretton who, in writing about Ancona and its environs, is purposely offering a portrait of 'the inner life and customs of a part of the Italian peninsula comparatively little visited, – untrodden ground, in fact, to the majority of English tourists'.[42] On a more political front, Morgan declares that the object of her work is to trace the result of the French Revolution on Italy because most people are unfamiliar with the history of the Italian republics; fortunately she keeps this somewhat ponderous intent in the background, and her book is much more interesting than it would suggest.[43]

Instruction on a smaller and more 'womanly' scale is another rationale for writing. Martin explains that she is merely trying to 'relate to one interested in all my details our everyday life while domesticated in Italy' (p. v) and also to give her friend her personal impressions of the state of religion and society in that country; her book may also be useful, she ventures modestly, to those families who are considering taking their children abroad for educational purposes. Taylor's 'Letters to a Younger Sister' have the same ostensible and properly feminine aim: since among all the works she has read on Italy none 'brings this country with all its interesting associations, within the reach of young people' (I, p. iii), she resolves that what was originally written for family benefit may be equally usefully offered to a wider, similar-aged audience. (Another, perhaps subsidiary, purpose is to inspire charitable feelings towards Roman Catholics – 'My desire has been to blend the amusement of a

personal narrative with an interest of a more important nature' [II, p. iv],
she remarks pedantically.) Sewell published her *Journal of a Summer Tour*
for like educational reasons, hoping to edify the local village schoolchil-
dren with it; unfortunately, as she herself admits, the project was not a
success, since in the main the style and content of the book are far too
sophisticated to be valuable to children.

Aware of possible charges of unoriginality in their accounts, the female
tourists also often considered it necessary to apologise for their modes of
presentation. In expressing their sense of a new or restored selfhood
emanating from their emotional revitalisation they were conscious of
how personal, often passionate, their responses were. Though in this
respect they had highly venerated literary models in Ann Radcliffe and
Madame de Stael (to whose works, especially the latter's *Corinne*, they
frequently refer), they felt obliged to devalue or explain away the
elements of sentiment in their own texts. Blessington, with perhaps
deliberate disingenuousness, thus dismisses her deeply felt reactions on
first seeing Rome: 'notwithstanding a pre-determination not to indulge in
the enthusiasm peculiar to female travellers, I confess it made my heart
beat quicker, and I was forced to suppress the expressions of delight that
rose to my lips' (II, p. 163). Shelley, describing her idyllic 'honeymoon' on
the Continent with the poet and Claire Clairmont in July 1814, apologises
for 'the enthusiasm of youth' which has so coloured her descriptions of
'the glaciers, and the lakes, and the forests, and the fountains of the
mighty Alps'.[44] Trollope, on the other hand, is more willing to argue
openly for the truth of emotional response; she agrees with those she
sardonically calls 'the lords of creation' (I, p. 179) that women's
judgement is always dependent on feeling rather than reason, but far
from seeing this as a limitation she defends its superior accuracy of
perception. Moreover, she herself indulges in passionate expression when
genuinely moved by what she observes.

Claims of special motivation and gender-related stylistic peculiarity
cannot of course disguise the element of conventionality or derivativeness
in certain areas of the travellers' responses and commentaries. As they
themselves admit, their aesthetic appreciation is often to a large extent
influenced by earlier commentators such as Starke, Eustace, Hall and
Forsyth and by creative writers, pre-eminently Byron. They also refer
frequently to painters, especially Claude Lorraine, Poussin and Salvator
Rosa, as a means of defining or encapsulating visual impressions – though
not without awareness of how art both verifies actuality (the colour of
Venetian buildings is exactly as Canaletto depicted it) and is transcended
by it (the Coliseum is more impressive than any representation of it). It is
perhaps, then, not surprising that the women's treatment of artistic or
architectural features contains some of their flattest and most unspecific

writing. Morgan's description of Santa Croce in Florence is a good example:

> The first burst of the long line of columned perspective, which offers itself as the nave of this magnificent temple is entered, is truly sublime. The rude massive rafters of its venerable roof, contrasting with the exquisite sculpture, and superb monuments, which rise along its lateral aisles! – the high altar in the centre of the noble space, with its burning tapers! – and, behind all, the skreened choir presenting its mysterious barrier, whence issues the solemn chant of the unseen monks – were images of a most imposing effect. (II, p. 79)

Despite the fulsomeness, there is a vagueness here which suggests that she has not really 'seen' the building in personal terms at all and has relied merely on conventional expressions of admiration. The style of the passage contrasts with much more vital writing where Morgan deals with more personally engaging or controversial matters. The same imprecision can be found elsewhere in the women's descriptions of churches, sculpture or paintings too well-known and well-documented to permit the writer's individual imaginative vision to make them come alive. This is perhaps partly the result of their feeling not only ill-equipped but also basically disinclined to write in areas or modes not naturally theirs. This was suggested by Trollope's contemporary critics, many of whom considered that her *Visit to Italy* was a less successful work than her previous travel books, in particular *Domestic Manners of the Americans*; her style, it was argued, was unsuited for dealing with the classical beauties of Italy and therefore the pungency and originality of the earlier work (which certainly aroused attention, whether admiring or disapproving) had been relinquished in the later one for a flatter, more conventional mode of writing.[45]

The representation of natural scenery is another area of commentary where derivativeness or lack of individual vision are evident. Again, the weight of previous literary tradition and the consciousness that originality is not only impossible but perhaps undesirable are largely responsible. Burke's theory of the sublime, taken up by Gothic and Romantic writers in their treatment of landscape, established a convention of 'nature writing' which emphasised the magnificent, the dramatic and the visually striking; at the same time, eighteenth-century notions of the pleasingly pictorial quality in the natural environment were still influential. Travel writers found themselves almost inevitably caught up in these traditions. Starke herself, in a guide purporting to be essentially factual, draws on a 'set' terminology when describing the Alpine scenery as 'awfully magnificent' and the mountains near Lucca as 'romantically picturesque'.[46] Later in the period, when such vocabulary was becoming increasingly outworn, the women travellers continued to rely on it for their effects. Martin calls the view from the top of Vesuvius 'sublime' (p. 92) and the hill-top town of Orvieto 'picturesque' (p. 204); Taylor describes the 'picturesque' desolation near Rome (I, pp. 95–6), and 'truly romantic' (II, p. 82) scenery at Salerno; and Jameson declares that if she had not visited Italy she would never have actually understood the meaning of the word picturesque.

Even while relying on such discourse, however, the women admit to its inadequacy. Blessington claims that she has vowed never to attempt to describe scenery, 'for all the descriptions that I have ever read, however accurate they may have been, have generally produced only a vague indistinct mass of images on my brain, rather fatiguing than gratifying' (I, p. 46); unfortunately, despite her observation, her own writing often fails to convey anything more distinct, as is illustrated by her depiction of an Alpine lake:

> This beautiful lake is bounded by verdant lawns, adorned with umbrageous trees, and flowering shrubs, and interspersed with picturesque villas; each of which looks the *beau ideal* of a delicious solitude. (I, p. 49)

The self-conscious 'literariness' of this passage gives no sense of an individually perceived scene. To some extent, of course, this absence of originality was related to external pressures. As Michael Sadleir has pointed out, Blessington's travel books were produced from her private journals, revised or re-written in order to make saleable works of the kind which the public wanted. Her *Idler in Italy* not only describes a tour which took place fifteen years earlier, but contains much conventional subject-matter and style, elements which he rather unkindly refers to as 'an answer to the prayer of some modern circulation-monger'.[47] But as he indicates, she herself resisted the temptation to turn her account into a self-pitying contrast between previous happiness and present misfortune (by 1839 she was widowed and without resources) – 'Instead, such alterations as she made were designed to convert a personal record into a bright narrative of foreign travel, with a deal of general feminine interest and as little individual application as possible'.[48] Indeed, it is likely that the desire to avoid the revelation of very personal and private feelings, as well as the wish to attract a wide readership, was in some measure responsible for the conventional elements in all the travellers' writing.

Some of them ironically foreground their descriptive derivativeness, aware of its partially strategic nature. Morgan mocks her own highly literary style, but must have recognised its appeal to readers such as Geraldine Jewsbury who praises her portrayal of Italian scenery because the 'descriptions remind one of Beckford's *Italy*, and the Italian novels of Mrs Radcliffe; especially of some of the pages in *The Mysteries of Udolpho*'.[49] Jameson, taking a refreshingly cool glance at the conventionally melancholic pose she has adopted, sensibly remarks the dangers of trying to be sentimental or 'poetical': on contemplating the Falls of Terni, for instance, she admits that she has exhausted her stock of fine verbal effects, and acknowledges that 'it *is* nonsense to attempt to image in words an individual scene like this' (IV, p. 30). Shelley (whose Romantic heritage naturally leads her towards the poetic and lyrical) slyly sends up the well-worn literary terminology which she uses in her own text:

> It is always satisfactory to get a picturesque adjunct or two to add interest when, with toil and time, one has reached a picturesque spot. (I, p. 50)

Awareness of literary constraints does not however preclude individuality or richness of personal vision. Where the women are fully engaged by the scene or event before them, they make it come alive for us with all the freshness of immediate perception. We have already seen how Venice calls forth some of their most effectively impassioned writing; scenes of a different kind produce some equally striking and sharply observed passages. This is particularly the case where people form part of the environment, since here the response is less conditioned by preconception and a more original rendering is possible. Jameson's description of her visit to Vesuvius is a good example:

> the landscape partially lighted by a fearful red glare, the precipitous and winding road bordered by wild-looking gigantic aloes, projecting their huge spear-like leaves almost across our path, and our lazzaroni attendants with their shrill shouts, and strange dresses, and wild jargon, and striking features, and dark eyes flashing in the gleam of the torches, which they flung round their heads to prevent their being extinguished, formed a scene . . . so extraordinary . . . that my attention was frequently drawn from the mountain, though blazing in all its tumultuous magnificence. (IV, p. 145)

The excitement conveyed here may be compared with a similar dramatic vitality in Kemble's account of the Easter festivities in Rome, in her *Year of Consolation*. Her treatment of the milling crowds at the Carnival in their bizarre costumes and 'fantastic and grotesque gaiety' (I, p. 158) and of the illuminations at St Peter's with the hordes of spectators forming a 'compact blackness' (II, p. 2), the sea of upward-looking faces lit up by the lights, reveals her intense involvement in the events and her thrilling sense of the living variety all round her. The striking liveliness of this kind of writing, as well as depending on the individual's capacity for observation and relay, is also due to a particular interest in the human aspect of the foreign environment, a significant feature in women's travel texts.

Other aspects of the travellers' accounts express even more clearly a specifically female consciousness or 'voice', evident in both their choice of subject-matter and their consequent attitudes. In the latter they are often surprisingly iconoclastic, showing a willingness to challenge authoritative opinion, which represented the domination of public and patriarchal assumptions in their lives. Accustomed to deferring to male opinion at home, many obviously saw their foreign sojourns as an opportunity to articulate a more individualistic response, even in well mapped out spheres. So while dutifully following the guidebooks – most of which were by men – through the maze of Italian artistic riches, they often refused to accept their definitive pronouncements. In this, they had an eminent model in Starke herself, who for all her efficient categorisation of worthwhile sights (signalled by her somewhat startling code of prefatory exclamation marks, increasing according to artistic merit), is quite prepared on common-sense grounds to challenge received opinion; to her, for instance, trees painted on the ceiling of a Venetian palace are quite 'absurd' (II, p. 203).

Later female tourists display the same independence of thought. Morgan, determinedly individualistic about political, social and religious matters, has no hesitation in debunking what seem to her foolish artistic judgements; so the revered Eustace's comments about Turin are 'false, flimsy, and pompous', showing 'his utter ignorance of Italy' (I, p. 105). In general, she has little time for art critics and antiquarians, preferring to rely on her own often unorthodox opinions and briskly speaking out where she finds accepted models of aesthetic excellence personally unsatisfactory. Thus for all its splendour, the Medici chapel in San Lorenzo, Florence, is 'by far the most tasteless edifice in Italy' (II, p. 96); the Pantheon in Rome, with its absurd added towers is 'the very perfection of bad taste' (II, p. 347); her first impression of St Peter's is of 'utter disappointment' (II, p. 376) (a view shared by many of these travellers); and the Capitol, imaged in literature as a grand classical site, is actually 'scarcely larger than the usual space allotted for the lantern-house and dusty garden of a London citizen' (II, p. 355). Even where she admires, her admiration is more personal than conventional. The famous Venus de'Medici in the Uffizi – a sculpture which seems to have had particular significance for women visitors to Italy, perhaps because it was seen as embodying ideal womanhood – delights her chiefly because the 'tiny goddess' is only four feet eleven inches tall, inspiring all 'short ladies and "dumpy women"' (like herself) to say a grateful prayer at her shrine (II, p. 173).

Eustace comes under attack from Shelley and Jameson. Shelley mocks Eustace's *Tour through Italy* for its absurd misrepresentations – 'among other select specimens of his way of think[ing] he says that the Romans did not derive their arts and learning from the Greeks – [and] that the Italian ladies are chaste and the Lazzaroni honest and industrious';[50]

youthful arrogance may be partly responsible for this sweeping judgement, since it was written on Shelley's first trip to Italy in 1818 when she
was in her early twenties. Jameson, reading Eustace at the Falls of Terni,
tells how she 'quickly threw down the book with indignation, deeming all
his verbiage the merest nonsense I had ever met with' (IV, p. 30). She too
voices her own opinions on notable artefacts: though she finds the Venus
de'Medici wholly satisfying, Michaelangelo's statues of Night and Day in
San Lorenzo affect her 'disagreeably' (III, p. 296), while one of his
generally accepted masterpieces, a portrait of the Virgin, with her 'brick-
dust coloured face, harsh unfeminine features, and muscular, masculine
arms, give[s] me the idea of a washerwoman' (III, p. 297), an honestly
expressed if somewhat naïve opinion which she was to revise later. Like
Jameson, Kemble also comments freely on artistic representations which
personally displease her. Stoutly maintaining that 'there are certain
provinces of criticism which belong even to those who know little of the
mechanical rules of art, or the technical terms by which they are
expressed', she has no hesitation in declaring that Raphael's Fornarina is
altogether 'a stupid-looking, staring handsome creature, whose regular
features and rich colouring present, nevertheless, a most unattractive and
unlovely countenance'; she also asserts that the baldachin or canopy over
the high altar in St Peter's reminds her of a four-poster bed, while the
little altars in the church of Santa Maria degli Angioli in Rome look like
'little cabinets at a French restaurant, with vile painted marble pillars'.[51]

Even the more conventional-minded travellers were prepared to refute
orthodox judgements. Taylor, in general echoing guide-book admiration
of Italy's scenic and artistic beauties, dislikes the 'magpie appearance' (I,
p. 27) of the black and white marble of Pisa and Florence cathedrals and
finds the gigantic statue of God mourning over the body of Christ in the
latter 'revolting' (I, p. 56). She also considers the Vatican a 'shapeless pile'
(I, p. 133), an opinion reiterated by Sewell who thinks it looks like a
factory or hospital, though, she muses, its library would certainly make a
good ballroom.[52]

Some of this iconoclasm may embody self-doubt, lack of real interest,
or a more pragmatic approach to foreign commentary. Holmes, for
instance, making comments that she says may be considered 'sacrilege'
(II, p. 272), makes it clear that her inclinations were far more towards the
outdoor equestrian life than the world of art galleries and aesthetic
criticism. She briskly dismisses 'the monstrous dome' and 'heavy and
ungraceful' (II, p. 272) Baptistry of Florence cathedral and is splendidly
irreverent about Ricci's monument to Dante in Santa Croce:

> [The figure of] Italy stands bolt upright folded in a blanket, and with a
> tower on her head, one arm stretched upward, the other holding a sceptre,
> resembling the pole of a French bed. (II, p. 315)

Trollope's similar bluntness may be partly due to her shrewd awareness that having achieved profitable notoriety by her previous published outspokenness it would be a pity to abandon such a successful position. Unapologetic about 'all the heterodoxy which may follow . . . [because] I have been too long in the habit of speaking of all things as they appear to me, to be able to change it now, even if I wished to do so' (I, p. 2), she peppers her artistic commentary with wittily astringent observations. The leaning tower of Pisa is 'to my fancy little better than a curious deformity' (I, p. 78); the interior of Florence cathedral is 'most abominably ugly' (I, p. 98); without the name of the artist appended to it Michaelangelo's 'Holy Family' 'would not be considered worth five pounds by any collector in the world' (I, p. 131); and the octagonal cupola of the Medici Chapel recalls 'disagreeably the idea of one of those angular tabernacles which young ladies often construct in pasteboard to enshrine their embroidery' (I, p. 182). If this is to some degree diplomatic mockery, however, it also endorses Trollope's firm conviction that personal evaluation is the most honest approach to art; though aware of 'my own deficiencies' (II, p. 323) in terms of critical expertise, she will not parrot what seem to her false or pretentious assessments, resisting the female tendency to disclaim or disguise individual opinion.

The actual objects of their attention are particularly indicative of the female-oriented vision of these tourists. All tourists to Italy of course commented on those natural and artistic beauties which by the mid-nineteenth century had become mythologised for visitors – the brilliance of the Naples coastline, the huge dimensions of St Peter's, the view over Florence from Fiesole – and these women are no exception. But more significantly they frequently seize on aspects of the Italian environment which speak especially to their own sex. Like all the female travellers, they frequently note items of a domestic nature. The remains at Pompeii and Herculaneum, for example, were of particular interest to them, enabling them to reflect on the contrasts between a past civilisation and their own. The lack of privacy in the open-plan layout of rooms at Pompeii particularly struck Trollope and caused her to reflect on the importance to women of her day of having some 'retreat that they may call their own *par excellence*' (II, p. 227). The visitors were also fascinated by the relics in the Borbonico Museum at Naples, such as cooking utensils, furniture and toilet items. Taylor had fun in speculating how a 'modern belle . . . would perhaps be puzzled to adorn herself for a ball at the toilette-table of a Pompeian lady; she might mistake the large and clumsy pins for skewers' (II, pp. 54–5), and Martin observes that the women's combs are worse than the ones now used for horses. Even more than the domestic arrangements of the dead and living Italians, the appearance, behaviour and conditions of the local women themselves were of universal concern.

Though as tourists they were interested in Italian female portraiture, the travellers were more personally drawn to the living representatives of their sex. Their attitudes towards them were ambivalent, however. The Italian women were less evidently 'foreign' than those in more exotic or unfamiliar cultures – as we shall see, the North American Indians or the Japanese Ainu represented the 'other' far more distinctively to European eyes. But in some respects the indigenous population still offered the visitors an image of the alien with which they had to come to terms. The female peasantry, whose bright clothes, striking head-dresses and unusual ornaments they often remark, embodied for them not only the general gaiety of the Italian scene which they found so appealing, but also all the colour and vitality which the Victorian woman had been taught to distrust. Moreover, Taylor's observation that Englishwomen's costumes rendered them to the staring local women 'objects of no less attention to them than they were to us' (II, p. 4) highlights the sense of unease which the travellers experienced in being themselves regarded as oddities. Thus while on the one hand they leant towards identification with their own sex, on the other they sought to distance themselves from the threat of disorientation which this might involve.

The most successful method of achieving separation between the self and the observed other is to objectify the latter so as to dehumanise it and 'fix' it in a preconceived image, a reaction characteristic of the inbuilt imperialism of most nineteenth-century travellers, even the more sympathetic female ones. One way in which the ladies attempted this objectification was to approach foreign womanhood in terms of an artistic ideal. Blessington, for instance, constantly praises the Italian women she sees for their likeness to antique statues or rural nymphs in paintings; she admires a group filling their jugs from a village fountain at Castellamare as items in a rich tapestry. Like Blessington, Trollope defines the beauty of some Italian peasant girls exclusively according to aesthetic criteria:

> [They had] an air of *historique* picturesque perfection that really approached very nearly to the *beau ideal* of beauty as it may be seen in the Madonnas of Raphael . . . having a look so indescribably resembling an Italian work of art, that I fancied I must have known their nation had I met them in a land the farthest removed from it. (I, p. 246)

Others, too, draw on artistic sources of evaluation in comparing female costume or features to figures in classic Italian paintings. Seeing these people as art thus comfortably and respectably marginalises them.

An alternative way of approaching the alien is to define it as savage or barbarous, undermining or mocking those elements which threaten familiar assumptions. Here, many of the women, albeit fleetingly, display the moral righteousness or racism of a self-aggrandising nation. So Starke, while noting the attractiveness of the Tuscan Contadine, expresses her doubts about the kind of power which such 'natural' beauty confers. Martin, too, though amused at the sight of peasant women riding donkeys with legs uncovered to the knees, chooses to see it as suggestive of general Italian female 'looseness'. The difficulty of accepting unfamiliar images of womanhood sometimes reveals itself in the unsympathetic objectivity of colonial discourse, seeking divorce from abhorrent models of humanity. Holmes, for instance, describing the physical deformities among the inhabitants of the Italian Alps, speaks in tones of disgust about one such 'hideous' goitre-afflicted cretin:

> One passed us with the usual vacant grin and dead eye, and uttered a yell which startled the horses; the wretched object wore a petticoat, and we could not tell whether it were male or female. (II, p. 85)

Deliberately using neuter pronouns, she makes it clear that for her the deformed represents the sub-human. Elsewhere she similarly dismisses what to her prejudiced eye is unfeminine vulgarity – 'the women wear the small straw hat with turned-up brim, ornamented with brilliant ribands of gold and silver tissue, which shows off in all their ugliness their unwholesome complexions and ill-formed features' (II, p. 92). Taylor is more taken with Italian female dress, but still qualifies her admiration by well-learnt home values. So the women at Mola 'wear their hair in a peculiar manner, and, were they more cleanly in their persons, it would be beautiful' (II, p. 9). The same kind of dissociated assessment, based on a complacent superiority, is found in Eastlake's descriptions of northern Italian women: the old ones are hideous, the girls 'have that common, uneducated look – mincing and servant-maidish . . . and the middle-aged women are over-stout, have sore eyes and mustaches, wear their hair entirely turned back under their bonnets and are the most impudent-looking creatures you can conceive' (II, p. 18). This may be amusing, but any potential sisterly sensibility has been subsumed by imperialistic, middle-class attitudes.

In contrast, Kemble is more sympathetically responsive to alternative images of womanhood. She not only frequently draws attention to examples of female beauty, but also seems especially attracted to those figures who represent a freedom which is both foreign and alluring to her. She creates a tableau of colourful vitality with her description of the local girls on the steps of the Piazza di Spagna in Rome, 'in the picturesque costume of the lower orders here, with splendid heads and shoulders, and scarlet jackets, and daggers thrust through the braids of their hair . . . [who] sit and stand, and lounge and loll in the sun, shouting, laughing, gesticulating, or dozing like cats with half closed eyes' (*Year of Consolation*, I, p. 132). The vigorous excesses of her prose show how attractive she finds the unashamedly sensual suggestiveness of the scene. There is a similar almost envious admiration in her vivid description of three girls she encounters at Tivoli,

> walking with intertwined arms and bare heads, whose beauty was extremely remarkable; as they went singing and laughing down the street, they would have formed a splendid study for a painter, with their fine heads and full figures and free reckless bearing; they looked dirty and saucy, but most eminently picturesque. (II, pp. 86–7)

Here, the artistic metaphors do not detract from the sense of felt physicality which the passage conveys.

It is also interesting that Kemble is one of the very few female Italian tourists who comment on masculine beauty. This of course is a topic fraught with danger. Victorian women could not admit to – indeed were not supposed to have – any physical feelings towards the opposite sex. The travellers were thus constrained by their awareness of what it was 'proper' for them to note, as well as perhaps reluctant to venture into an area which might involve the arousal of disturbing emotions. Kemble, brought up in a family which though highly respectable had strong links with the more robust eighteenth century, unabashedly points not just to the attractiveness of male costume but also to striking bodily features. She declares openly that 'it is only in Italy that I have seen men's faces as positively beautiful as women's, and that frequently' (II, p. 218) and she details this beauty. Young lads in Rome have 'blue-black locks falling all round the most wonderful eyes ever beheld' (I, p. 132); an old peasant has eyes gleaming 'like coals of fire' (II, p. 213) out of his tangled hair; and mule and cattle drivers in the Campagna are notable for their 'brilliant colouring and vivid expression peculiar to this singularly handsome race', their tight breeches and leather gaiters showing admirably their 'straight and well-proportioned limbs' (II, p. 215). There is an unashamed sexual pleasure here, a delight in male physical virility, expressed even more openly in Kemble's other descriptions of Italian peasants. There is no aesthetic distancing in her fascination with an old herdsman, 'his open shirt showing a brown brawny breast covered with curling silver hairs' (II, p. 184), or with the brutal earthiness of the village men treading grapes:

> . . . the hideous-looking red-brown scum, in which a hairy, sweating, brawny peasant prances, with his breeches rolled more than half-way up his thighs, and his limbs besmeared as though with blood, [in] the revolting-looking contents of the huge vat, in which he takes his exercise. (II, p. 196)

When the travellers did not feel threatened or disturbed by the 'otherness' of the foreigners, they responded with far more warmth and understanding. They exhibit, for example, what may be considered a particularly womanly compassion towards the impoverished lower classes. Trollope notes that on the way to Rome she has seen 'a sadder picture of human misery, ignorance and destitution than I have ever witnessed . . . except perhaps among the manufacturing population of Manchester' (II, p. 162), and Sewell, equally upset by the general air of degradation and sickliness among the Roman poor, confesses to a sense of helplessness in being unable to ease their lot. Their observations frequently include an urgent plea for improved conditions, though in this the more firmly Protestant of them cannot resist placing the blame for the suffering on the iniquities of Roman Catholicism.

More particularly, their interest in the conditions and circumstances affecting Italian women foregrounds what may be called a 'feminine voice' in their writing. One instance of this is their awareness of how the physical conditions of Italian life are especially hard on women. Kemble can again be singled out here for her perception of the harsh realities beneath the surface attractiveness. Her description of the female inhabitants of hill-top villages near Frascati succinctly undermines naïve aesthetic apprehension of the foreign environment:

> admirable as the groups [of women at wells] often are at these picturesque watering-places, and beautiful the antique form of the copper vessels which the women bear on their heads returning from them, it grieves my heart to meet them, as we do perpetually in our rides, toiling thus burthened up the steep ascent. (*Year of Consolation*, II, p. 210)

Discussion of the socially and educationally restricted existence of Italian women is also a significant element in the travellers' accounts, often somewhat clumsily interpolated, but presented with an energy that not only relieves the more pedestrian quality of their conventional commentary but reveals their deep engagement with the issue. In their concern, they are both expressing natural interest and implicitly evaluating their own positions, as the contrast between their state and that of women in another regime is forced upon them. Here, pre-established views of a different kind operate, the more radical tourists being critical of sexual discrimination in Italy, while others are not so committed to change. But even the less adventurous observers feed into their texts an enlightened sense of womanhood. Martin enlivens her rather tedious itemisation of well-known sights with brisk criticism of the general ignorance of Italian women and warm praise for Murat's institution for the education of orphaned girls. Blessington, too, notes with cautious approval the unusual fact of there being women students at Padua University, though her deeply ingrained conservatism prevents her from accepting the general principle with any enthusiasm; for her, 'the advantages to be derived from a scientific education, and an admittance to a university, would . . . be more than counterbalanced by the loss of that feminine delicacy and timidity which constitute the most attractive charms of woman' (III, p. 111).

The most feminist oriented exploit their representation of foreign experience in order to express their political views. Morgan and Trollope, for example, both independent and outspoken women themselves, voice their disapproval of the curtailment of female freedoms in Italy, and, later in the period, Cobbe, an energetic campaigner for Women's Rights at home, is specifically concerned with telling her readers how much the condition of Italian women needs reform. Morgan shows a particular concern for developments in women's education. She highly approves of institutions such as Bologna University which have opened their doors to women, and eagerly describes the establishment in Italy of a 'new and liberal system of education, raised upon the ruins of that demoralizing bigotry, which was calculated to make women concubines and devotees, but which could not produce good wives and mothers' (I, p. 196). Firmly pro-Republican in her sentiments, she commends Napoleon not only for his Alpine roads and his respect for Italy's culture, but also for his recognition of 'how powerfully women contribute in determining the character of society; and how much a generation of well-educated females must contribute to raise it' (I, pp. 196–7). She commends the female seminary at Milan for combining the teaching of domestic arts with that of languages, arts, sciences and literature, convinced that Italian women's dormant abilities will be awakened by the right stimuli. Morgan was no revolutionary feminist – like so many women of her generation concerned with the position of her own sex, while arguing for new attitudes she believed that women's talents were for 'developed sensibility' (II, p. 26) rather than abstruse learning, and that the duties of wife and mother were paramount – but she uses her encounter with Italy to articulate her championship of female self-development and free expression.

Morgan's experiences also compelled her to take stock of her own and her countrywomen's circumstances, and this was true of many of the other travellers. They found that confrontation with the foreign culture made them grateful for their own, albeit relative, advantages. Few actually obtained first-hand knowledge of Italian women's lives, since it was almost impossible for British visitors to gain intimate access to society here and the language was usually a barrier. But despite this, they took a committed and evaluative interest in what touched them personally as women. Of central importance was the significance of the female married state in Italy. Morgan notes sympathetically the especially miserable position of unmarried Italian women, imprisoned either in dreary homes or in convents, fates which mercifully were not the only alternatives for English spinsters. Married Englishwomen, too, she argues, are more fortunate than their Italian counterparts, who are often reduced to demeaning role-playing, as in the 'degraded' society of Venice, where wives, deprived of the means of exercising wholesome influence, are merely slaves or sultanas, 'destined to serve or to sway by the worst of means' (III, pp. 401, 2). Eastlake observes how the over-protection of young unmarried Italian women denies them the opportunity to develop firm moral principles which will serve them after matrimony and Kemble, scornful of the Italian theory that women are not to be trusted, also recognises how rigid supervision in youth here encourages unchastity later. Shelley reminds us that she is Mary Wollstonecraft's daughter when she discusses Continental female society. Much valuing her own freedom to travel, she too deplores the constrained and unrespected position of Italian women and is particularly dismayed by the inanity and boredom of upper-class female Venetian life in which the poor creatures spend their time eating ices in the Piazza and chatting idly, with no sources of reading matter or acquisition of knowledge. She also sees how matrimony has become a debased ideal in Italy, commenting wryly, 'unmarried women all over the Continent have so much the worst of it, that few remain single' (II, p. 109) – though she adds, with rueful honesty, 'It does not strike me that, as regards daughters who survive their parents, things are much better managed with us' (II, p. 110).

Gretton, who had more direct access to mid-nineteenth-century society in a small Italian town, devotes a considerable portion of her narrative to female roles and circumstances. Though she laughs at the formality of rules and etiquette in Ancona, she both pities and disapproves of the restricted lives led by women here, who with nothing to do except fancy-work, a little reading and entertaining, can only look out of their windows and breathe an atmosphere which is morally as well as physically injurious to them. Blaming the system of arranged marriages and 'their defective method of education' (I, p. 36), she makes implicit comparisons with the preferable state of things in England, as her grim picture of Italian spinsterhood makes clear:

> Dressed with scrupulous plainness, seldom or never taken into company, rarely appearing out of doors, except for a drive in a close carriage, or to go to mass, or to call on some old female relation – without the advantages of a cultivated mind or literary resources – the condition of our Italian unmarried woman is as cheerless and insignificant as it is possible to conceive. (I, pp. 41–2)

More directly, Gretton offers some pertinent contrasts between her own position and that of the Anconian women. Reporting a visit to a neighbouring family whose eldest daughter is an eccentric and unhappy spinster, she reminds herself and us of the benefits of a society in which females are not regarded as totally inferior, girls can to a large extent choose their marital status and to be unmarried is no disgrace. In her case, exposure to the foreign environment has taken her to some reassuring conclusions about her own circumstances.

The same is true for Cobbe, whose aim is to put down 'the facts concerning the new order of things' (p. 11) in Italy. Like Shelley, she remarks the paucity of unmarried Italian women, commenting cynically that the female objective is to get a husband at all costs, 'the only question being, whether he is a little younger or older, richer or poorer' (p. 137); and she bitterly attacks the social injustices suffered by women here. She is particularly hostile towards southern European society where women 'have been left to grope among whatever superstitions their confessors and directors [choose] to teach them' (p. 248), and her use of capitals reinforces her message that where females are so degraded and unenlightened 'the NEMESIS of WOMAN has come indeed' (p. 250). Her ardour, deeply sympathetic though it is to the female cause, reminds us how political stance can determine not only the discourse but also the focus of travel writing. Cobbe, perhaps seeing what she knew she would see, has shaped her responses according to her personal perspective, which in her case has made her aware not only of the iniquities suffered by Italian women but also of her own better fortune in at least being able to fight at home for the rights of her sex.

Observation of the foreign in this area, as much as in the aesthetic sphere, was thus controlled by preconception, only here the conclusions reflect back to the travellers themselves. If many aspects of their Italian experiences touched their subconscious and awakened them to undreamt-of worlds within, matters specifically pertaining to them as women provoked re-evaluation of many of the fundamentals of their own society. For some, this merely reinforced their established standpoints; indeed, generally speaking, Italy did not produce the radical disturbance of attitude experienced by women travellers in the East. But for others, however indirectly, such re-thinking may have changed their lives. They certainly carried their treasured memories back home with them, the magic land indelibly engraved on their minds.

3

North America:
a new world

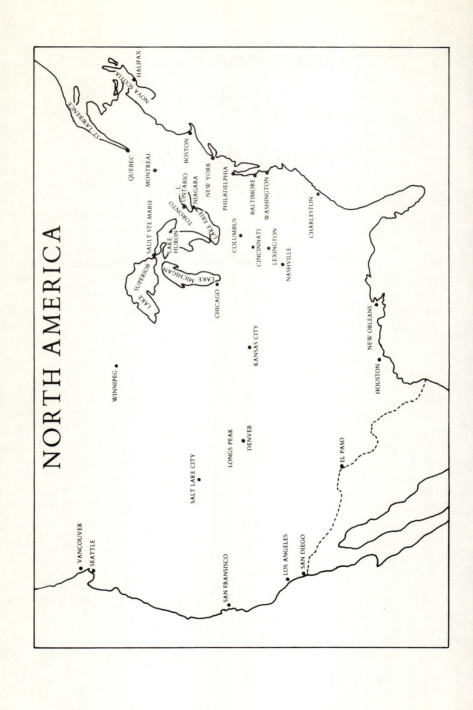

NORTH AMERICA

ST. LAWRENCE

NOVA SCOTIA

HALIFAX

QUEBEC

MONTREAL

BOSTON

NEW YORK

PHILADELPHIA

L. ONTARIO

NIAGARA

BALTIMORE

WASHINGTON

TORONTO

LAKE ERIE

COLUMBUS

CHARLESTON

SAULT STE MARIE

LAKE HURON

CINCINNATI

LEXINGTON

NASHVILLE

LAKE SUPERIOR

LAKE MICHIGAN

CHICAGO

WINNIPEG

KANSAS CITY

NEW ORLEANS

HOUSTON

LONGS PEAK

DENVER

EL PASO

SALT LAKE CITY

VANCOUVER

SEATTLE

SAN FRANSISCO

LOS ANGELES

SAN DIEGO

'[As] I stepped upon those shores on which the sanguine suppose that the Anglo-Saxon race is to renew the vigour of its youth, I felt that a new era of my existence had begun.'[1] Such was Isabella Bird's reaction as she crossed into the United States from Canada at Portland, Maine, on her first visit to North America in 1854. Her idealistic enthusiasm, tinged with a note of conscious irony, encapsulates what that country meant to the nineteenth-century traveller. It also marks the contrast between this response and that of the tourist in the Old World. The women who went to America took with them a rather different set of expectations and assumptions from those who visited Italy. Whereas the latter country beckoned them as the land of dreams, the former seemed another kind of Promised Land. The New World represented to them less the fulfilment of youthful longings inspired by literature and art[2] than an arena where more pragmatic and socially oriented beliefs could be tested. Pre-existing familiarity here, too, was not only of a more factual nature, but also critically sharper (as we shall see, all the travellers were aware of the often misleading reports circulated by previous visitors) and so to go to America was to measure foreknowledge against actuality in a more rigorous way. The political and social links between England and North America, as well as the ostensibly common language, also helped to ease their entry into the new environment and give them more confidence about assessing it. At the same time, more than Italy, the continent offered in physical terms opportunity for exploration and discovery involving self-testing in an 'uncivilised' and sometimes hostile natural landscape, unmediated by historical or cultural association. The challenge, both feared and desired, often demanded considerable bodily and spiritual readjustment.

By the early nineteenth century, visitors to the United States and Canada were by no means uncommon and the main tourist routes had been established: travellers usually started from Halifax, Nova Scotia, or New York, and took in the major eastern and southern cities including Boston, Philadelphia, Baltimore, Washington, Charleston and New Orleans, then turned northwards via the Mississippi and Ohio rivers to Cincinnati and back across to Buffalo and Niagara, returning through New York State; some made a detour to see Chicago, Detroit and the

Great Lakes, as well as parts of eastern Canada. It was, however, still relatively unusual for women tourists to go there, as Fanny Kemble points out in the late 1870s, contrasting the early and later decades of the century in this respect:

> 'A trip', as it is now called, to Europe or America, is one of the commonest of experiences. . . . But when I first went to America, steam had not shortened the passage of that formidable barrier between world and world . . . Few men, and hardly any women, undertook it as a mere matter of pleasure or curiosity.[3]

It was even rarer for women to travel without the protection of a male escort. When Frances Wright and her sister first went to America on their own in 1818, for instance, the local press called amazed attention to their independence. Most female visitors, even in the later period, had at least one man in their party to cushion them from the roughness of New World travel. Kemble herself made her first trip in 1832 with her father and aunt on their fund-raising acting tour, though on subsequent transatlantic journeys she was often on her own, apart from her maid and two small daughters. Marianne Finch, who visited the States in 1850, also went under the care of the paternal wing. Husbands figure largely as fellow-travellers: the sisters Catherine Parr Traill and Susanna Moodie took off for the Canadian outback in 1832, newly wedded to prospective immigrants; Barbara Bodichon went to America on her honeymoon in 1857; Matilda Houston, Margaret Hall and Isabella Trotter were all accompanied on their mid-century American tours by spouses who made the decisions and arrangements (Trotter writes to her daughter at home that 'Papa' keeps her in happy ignorance of each succeeding destination). Where there was no male protector, chosen females usually filled the position: Harriet Martineau took with her a companion, Louisa Jeffrey, a lady 'of very superior qualifications', whose expenses she paid in return for her assistance as 'companion and helper'[4] and who was especially helpful over difficulties connected with Martineau's deafness; Bird was enabled to visit the United States at the age of twenty-three by joining two female cousins on their way back to their father posted in Prince Edward Island; Marianne North sailed to Boston in 1871 with the woman friend who had asked her to spend the summer with her in America.

As Kemble suggests, some kind of ostensibly utilitarian or respectable 'purpose' was a more common reason for going to the New World than pure leisure, although, as has already been noted, such orthodox motivation could conceal a deeper desire for self-pleasing. The travellers can be divided roughly into three groups here – the pragmatists, the idealists and the pleasure-seekers. The pragmatists include those like Traill, Moodie, Kemble and Anna Jameson, whose overt motive was family duty rather than choice, Traill and Moodie the loyal helpmeets of their emigrant spouses, Kemble the supportive daughter and Jameson the reluctantly obedient wife going to join her semi-estranged husband in Canada. Others went to America in seach of health, a venture often thought to be more beneficial than a trip to Europe because it involved a long sea voyage. The idea of travel to the United States was first suggested to Martineau by her urgent need for two years' 'rest and recreation'[5] after nearly prostrating herself to complete her massive *Illustrations of Political Economy* in 1834, and Bird began the pattern of her travelling life when she made her first transatlantic journey on the recommendation of her doctor.

The idealists are those who went to America with theoretic or visionary ideas which they wished to match against actuality or to implement practically. The earliest of such was Wright who, having read Carlo Botta's history of the American Republic in her late teens and imaging the New World as 'the theatre where man might first awake to the full knowledge and full exercise of his powers', made it her 'fixed but secret determination' not only to visit the country but to set up a colony where her principles of social liberation and equality could operate. Not surprisingly, her missionary inspiration, plus her desire to remove some of the current unfavourable opinions of the new republic – she was angered by those English visitors who, having partaken of American generosity, 'afterwards, at their leisure, with better opportunity, jeer at the manners and traduce the character of the people whose hospitality they have shared' – make her a somewhat partisan observer and interpreter:

> What other land is there that points not the imagination back to better days, contrasting present decay with departed strength, or that, even in its struggles to hold a forward career, is not checked at every step by some physical or political hindrance?[6]

Some of her visionary enthusiasm spilled over onto Trollope who, as we have seen, initially set off for America hoping to assist her friend at Nashoba. On discovering, however, that 'every idea I had formed of the place was as far as possible from the truth' (*Domestic Manners*, p. 19), she quickly packed her bags and went on to Cincinnati where she hoped to make money by setting up a dry-goods bazaar – as it turned out, another piece of idealism doomed to failure.

Martineau's idealism, a stronger force than her more utilitarian motives, was less visionary. She tells in her *Autobiography* how Lord Henley, on hearing that she was proposing to travel, suggested as a 'good reason' why she should go to America that she might investigate and describe those 'principles of justice and mercy' which the Americans promulgate 'in their treatment of the least happy classes of society' (I, p.

270). Already a staunch opponent of slavery, Martineau acted on Henley's recommendation in order to examine this hated institution, as well as 'because I felt a strong curiosity to witness the actual working of republican institutions'.[7] Her respectably intellectual motivation, however, was reinforced by more ascetic personal idealism. Worried that her alluringly easy life of indulgence and flattery was making her irredeemably selfish, she admits to

> my purposes of self-discipline in undertaking [my American travels]. Fearing that I was growing too much accustomed to luxury, and to an exclusive regularity in the modes of living, I desired to 'rough it' for a considerable time. (*Autobiography*, II, p. 85)

Her enjoyment of 'roughing it', so evident in her subsequent accounts, is thus irreproachably 'covered'; Martineau made the social assessment she had come for, but her trip was clearly far from being one long penance.

Others who travelled with idealistic motives were similarly concerned with the operation of social and moral principles in America. Like Wright, Mary Duncan, a visitor in the early 1850s, wanted to confirm her conviction that previous English accounts of the country were unjust and injurious, and to substantiate her belief in Christian brotherhood between the two nations. Finch and Bodichon, too, on what were primarily pleasure trips, were anxious to obtain and relay information about important American issues, especially slavery and women's rights; both went to hear anti-slavery sermons by Theodore Parker and Lucretia Mott and Finch attended some of the debates at the first and second National Woman's Right Conventions at Worcester, Massachusetts, in 1850 and 1851.

A few of the women were more solely and unashamedly self-indulgent in their undertaking. Hall, accompanying her husband Captain Basil Hall, whose subsequent book (1829) caused almost as much stir as Trollope's was to,[8] aimed merely to enjoy herself. More sybaritically, Houston took two pleasure trips to America, the first a voyage in the early 1840s to the southernmost states bordering the Gulf of Mexico, via Madeira, Barbados and Jamaica, in her husband's luxurious yacht, the *Dolphin*, the second a slightly more strenuous visit several years later, penetrating further into the country. Personal enjoyment was her main purpose, though apparently the Americans found this hard to believe – she reports a conversation with a New York merchant in which 'as usual, it was quite a matter of wonderment to him that we could be travelling in America with any object beside that of business'.[9] She does, however, add the rider that the voyage in particular was 'undertaken principally in search of health for me'.[10] Inherent passion for foreign experience was as much as anything responsible for taking others to America. Lady Emmeline

Stuart-Wortley, transporting a supposedly delicate daughter not only all over the United States but to Mexico, Panama and Peru as well; Bird constantly on the move from one region to another; North, left on her own after the death of her father, her previous travelling companion, setting off again to paint the exotic American plants and scenery (though confessedly suffering from the common delusion that North America was quite close to the tropics)[11] – all saw the New World as a place for discovery and personal enrichment.

The excitement of going to America began with embarkation at the port of departure, if not before (Houston and her husband, for instance, had a hair-raising ride in a 'fly' through the streets of Liverpool to the dock, with their eight trunks precariously balanced on top, convinced that they were about to miss their steamer), since the voyage itself was an intrinsic part of the adventure. It is perhaps because of this that most trans-Atlantic tourists spend longer than their European counterparts on describing how they got to their destination. A long sea voyage was a novelty, fraught with potential danger, and an appropriate introduction to much-anticipated new experience.

Various routes were available to the tourists. Most crossings were from Liverpool and went either to Boston or New York, usually stopping first at Halifax, Novia Scotia to let off the Canadian immigrants. Some travellers left from other ports: Jameson sailed from Portsmouth; Trollope sailed from London; Traill sailed from Greenock. In the early days of the century the mode of transport was sailing-ship, but the introduction of steam on the trans-Atlantic route in 1838 revolutionised travel between Britain and the United States. In 1840, the British and North American Royal Mail Steam Packet Company (which became the Cunard Steamship Company), having secured a mail contract, began a regular fortnightly service with four paddle steamers and by 1848 was running eight boats on a weekly mail service to Boston and New York, with an accompanying dramatic reduction in the duration of the voyage. Under sail, the average length was thirty days, though a bad crossing could well be over forty (Martineau's was forty-two) and Trollope's, admittedly all the way to Balize, at the mouth of the Mississippi, took seven weeks; under steam, the time was halved, the voyage to Halifax about ten days, with another couple of days to get to Boston or New York.

The relief which the advent of 'those blessed beings – the steam ships, those Atlantic angels of speed and certainty' brought to a bad sailor like Kemble was enormous. The general ease and comfort of trans-Atlantic travel improved greatly as the century progressed, and as she points out, the differences between the 1830s and the 1880s in this respect were almost unimaginable: then, the traveller could expect danger, difficulty and delay and, with fewer ships and no transatlantic telegraph, the 'distance between the two worlds, which are now so near to each other, was . . . immense';[12] now, fifty years later, 'crowds . . . throng the great watery highway between the two continents'.[13] Stuart-Wortley also observes the relative ease of modern (i.e. mid-century) travel to the United States, feeling reassured by and full of admiration for the progress of civilisation in this respect:

> In my transatlantic travels, I do not feel so far away from home as I thought I should; the Cunard steamers are so regular and rapid in their passage, they are now generally here to the day they are expected. What a fast age we live in![14]

What, one wonders, would she have made of a trip across the Atlantic at the speed of sound? Bird, too, brushing off warnings from her friends about the possible perils of the sea-crossing, has equal praise for the speed, safety, and efficiency of the Cunard steamers, though admitting that she would have liked the chance to have sailed in a clipper (p. 458).

Women crossing on their own could expect some annoyances, such as the lack of privacy which so appalled Jameson –

> Only imagine the horror of being confined for 35 to 40 days in a space of six feet square with a stranger, to sleep, to undress. I believe I had rather make the voyage in a long boat.[15]

– though all these travellers could afford passenger fares, and did not have to suffer like the poor emigrant women in steerage. But enjoyment of the voyage depended essentially on two things – the other passengers, and the traveller's state of health. The former provided Martineau and Bird with good entertainment, but others were not so lucky. Jameson complains that her fellow voyagers are not at all exciting and that there are too many noisy children. Houston finds hers selfish, demanding and boring; in particular, the 'double distilled dulness of English exclusiveness' among her countrymen contrasts markedly with the gaiety of the Americans, fortifying themselves with brandy cocktails and 'when subjected to unavoidable sea-going annoyances, such as receiving the contents of their soup plates in their laps, or the candles against their noses' (*Hesperos*, I, p. 14), laughing even more. Bird was unfortunate enough to be allotted a most uncongenial state-room companion, a coarse and drunken Englishwoman who had lived for some years in New York 'and who combined in herself the disagreeable qualities of both nations' (p. 10).

More crucial to enjoyment was whether or not the traveller suffered from sea-sickness. Trotter made no attempt to fight the dreaded malaise; utterly prostrate by mid-Atlantic, she declared herself quite unable to contemplate going up on deck and reclined in her cabin for the rest of the journey. Hall was also very sick on the crossing, but was at least able to laugh at the absurdity of the situation as she herself, her little daughter, Eliza and Eliza's nurse were all thrown together on the floor of the Ladies' Cabin by the force of the waves. Jameson, with the kind of histrionic self-presentation which we have already seen in her earlier work on Italy, describes the awful experience of being stranded by a bad storm off the Isle of Wight for nearly a week – 'all this time I was almost insensible to every thing but intense suffering; I think one could hardly suffer more and live'. She too, though, was capable of seeing the funny side of it:

> sometimes in the midst of all, a sense of the ludicrous and the grotesque comes across me and I could laugh if I were not too utterly miserable.[16]

Martineau, on the other hand, with characteristic determination to enjoy every moment of the voyage, refused to be deterred by her initial bout of sea-sickness; rapidly on her legs again, she went up on deck to get fresh air and was soon feeling quite exhilarated enough to decide that 'a voyage is the most pleasant pastime I have ever known'.[17] Minor irritants bothered her as little; other less stalwart souls, lying on their beds of sickness, found it harder to ignore creaking timbers or doors which would not stay shut.

Kemble, as has already been indicated, was a genuinely bad sailor, and though she tried hard to cope with her sickness by occupying herself was usually laid low for most of the journey. She describes two particularly horrendous crossings. The first took thirty-seven days, during which she was almost totally confined to her bed and arrived in New York looking like a ghost; the other, in May 1843, took only fifteen days but she was dreadfully ill the whole time, in a high fever for ten days, able to swallow only iced water and two glasses of calves' foot jelly, and so weak when they docked at Halifax that she scarcely had the strength to write a note to her father back home.

The few who suffered no ill-effects were of course able to get the most out of the voyage. Houston seems to have had an Amazonian constitution, and is very smug about her own immunity to sea-sickness during a period of gales:

> the sea was gradually lashed to mountain height, and the ship rocked, and rose, and plunged, causing all the ladies, with but *one* exception to quit the scene of action, and to bury themselves and their apprehensions in the solitudes of their respective berths. Sad, and weary to *them*, must have been the days of our watery pilgrimage! But there was no dulness or tedium for those in health. (*Hesperos*, I, pp. 12–13)

Bird, another who was untroubled by the malaise, also derived amusement from the sight of 'diligent peripatetics . . . extended on sofas, or feebly promenading under the shelter of the bulwarks' (p. 461).

The travellers' response to more serious events at sea gives some indication of their subsequent reactions to the physical and mental challenges of America. Ocean storms (which in this period certainly presented the possibility of real disaster) called up all their resources and in many cases awakened highly emotional feelings. Despite her depiction of herself as a helpless invalid, able only to be carried up on deck and laid on pillows, Jameson clearly quite enjoyed her storm, as the somewhat melodramatic description of the shrieking winds and roaring waves which she sent to her friend Ottilie von Goethe makes clear. Sarah Maury, travelling for her health but little improved by having been sick for thirty-seven hours during a fierce gale, had herself tied to a chair on deck and was soon relishing the excitement of high seas and brilliantly coloured water. Her response to a second storm indicates even more strikingly how for her the experience represented physical release and energising engagement with a strong external force: lashed to a capstan and clinging to the rigging, she declares herself exhilarated by the feeling of 'uncontrolled and unlimited power'[18] which the huge waves give her. The intrepid Martineau responded similarly to the challenging excitement of a storm at sea. She too had herself lashed to the post of a binnacle on deck, from where she could enjoy 'the whole of the never-to-be-forgotten scene' (*Retrospect*, I, p. 28), quite untroubled by any fear of danger.

Surprisingly, it is the long-suffering Kemble who most vividly describes the powerful effect on her of such wild weather, as she tells of her spirits stirring in sympathy with the vast motion of the waves. Her most memorable experience was of a formidable tempest which lasted for nearly four days. She records her sudden certainty that she would be drowned, followed by that phenomenon said to be common to all in a similar situation: her whole past life was 'suddenly held up to me as in a mirror, indescribably awful, combined with the simultaneous acute and almost despairing sense of *loss*, of *waste*, so to speak, by which it was accompanied';[19] though finally her sense of terror vanished, she remained aware that she had reached one of the most extreme points of psychological experience.

Their appreciation of less dramatic aspects of the voyage also indicates the women's capacities for responding to a new environment. Trollope speaks for many in declaring how rewarding the journey had proved to her:

> In truth, to those who have pleasure in contemplating the phenomena of nature, a sea voyage may endure many weeks without wearying. Perhaps some may think that the first glance of ocean and of sky shew all they have

to offer; nay, even that first glance may suggest more of dreariness than
sublimity; but to me, their variety appeared endless, and their beauty
unfailing . . . never, while I remember any thing, can I forget the first and
last hour of light on the Atlantic. (p. 3)

Unfamiliar phenomena of nature such as the silvery islands made by
moonlight in the night fog, phosphoric light on the waves and strange
creatures like Portuguese men-of-war, dolphins and flying fish caught
their attention and inspired some of their most colourful writing; eagerly
drinking in such sights, they anticipated the further wonders which
awaited them in the New World.

After arriving in the New World, other kinds of hardship and
discomfort awaited the woman traveller. First there was the matter of
getting from place to place. Although all the tourists journeyed partly by
road, in the earlier part of the century the most common method of
transportation within America was by water, the Mississippi and Ohio
rivers providing the main links between north and south, and the St
Lawrence and the Great Lakes the chief means of communication in the
mid-west and Canada. By mid-century, however, American railroads,
first introduced in 1828, had already opened up large expanses of the
continent in the east and south and in 1869 an all-rail connection was
complete between the east and San Francisco; other trans-continental
routes developed in the next two decades, through both the northern and
southwestern states, making it possible for a traveller such as North to
cross and re-cross from Atlantic to Pacific coasts in the 1870s and 1880s
almost entirely by train.

For most travellers the novelty of their wanderings outweighed the
discomforts, though there was often a great deal to be laughed off. The
most uncomfortable, if not the most potentially dangerous, mode of
travel was overland by road; though, unlike in Italy, there was no
thrilling prospect of brigand attack to be looked for, bumps and bruises
could certainly be anticipated and complaints about dismal conditions are
almost universal. Worst of all were the so-called 'corduroy roads' –
tracks made from logs laid side-by-side – which traversed the remoter
regions of forest and prairie. On her way to her Canadian settlement,
Traill travelled on one such road, seated on carpet-bags and trunks in a
box-like conveyance whose pegged sides kept jumping out; at one point
there was such a lurch that the driver was thrown out into the mud,
followed by parcels of flour and salt pork. Kemble suffered similar
discomfort in the south; and Bird, describing the same experience in the
mid-west, notes an additional disagreeable aspect of such a journey – the
constant jolting brings the passengers' faces unpleasingly close to one
another. Roads across the Alleghenies seem to have been equally bad: all
travellers here grumble about having their heads continually knocked

against the roof of the carriage and Vicky, Stuart-Wortley's twelve-year-old daughter, observes that only by stuffing cloaks and shawls under the seat and at the sides were they able to make themselves tolerably comfortable. Road travel in winter could be just as bad, even though the snow cushioned the worst of the ruts, and sleighs broke down less frequently than carriages. Jameson was tossed out of hers on the way to Niagara, and the return route on a narrow track across a frozen lake had its potential perils. Moodie describes ruefully how, in the same region, the sledge carrying their household goods to their new Canadian abode overturned on a fallen pine-tree, smashing all their crockery and china.

Even the most indefatigable voyagers could not always make light of their discomfort. Jameson, prepared for most exigencies once she had left Toronto, found travelling on awful roads in the Canadian interior not only utterly exhausting, but also depressing because of the endless forests:

> to be dragged along in a heavy cart through their impervious shades, tormented by mosquitoes, shut in on every side from the light and from the free air of heaven . . . was to bring down the tone of the mind and reflections to a gloomy, inert, vague resignation, or rather dejection.[20]

Only Martineau was wholly unperturbed by all the mishaps she encountered, retailing with evident relish how the carriage was constantly breaking down, forcing the passengers to walk (marching briskly on ahead, she watched with amusement the others struggling behind in the mud). In her *Retrospect of Western Travel*, she devotes several pages to a vividly dramatised sketch of a typical long road journey – the bumps and joltings, the drowsy passengers temporarily stirred by the prospect of supper, the frequent disembarkation when conditions got too rough and the attempt to snatch a couple of hours' sleep at a wayside inn in a draughty room with no sheets on the bed. But after all this, she concludes cheerfully, in the morning 'you wonder where your fatigue is gone. As the day steals through the forest, kindling up beauty as it goes, the traveller's whole being is refreshed' (I, p. 213).

Rail travel was the least novel mode of transportation for most of the tourists and generally gave less cause for complaint, though Trotter, before experiencing the luxury of crossing the Alleghenies in a private car loaned by the director of the railroad, observes with some distaste that because of the American system of unclassified accommodation the visitor had to share the carriage with people who at home would have travelled third-class. Dirt and over-heating – the latter particularly trying to the British tourist's mania for fresh air, since opened carriage windows were promptly closed – are also often remarked. On the whole the experience was enjoyable. Trotter notes admiringly that altogether she covered over 5,500 miles by rail, with only one late arrival and one breakdown. North, crossing from San Francisco to New York in 1881 via southern California, Arizona, New Mexico, Kansas City, St Louis, Washington and Philadelphia, is full of praise for the clean, comfortable Pullmans 'where I could have a good wash unhurried, and a good bed to rest my weary bones';[21] she was especially impressed by the fact that her ticket cost only £30 and was valid for twenty years.

Boat travel was a more notable undertaking. Some travellers found prolonged voyages up the Mississippi or on the Great Lakes very monotonous, but most were enthralled by the prospect of spending time in such 'a dream of enchantment . . . Aladdin's palace on fire',[22] 'an Eastern palace, a vision of the Arabian nights',[23] as they call the river steamers. This mode of transportation also had its dangers – Bird, for instance, experienced a severe storm on Lake Ontario, and tales of burst boilers and collisions are rife – but its main drawback as far as women travellers were concerned lay, ironically enough, in the arrangements made especially for them. Although Stuart-Wortley and Vicky enjoyed the luxury of a richly furnished ladies' cabin on the steamer carrying them to New Orleans, their experience was unusual. Martineau was so disgusted by one on a New York canal boat that she considered sitting up all night on deck in the rain instead. Others found conditions equally unpleasant. Sharing the cabin with uncongenial and over-numerous company could be disagreeable, especially for the fastidious, and the facilities often left much to be desired. Houston was horrified to discover that the ladies' washing-room on the famous 'Ben Franklin' contained only three basins, one towel and one communal comb; and the eternally enthusiastic Vicky notes laconically that on the daytime journey from Cincinnati to Louisville, 'we had found out that there was a multitude of cockroaches in our pretty cabin, which would have been very disagreeable at night'.[24] Even Kemble's usual sang-froid deserted her in this situation:

> what with the vibratory motion of the rocking-chairs and their contents, the women's shrill jabber, the children's shriller wailing and shouting, the heat and closeness of the air, a ladies' cabin on board an American steam-boat is one of the most overpowering things to sense and soul that can well be imagined.[25]

Sometimes the women found it easier to laugh than cry about such circumstances. On an occasion when Martineau and her companion were the only two ladies on a crowded boat from Detroit to Buffalo they had to share their cabin with a stout man, and she gleefully relates how they made a partition with a counterpane fastened by four forks. Finch chuckles about a similarly bizarre occurrence when she had to cross a makeshift gentleman's dormitory in order to reach the ladies' quarters which were concealed behind a red curtain.

Whatever the means of transportation, however, the most significant aspect of it was that in America a woman, even on her own, could travel in ease and safety, untroubled by apprehension of danger or unwelcome attentions, in a way that would have been quite impossible in Europe.[26] Jameson, making her solo journey into the Canadian interior, was escorted by a series of settlers whom she had never met before, and fearlessly enjoyed a meal in an isolated tavern in the company only of two backwoodsmen, who were 'rude but not uncivil' (*Winter Studies*, II, p. 137). She was also grateful for the tact of her all-male escorts on her canoe trip back to Toronto (on which she was the only woman out of twenty-two voyagers), who pitched her tent 'at a *respectful* distance from the rest' (III, p. 326) and helped her to find a secluded little creek where she could perform her morning toilette, though on this journey she did purportedly carry a small stiletto with her in case of need.[27] She, like North in California some thirty years later, was not troubled either by the fact that she could not lock her bedroom door at her overnight lodgings.

Most of the travellers note how freely and confidently ladies could go around in the United States. For Martineau, this was one of the real benefits of her visit:

> the national boast being a perfectly true one, – that a woman may travel alone from Maine to Georgia without dread of any kind of injury. For two ladies who feared nothing, there was certainly nothing to fear. We had to 'rough it' sometimes, as every body must in so new and thinly populated a country; but we always felt ourselves safe from ill usage of any kind. (*Autobiography*, II, pp. 85–6)

She was particularly immune from anxiety on this score, as is clear from her account of an adventure one night in a New Orleans hotel. On this occasion her companion whispered to her that there was a man without any shoes walking about in their bedroom; though owning to momentary fear, Martineau, protected by her deafness, resolutely went back to sleep, her coolness justified by their subsequent discovery that the intruder was a large wandering dog. On her canoe trip, Jameson was similarly relieved to find that her nocturnal would-be attacker was actually a cow which had got its nose stuck under the wall of her tent, while Bird, momentarily scared by nocturnal scuffling and breathing under the floor of her lonely Rocky Mountain cabin, was grateful that they emanated merely from an energetic skunk, harmless to her person if not to her senses. Bird's experiences in this isolated spot confirmed the assurances she received that it was quite safe for a lady alone in the 'uncivilised' West, and that even in a lumbering town she might be 'sure of respect'.[28] Though she carried a loaded revolver with her she never needed to use it, and she was quite confident about accepting the companionship of any man she met on her lonely rides through the Rockies. And however much of a desperado her 'Rocky Mountain Jim' was, as she stresses he always treated her with the greatest courtesy and consideration.

Kemble confirms such observations, noting that America was a much safer place than Italy with regard to

> the honour and security in which a woman might traverse alone from Georgia to Maine . . . certain of assistance, attention, the most respectful civility, the most human protection, from every man she meets, without the fear of injury or insult.[29]

Moreover, she adds, 'women can walk . . . with perfect safety, by themselves, either in New York, Philadelphia, or Boston'.[30] For Houston, an additional advantage was that there was nothing improper in unaccompanied ladies 'avail[ing] themselves of the escort of any polite stranger they may happen to meet with on the journey', and that having done this they 'will meet with nothing but respect and attention the whole way' (*Hesperos*, I, pp. 77, 185).

Rail travellers in particular found this to be the case. For many of them, the female freedom thus conferred highlighted the contrast between home and abroad, as Bird explains:

> We must be well aware that in many parts of England it would be difficult for a lady to travel unattended in a second-class, impossible in a third-class carriage; yet I travelled several thousand miles in America, frequently alone, from the house of one friend to another's, and never met with anything approaching to incivility. (*The Englishwoman*, p. 94)

North also experienced the special courtesy shown to women by railway staff and male passengers alike. While journeying alone from Niagara to Pontiac, Illinois, she had to board a very crowded train full of 'such a rough lot, – they could not have been rougher, – but they seemed to know I was a lady, and gave me a seat to myself and no annoyance' (*Recollections*, I, p. 60). She found the same true of the trains out west, where she once had to travel by freight train, a proceeding about which the local baker's wife was very dubious:

> If it was full they might be a rough lot, she said; women hardly ever went that way. However, I risked it, and was most comfortable, and hospitably treated in the one carriage, the guard's van. (I, p. 61)

It is not hard to understand how joyfully these women responded to the liberty which America represented to them in this respect.

One of the *desagréments* of American travel from which the female tourist was not safeguarded, however, was bad hotel and lodging-house accommodation, especially away from the main cities. Hotels such as the famous Astor House in New York or the Tremont in Boston usually more than adequately met the traveller's needs, but elsewhere it was a different story. All nineteenth-century visitors to the New World discovered something to complain of on this matter, but there were certain inadequacies especially trying for women. An important one was the general lack of privacy, especially in the larger hotels. Meals tended to be taken all together in one huge room, and as Stuart-Wortley – herself fortunately able to afford the luxury of dining in private – observes, it was very unpleasant for ladies to have to eat publicly in so immense and inhuman an environment. The immensity itself often bewildered them – Bird, staying in one such hotel, felt it was 'more like a human beehive than anything else' (*The Englishwoman*, p. 101) and North found the Palace Hotel, San Francisco, quite perplexing in its vastness. The dirt, inadequate toilet facilities and inedible food in such establishments were other sources of dissatisfaction to the women travellers but they were more prepared to laugh off shortcomings in these areas. Houston, for example, is ironic about 'the accumulated dust of years' (*Hesperos*, I, p. 38) in the room she was offered in a hotel in Newbury Port, Massachusetts and Bird can joke about an awful hotel in Chicago, in which her room was dark and cold, the bed was covered with a dirty buffalo-skin crawling with 'swarms of living creatures', several of the guests had fever, and dinner consisted of nearly raw boiled mutton, 'six antiquated fowls, whose legs were of the consistence of guitar-strings' and stewed tea, embellished by salt from a communal pot, served by 'brigand-looking waiters' (pp. 148–9). Wisely, she decided not to spend the night here but to catch the next available train out of town.

For much of the nineteenth century, to the visitor America meant New York, Boston, Philadelphia and New Orleans, in the same way as Italy meant Venice, Florence, Rome and Naples. But the parallel ends there, for a variety of reasons. The first is the nature of American cities at this time. Although urban growth proceeded at a phenomenal pace throughout the century, not until the later decades were there any sizeable centres of population beyond the eastern seaboard and the south. Outside these areas, too, there was little of cultural or historical interest to attract the European-oriented tourist, accustomed to apprehending a country through its buildings and artefacts, so visitors often had to readjust their expectations of the foreign here. Moreover, the large distances between the major cities meant that inevitably all travellers were exposed to the kind of landscape they would not come across at home, whether it was the swamps and rivers of the south, the extensive prairie lands of the midwest, or the huge lakes and forests of the northern territories, both American and Canadian. Encounter with the natural wilderness of a continent apparently hardly touched by 'civilisation' was thus an intrinsic

CITY OF HOUSTON IN THE 1840s
from Matilda Houston, *Texas and the Gulf of Mexico*, 2 vols (London, 1844)

element of their visits. The personal accessibility of this environment was more problematic than was the case in Europe. Not thoroughly pre-familiarised through aesthetic representation, it could bewilder observers since they had fewer referential 'givens' to guide their responses to it. While some of them welcomed the strangeness as part of the experience of difference to which they had looked forward in the New World, others, perhaps not fully prepared for what they were to find, shied away from it, seeking to demystify it and reduce the sense of alienation produced by the country's unrestrained and chaotic vastness.

Broadly speaking, the travellers can be divided into two groups here – those who essentially rejected or tried to familiarise the wilderness, and those who were drawn to its otherness. The first group, taking Europe as their standard, assessed it in terms relevant to their own culture or to their previous experiences of foreign landscape. Italy was a frequent touchstone of appreciation, especially with reference to America's brilliant blue skies and pure air. European places of 'known' beauty also provided reassuring analogies. Trollope, for instance, saw the noble mountain road through the Alleghenies as 'the Semplon of America' (p. 138) and many travellers fell in love with the Hudson river scenery in upper New York because it reminded them of the Rhine. More often, though, they sought to impose conventional literary or aesthetic images

NEW YORK CITY IN THE 1880s
from *Stanford's Compendium of Geography and Travel* ed. by Hayden and Selwyn
(London, 1883)

of beauty on the natural environment. Frequently they praise the landscape for being 'picturesque', 'romantic' or 'gothic', and the closer it approximated to the European ideal the more it pleased them. Trollope's initial distaste for the American environment as a whole was somewhat modified as the scenery on her northward progress away from the savage wilds of Wright's Nashoba settlement became increasingly 'picturesque'; with no sense of inappropriateness she puts the Ohio landscape in perspective:

> Often a mountain torrent comes pouring its silver tribute to the stream, and were there occasionally a ruined abbey, or feudal castle, to mix the romance of real life with that of nature, the Ohio would be perfect. (p. 23)

Her enthusiasm for the scenery north of New York similarly betrays its aesthetic origins – the 'magnificent confusion', 'unfathomed torrent' and 'darkening shadows cast over the abyss' combine to create the 'sublimity' of Trenton Falls (pp. 279–80). Houston similarly draws on cosily civilised terms to interpret the attractiveness of the Texan forest, with its trees 'so tastefully arranged by the hand of nature, that you could imagine yourself in a finely kept Engish park, where landscape gardeners and studiers of the picturesque had expended their utmost skill in beautifying the scenery' (*Texas*, II, p. 194).

Her observation points to another way of familiarising the natural environment – to look for signs of man's benevolent and practical intervention. For many of the women travellers, fear of the inaccessible could be diverted by focusing on cultivated nature, in harmony with humanity, not divorced or alien from it. Even Wright, used to the impenetrable and dreary southern swamps which so appalled Trollope, was pleased to see how the wilderness of upper New York had been transformed into a usefully beautiful paradise of lawns, fruit-laden orchards, grain-fields and houses. Traill and Moodie articulate a stronger and more deep-seated desire to domesticate the landscape. Since for them its strangeness represented not the pleasures of holiday exploration but potential permanence, they were especially anxious to find comforting comparisons with the homeland they might never see again. Traill immediately disparaged the absence of the picturesque in Canada: in both Quebec and Montreal not enough had been done with 'the romantic situation', and there were no enchanting roses and honeysuckle round cottage doors and windows. In the upper province, she happily observes, 'the scenery is more calculated to please, from the appearance of industry and fertility it displays', but her reactions grew gloomier nearer to their prospective habitation. The countryside around Coburg, where they settled initially, reminded her of Gloucestershire, but without 'the charm with which civilisation has so eminently adorned that fine country, with all its romantic villages, flourishing towns, [and] cultivated farms', while their immediate surroundings showed 'a want of picturesque beauty . . . that is so delightful in our parks and woodlands at home'.[31]

Her sister, who went to Canada at almost the same time, found it equally difficult to accept the alien character of the wilderness as she too travelled with her husband westward from Nova Scotia to settle first in Belleville, Ontario, then in the backwoods, where the Traills were already established. In her second book about her Canadian experiences, *Life in the Clearings*, Moodie expands on her initial conviction that there is nothing 'picturesque' about bush scenery with its endless forests punctuated only by ugly wooden fences. She looks longingly back to the Old World, deprecating the dreary uniformity of her present surroundings in which 'there are no green vistas to be seen; no grassy glades beneath the bosky oaks, in which deer browse', and no flowers to brighten 'the desolate wilderness'.[32] Her vocabulary, with its mixture of literary archaism and bleak literalism, reveals her unease before the vast reaches of raw nature in which she saw neither artistic beauty nor the controlling hand of man. A melancholy poem written at one of her lowest moments in the backwoods also reflects her antipathy, verging on panic:

Oh! land of waters, how my spirit tires,
In the dark prison of thy boundless woods;
No rural charm poetic thought inspires,
No music murmurs in thy mighty floods. . .

The swampy margin of thy inland seas,
The eternal forest girdling either shore,
Its belt of dark pines sighing in the breeze,
And rugged fields, with rude huts dotted o'er,
Show cultivation unimproved by art,
That sheds a barren chillness on the heart.[33]

Moodie came to accept some of the positive aspects of the wilderness, but her response on the whole remained sentimentally domestic. Tidy farmhouses and fruit-laden orchards continued to represent her ideal: Belleville, to which she and her husband returned after a disastrous spell in the bush, restored her with the pretty signs of civilisation, embodied in its 'smooth verdant plains . . . surrounded with neat cottages and gardens' (*Life in the Clearings*, p. 5); and en route to Niagara she was charmed by the gentle slopes, fine meadows and peach and apple orchards clustering round neat homesteads, in the English-looking landscape.

Such responses betray the women's fear of the alien in which the individual can find no comfortable place. As we have seen, many aspects of the North American wilderness threatened their sense of security. The huge and seemingly endless Mississippi could seem not only 'a most unpoetic and unromantic river',[34] but also a bewildering expanse of 'mud, and reeds, and floating logs, yellow fever, dampness and desolation'.[35] 'Not all the novelty of the scene, not all its vastness, could prevent its heavy horror wearying the spirits' (p. 15), complains Trollope, her choice of metaphor hinting at her sense of near-nightmare. She hated equally the 'unmeaning expanse' (p. 292) of Lake Erie; and the vast reaches of the Great Lakes similarly oppressed other travellers, unable to reduce the infinitude to graspable dimensions.

The primeval forest also awakened feelings of disorientation and terror. Traill and Moodie were frightened by its gloom and desolation, incapable of responding to the immensity of pines and rushing water with any sense of uplift. Trollope, too, found the endless trees both depressing and visually unpleasing, and though she makes light of an unfortunate brief expedition into the Cincinnati woods, during which the various mishaps included being bitten to pieces by mosquitoes and getting lost, her concluding resolve 'never to propose any more parties of pleasure in the grim stove-like forests of Ohio' (p. 69) reveals her deeper unease.

Others of the travellers were readier to embrace the challenge, psychological as well as physical, of the New World's uncompromising vastness. Not wishing their American tour to replicate European experience, they welcomed the difference from an ordered landscape which represented the regular pattern of their home lives. Kemble compares Italy and America in this respect; while admiring the 'human picturesqueness' of the Frascati region, which she was then visiting, she confesses that

> the *populousness* of this landscape is not agreeable to me. Absolute loneliness and the absence of every trace of human existence was such a striking feature of the American scenery that I am fond of . . . that the impossibility of getting out of sight of human presence or human habitation is sometimes irksome to me here.[36]

Many shared her view that man was destroying, not enhancing, the wilderness here and, like her, they valued the natural scene in proportion to its remoteness from America's ever-burgeoning 'progress'. As early as the 1760s Mrs Grant, a pioneering visitor, bemoaned that the Utopian beauty of Oswego, near Albany, was being threatened by the constant flow of greedy prospectors and land speculators. In the following century, when urban development had spread further, 'raw' nature was far more threatened by civilisation. In the late 1830s Jameson, admiring the still unspoilt view from Bear Hill, near St Thomas, Ontario, was apprehensive about its future – '[when] all this infinitude of animal and vegetable being has made way for restless, erring, suffering humanity – will it then be better?' (*Winter Studies*, II, pp. 172–3), she asks doubtfully. At about the same time, Kemble, soothing her deep misery about the slaves on her husband's Georgia plantation with the loveliness of the southern scenery, recognised that such an environment would not benefit from the intervention of 'the genius of man, and his perception of beauty'.[37]

Bird, making her first trip to America in the eager expectation of encountering its wilderness (a need for escape which increased as she grew older, and dominated her later travels), was only too anxious to get away from the evidence of human interference. For her the lonely beauty of forest scenery on Prince Edward Island made it a kind of 'fabulous Elysium' ('in enterprising England', she interjects sardonically, 'a town would have been built round it, and we should have had cheap excursions [to it]' [*The Englishwoman* p. 55]), while the attractiveness of both the primitive forest near Albany and the Hudson river scenery lay in the absence of any evidence of humankind. Nearly twenty years later, having returned to the United States as an explorer in the still relatively virgin West instead of as a conventional tourist, she got closer to fully realising her longings for the remote and unspoilt wilderness. On her way to her long-dreamt-of goal, Long's Peak in the Rocky Mountains, she writes home:

> The scenery up here is glorious, combining sublimity with beauty. . . . This
> is a view to which nothing needs to be added. This is truly the 'lodge in some
> vast wilderness' for which one often sighs when in the midst of 'a bustle at
> once sordid and trivial'. . . . This scenery satisfies my soul. (*A Lady's Life,*
> pp. 61–3)

Bird also voices what many of the travellers inherently recognised –
that empathy with America's natural spirit depended on rejection of
European preconceptions and values. For herself,

> An entire revolution had been effected in my way of looking at things since
> I landed on the shores of the New World. I had ceased to look for vestiges of
> the past, or for relics of ancient magnificence . . . and [had] become
> accustomed to a general absence of the picturesque. (*The Englishwoman,*
> p. 323)

Wright came to the same conclusion while in the 'truly sublime'
untainted natural world of the northern states:

> The lakes and rivers of this continent seem to despise all foreign auxiliaries
> of nature and art and trust to their own unassisted majesty to produce effect
> upon the eye and the mind; without alpine mountains or moss-grown ruins,
> they strike the spectator with awe. (p. 129)

As has already been suggested, the desire – so crucial to these women –
to reach the remote and to escape reminders of a constrained existence
could still be satisfied in nineteenth-century America. Many made
enterprising journeys into remoter territories. Grant and her mother,
travelling in the pre-Revolutionary period from Albany to Oswego in a
flat-bottomed boat, had the distinction of being probably the first women
'above the very lowest rank, who had ever penetrated so far into this
remote wilderness'. Relishing the exciting experience, the girl dreaded
its conclusion since, as she well knew, 'long tasks and close confine-
ment',[38] the lot of all well-brought-up young ladies, awaited her. In the
next century, similar pioneering was possible further afield. Jameson's
longing to 'take to myself wings and fly off to the west!' (*Winter Studies,* I,
p. 171), like Bird's impulse to go deeper and deeper into virgin territory,
is representative of the deep female urge for freedom (interestingly, the
phrase recalls Charlotte Brontë's 'wish for wings').[39] Jameson was almost
desperate to leave Toronto and start on her travels 'alone – alone – and on
my way to that ultimate somewhere of which I knew nothing, with
forests and plain, and successive seas intervening' (II, pp. 36–7). She saw
her solo trip into the interior of Ontario, planned in defiance of all
reported dangers, including 'white men more savage far' (II, p. 8) than
wild Indians, as a personal challenge in which she could vindicate her
own selfhood – 'I am just returned from the wildest and most extraordinary tour you can imagine, and am moreover the first Englishwoman

– the first European female who ever accomplished this journey',[40] she writes triumphantly on its completion. The venture climaxed in a bateau voyage to Sault Ste Marie ('the Ultima Thule' [*Winter Studies*, II, p. 34]) with the half-Indian Mrs MacMurray, wife of a local Anglican missionary, in which, apart from loving the primitive life-style, sleeping in the boat and eating camp-fire meals, Jameson enjoyed the first real peace she had experienced since coming to Canada, in an environment where isolation was not desolation:

> I cannot, I dare not, attempt to describe to you the strange sensation one has, thus thrown for a time beyond the bounds of civilised humanity, or indeed beyond any humanity; nor the wild yet solemn reveries which come over one in the midst of this wilderness of woods and waters. All was so solitary, so grand in its solitude, as if nature unviolated sufficed to herself. Two days and nights the solitude was unbroken; not a trace of social life, not a human being, not a canoe, not even a deserted wigwam, met our view. Our little boat held on its way over the placid lake and among green tufted islands; and we its inmates, two women, differing in clime, nation, complexion, strangers to each other but a few days ago, might have fancied ourselves alone in a new-born world. (III, p. 163)

On an extended return voyage, she again drank in the 'feeling of remoteness, of the profound solitude' (III, p. 320). Jameson's experience had such a profound effect upon her that back on land she could not adapt to normal existence – 'nine nights passed in the open air, or on rocks, and on boards, had spoiled me for the comforts of civilisation, and to sleep *on a bed* was impossible; I was smothered, I was suffocated, and altogether wretched and fevered; I sighed for my rock on Lake Huron' (III, p. 340). In the same way, Bird found it impossible to adapt to life back in the western towns after leaving the emptiness of the Rockies.

Such an experience offered the woman traveller a rare chance to enjoy pure 'being', as well as a means of self-testing. The environments which made the most dramatic impact in this respect were those of mountains and water, both emblematic of limitlessness and unrestrained power. Only Bird fully penetrated the former, but all either journeyed by water or encountered it scenically at some time during their travels. Interestingly, their responses are often similar to those of the tourists who were so bewitched by the watery beauty of Venice, seen from its canals, though in America their engagement was normally more passionate. Jameson was not alone in feeling that she had entered a new existence while being carried across the Canadian lakes. Kemble, drifting in a canoe through the swamps of Georgia, experienced 'a sort of dreamy stillness . . . creeping over the world and into my spirit',[41] and Moodie could momentarily forget her dislike of the Canadian outback in a canoe trip to a nearby lake. Martineau articulates more directly the symbolic

significance of such release from normality, perceiving the occasional
lonely canoeist on the Mississippi as representative of a spiritual existence
in which 'life would become tolerable . . . only by the spirit growing into
harmony with the scene, wild and solemn as the objects around it'
(*Retrospect*, II, p. 23).

The sense of new being, experienced here as a kind of transcendental
loss of personality, was felt more urgently in the encounter with water in
its more dramatic forms. The most notable instance of this, as we shall
see, is their reaction to Niagara, but elsewhere too the vigour of their
writing suggests a sense of identification with the elemental. Grant
suddenly breaks the even tenor of her narrative to describe with
breathless excitement the breaking up of the ice on the Hudson: 'the lofty
banks . . . were now entirely filled by an impetuous torrent, bearing
down, with incredible and tumultuous rage, immense shoals of ice; which
. . . falling together with an inconceivable crash, formed a terrible
moving picture, animated and various beyond conception' (p. 270). Even
the rational Martineau was moved almost to tears by the sight of the
waves of Lake Michigan, 'that enormous body of tumultuous waters',
breaking on the shore (*Society*, I, p. 175).

There is oblique self-identification in Jameson's representation of the
Sault rapids as a changeable woman:

> as they come fretting and fuming down, curling up their light foam, and
> wreathing their glancing billows round the opposing rocks, with a sort of
> passionate self-will, they remind me of an exquisitely beautiful woman in a
> fit of rage, or of Walter Scott's simile – 'one of the Graces possessed by a
> Fury'. (*Winter Studies*, III, pp. 172–3)

In a more direct way, she had already aligned herself with this volatile
energy when she daringly braved the rapids in a canoe propelled by a
dextrous Indian through a narrow, twisting two-foot wide channel
between the rocks; exhilarated by the potential danger, she reacted with
intense emotional and physical pleasure – 'I can truly say, I had not even a
momentary sensation of fear, but rather of giddy, breathless, delicious
excitement' (III, p. 199). Bird experienced the same thrill when the boat
taking her from Toronto to Montreal ran the rapids at Galouse and La
Chine, on the St Lawrence; the broken syntax and shifting tenses of her
recall reveal her almost uncontainable excitement as she re-enacts the
boat's progress:

> we dash straight down upon rocky islets, strewn with the wrecks of rafts
> . . . Still we go on – louder roars the flood – steeper appears the descent –
> earth, sky, and water seem mingled together . . . we reached the ledge – one
> narrow space free from rocks appeared – down with one plunge went the
> bow into a turmoil of foam – and we had 'shot the cataract' of La Chine.
> (*The Englishwoman*, p. 143)

NIAGARA FALLS AS PAINTED BY MARIANNE NORTH IN THE 1870s
from *A Vision of Eden* (Exeter, 1986)

Kemble's equally passionate response to a waterfall near Philadelphia reminds us of Morgan's intensely physical reaction to the Venus de 'Medici, though here there is an even stronger sense of unwilled loss of self:

> for a moment my breath seemed to stop, the pulsation of my heart to cease – I was filled with awe. The beauty and wild sublimity of what I beheld seemed almost to crush my faculties, – I felt dizzy as though my senses were drowning . . . I could have stretched out my arms, and shouted aloud – I could have fallen on my knees, and worshipped – I could have committed any extravagance that ecstasy could suggest. (*Journal*, I, p. 268)

The unashamed sexuality of her writing, expressing abandonment to an irrational force, reveals the power of inner feelings which she cannot directly articulate, and in this it prefigures her response to Niagara.

For early and mid-nineteenth-century visitors, Niagara itself represented the apotheosis of their encounters with 'uncivilised' America. Like Vesuvius, it exemplified all the supreme magnificence of untamed nature, mysterious, alluring and challenging, and indeed several of the women who had previously travelled in Italy connect the two sights in this regard. The young Victoria Stuart-Wortley comments that the raging water reminds her of the tumultuous eruption of the volcano which she had seen the previous year, while Kemble, more melodramatically,

NIAGARA IN THE 1880s
from *Stanford's Compendium of Geography and Travel* ed. by Hayden and Selwyn
(London, 1883)

claims that the whirlpool of Niagara is one of the only three places she
knows which have given her the impression 'of being accursed, and
empty of the presence of the God of nature', the other two being 'that
fiery, sulphurous, vile-smelling wound in the earth's bosom, the crater of
Vesuvius, and the upper part of the Mer de Glace at Chamouni'.[42] Even
by the early years of the century, Niagara was well-established in the
tourist's statutory list of 'sights': on her trip there in 1818, Wright
commented wryly that the spot had now become so popular and the road
there so good, that the visitor was hard-pressed to find a less-frequented
route which would preserve 'the awe with which this scene of grandeur is
approached' (p. 124); and sawmills, drug-stores and hotels were beginning to encroach on its environs, much to the disgust of many observers.
Nevertheless, it had lost none of its inherent fascination and was still
considered 'one of the wonders of the world'.[43]

Encounter with Niagara was both passionately desired and anticipated
apprehensively by the women travellers. Generally speaking, as has
already been indicated, America was not associated with the same
fulfilment of romantic aspiration and youthful dreams as was Italy, but
the Falls were an exception. Here, their imagination had already been
fired by earlier accounts, and expectation could merge with personal
desire. Trollope, finally on her way to Niagara after a disappointing two
years in the States, declares that it was 'the object, which for years, I had
languished to look upon' (p. 284), while for Jameson, pining unhappily in
Toronto, it was 'a thing to be imagined, hoped, and anticipated –
something to live for' (*Winter Studies*, I, p. 82). The accounts of the long-
awaited moment ring with excitement, and dramatically re-enact the
intensity of anticipation. Houston, having limited sightseeing in Albany
to one day because of her impatience to reach 'the wonder of the western
world' (*Hesperos*, I, p. 88), voices the feelings of many women travellers
on finally getting to Niagara:

> To obtain a sight of this mighty wonder had been, from my earliest years,
> one of the most eager, but, at the same time, the most hopeless longings of
> my mind! How nearly impossible, how vain and wild, had ever seemed to
> me the realization of that intense wish! (I, p. 122)

She was so worked up to 'a perfect fever of expectation' (I, p. 123) that
she almost dreaded the accomplishment of her desires; and her breathless
narration of her hasty progress from the station, through the Fall-side
hotel[44] to the water itself, without waiting for carriage or guide, climaxes
at the moment of actual encounter – 'and so, with a beating heart, I
approached Niagara. One sudden turn in the narrow path, and it was
before us! – before us in all its tumultuous grandeur and unequalled
magnificence!' (I, p. 124).

In her even more heightened account of the same eagerly anticipated moment, Kemble consciously exploits all the potential drama of the situation. She gives two versions of the event, one in her *Journal*, published in 1835, the other in her later *Record of a Girlhood* (1878), which itself draws on letters which she wrote at the time. In the former, she builds up the reader's suspense by depicting her own:

> My mind was eagerly dwelling on what we were going to see: that sight which [Trelawney] said was the only one in the world which had not disappointed him. I felt absolutely nervous with expectation . . . [when I heard] the voice of the mighty cataract . . . [a] frenzy of impatience seized upon me; I could have set off and run the whole way.

Kemble's prose almost stumbles over itself with its own fervour, and she carries us along with her frantic momentum as she describes how, without staying for anyone else, she leapt out of the carriage, rushed through the hotel hall and garden, down a steep and narrow rocky footpath and sprang on to the Table Rock where finally, at the brink of the abyss, 'I saw Niagara – oh God! who can describe that sight?'[45] At this point, with a deliberately tantalising (and literal) cliff-hanger, she breaks off and the *Journal* ends. In the *Record of a Girlhood*, however, Kemble allows us to share her vision, as she follows up her prologue (which up to this point in the later work is an almost word-for-word repetition of the earlier version) with an extended and powerful depiction of the Falls themselves which, as we shall see, conveys all the passion of her response.

Confrontation with Niagara symbolised a process of self-discovery for many of these women, both bodily and psychically. Though less physically challenging than Vesuvius, the Falls could provide excitement and a sense of risk for the adventurous lady tourist not content with merely viewing them from the safety of the American or Canadian bank. Walking under the rapids themselves, for example, was a thrilling and potentially dangerous undertaking. The more intrepid women, forewarned by stories of visitors swept to their deaths after one false step on the slippery path, were at once frightened and allured by the expedition. For Finch, at Niagara in the 1850s, going behind the Horseshoe Fall was 'unspeakably fearful'.[46] Tightly clinging to the wet rock, she was conscious of a new personality being drawn out of her – 'Half drowned and deafened, I emerged with a deeper feeling of awe than I ever experienced before' (p. 367). Houston, making the same trip a few years earlier, nervously negotiating the slippery ledge with the tottering Table Rock suspended over her head, was also caught up in the 'wild magnificence' (*Hesperos*, I, pp. 126–7) despite her fear.

The feeling of risk presented an almost attractive challenge. For

Wright, damp and breathless after her descent down a shaky and slippery ladder in order to get a closer look at the Falls, the sense of achievement, as well as the magnificence itself, more than compensated for the physical discomfort; even the apprehension that the Table Rock might fall on her made her only the more appreciative of how here 'the sublime is wrought to the terrible' (p. 127). Jameson's prophecies of the therapeutic effects of the Falls were self-fulfilling. Initially disappointed with the spectacle, she found that the physical rigours awakened her torpid spirits. Making her first visit to Niagara in the depths of a Canadian winter, she resolutely equipped herself with crampons and strode through the ice and snow to the Table Rock, the very effort totally converting her disillusion to awe at the 'wild and wonderful magnificence . . . [of] the dark-green waters, hurrying with them over the edge of the precipice enormous blocks of ice' (*Winter Studies*, I, p. 89). Martineau experienced the same thrill from going behind the falling water in June 1836. Garbed in the 'extraordinary . . . mountaineer sort of costume' (*Retrospect*, I, p. 103) in which the adventure had to be undertaken, she quickly found the best way to cope with the wind and spray ('It was to hold down the brim of my hat, so as to protect my eyes from the dashing water, and to keep my mouth shut' [I, p. 104], and started off intrepidly along the wet ledge, which at that time had no rope to assist the creeping pilgrims. Determined to touch Termination Rock – the goal for all who attempted this route – she ignored the signal from the guide to turn back, confident in her own abilities:

> it was no time and place to be stopped by anything but impossibilities . . . I made the guide press himself back against the rock, and crossed between him and the caldron, and easily gained my object. (I, p. 104)

Interestingly, as she herself admits, it was the very harshness of the conditions which drove her on – 'If all had been dry and quiet, I might probably have thought this path above the boiling basin dangerous, and have trembled to pass it; but amid the hubbub of gusts and floods, it appeared so firm a footing that I had no fear of slipping into the caldron' (I, p. 104). As with the others, the physical challenge inspired a new consciousness of physical and spiritual potential.

The travellers' re-creation of their experience of Niagara reveals the ambivalence of their response. On the one hand, it is noticeable that in almost every case the visit to Niagara produces some of the most highly charged writing in their texts. When dealing with Niagara even the most dispassionate or fact-oriented commentators substitute for a 'male' register of analytical reportage a more instinctively emotional – and arguably 'feminine' – mode of expression. Thus though Wright focuses largely on the social and political aspects of the New World and on the whole ignores the natural environment, at Niagara her writing changes dramatically as she images 'the dazzling white of the shivered water' (p. 125) and the heavy columns of the falls 'like fixed pillars of moving emerald' (p. 126) which have so stirred her. Similarly, in Martineau's two works on the States, there is a notable change of style as she moves from discussion of American social, industrial, and political life, to a rendering of the Falls' powerful effect on her:

> While I stood in the wet whirlwind, with the crystal roof above me, the thundering floor beneath, and the foaming whirlpool and rushing flood before me, I saw those quiet studious hours of the future world when this cataract shall have become a tradition, and the spot on which I stood shall be the centre of a wide sea, a new region of life. (*Society* I, p. 108)

Such writing indicates deep emotional engagement with the scenic magnificence. On the other hand, however, Niagara could create in the observer a fear of disorientation, and some commentators found it hard to come to terms with its potent and often traumatic influence. Many responded initially with bewilderment or confusion; and their written representations reflect not only Kemble's recognition that it was nonsense to write about it 'because it is quite unspeakable . . . words cannot describe it nor can any imagination, I think, suggest even an approximate idea of its terrible loveliness',[47] but also their inability to comprehend fully their own reactions. Thus they enact various literary strategies in an attempt to familiarise it and defuse some of its disturbing power.

Several of the writers seek to reduce their experience to manageable proportions by retailing facts about the Falls, such as its dimensions and the history of exploration there, a mechanism which relies on the validation of orthodox authorities and obviates the personal. Other travellers adopt the protective – and, as Houston wryly points out, currently fashionable – pose of disappointment, though most go on to admit that the fulfilment of expectation here was gradual and cumulative, not instantaneous. Jameson, for instance, counters her initial and somewhat calculatedly self-dramatising disenchantment – 'the reality has displaced from my mind an illusion far more magnificent than itself – I have no words for my utter disappointment' (*Winter Studies*, I, p. 82) – with a confession of subsequent enthusiasm. Trollope's attempt to deal with this potentially unsettling encounter is particularly interesting. During her unsatisfactory two years in America she had found little to admire, and at Niagara, despite her declared excitement of anticipation, she resisted instinctive openness to one of the country's marvels. So although she purports to be initially overwhelmed with wonder, terror, and delight, she spends no time in detailing these emotions but quickly backs off into a securely rational conclusion:

> I dare not dwell on this, it is a dangerous subject, and any attempt to
> describe the sensations produced just lead direct to nonsense. (p. 285)

Significantly, the remark itself indicates both her subconscious fear of
Niagara's power and her need to dismiss the implications of that fear.

Another method of familiarising the disturbing or inexpressible is to
implement conventional literary phraseology. Thus Niagara is variously
described in terms of its 'sublimity', 'awful beauty', 'terrible majesty' and
'manifold perfections and glories'; the Falls themselves are 'stupendously
magnificent' and 'fearfully beautiful', and their 'silvery torrents' make
'fantastic wreaths'. Fantasy takes over, too: drops of water become
'silvery stars or beams of light', the rapids resemble 'snowy robes and
feathery wreaths',[48] and the falling cataract is like the walls of a fairy
palace. Even the pious apprehension of it in terms of a great and
unfathomable sacred mystery or emblem of God's power ('one glorious
natural temple', a 'shrine' awaiting 'worshippers')[49] utilises a referential
system which formalises and objectifies the individual response.

The individual's voice is never wholly negated by such strategies,
however. The sight of Niagara awakened in all the women suppressed or
dormant emotions which, albeit obliquely or unconsciously, they were
impelled to articulate. In depicting the water's violence, for example – to
them symbolic of free and boundless energy – they draw on physical,
often sexual, imagery, to express their own desire for personal release.
The impulse to identify with the scene before them often involved
discovery of a new psychic self. Finch expresses an almost desperate
desire to precipitate herself into the turmoil – 'anything to *know* it – to *feel*
its power' (p. 365) – and to become 'inseparably united' (p. 368) with it.
Her passionate response is imaged in her depiction of the Whirlpool, its
tortured waters trying to 'escape from their narrow prison-house' (p.
369) as a tormented creature, an apt embodiment of her own frustrated
longings and desire for freedom. Stuart-Wortley, attracted, disturbed,
and excited by the tumult of a thunderstorm over the Falls, expresses
more directly her feeling of being taken over by 'this surpassing and
astounding marvel of creation' (I, p. 25):

> the great cataract goes sounding through all one's soul, and heart, and mind,
> commingling with all one's ideas and impressions, and uniting itself with all
> one's innermost feelings and fancies. (I, p. 26)

Bird, too, in describing the tortured violence of the rapids, enacts her
passionate identification with the scene before her:

> The turbulent waters are flung upwards, as if infuriated against the sky. The
> rocks, whose jagged points are seen among them, fling off the hurried and

foamy waves, as if with supernatural strength. Nearer and nearer they come
to the Fall, becoming every instant more agitated; they seem to recoil as
they approach its verge; a momentary calm follows, and then, like all their
predecessors, they go down in the abyss together. (pp. 223–4)

Characteristically, Jameson and Kemble most passionately identify
with the natural environment here. Drawing on images of freedom and
sexuality, they express their own sense of released energy, inspired by the
almost mesmeric effect of Niagara upon them. Jameson, shaken out of her
lethargy by closer encounter with the rushing waters, was irresistibly
drawn to them in a fascinated submission which was both exciting and
disturbing. On her second visit in the summer of 1837 she was even more
aroused, as her description indicates:

the ocean lashed into breakers . . . the foliage and the foam of the leaping
waves mingled together and the splendour of colour and light over the
whole, render it one of the most wonderful scenes I ever beheld.[50]

Recalling her solitary vigil at Table Rock in the moonlight, she images
'those wild, impatient, tumultuous rapids' (*Winter Studies*, II, p. 67) as a
terrible creature, a tiger at play, which hypnotises her into a volitionless
state yet also arouses in her intensely physical feeling. It is not hard to
recognise the personal implications of her response in the context of her
recent awareness that her marriage was beyond redemption: the waters,
'whirling, boiling, dancing, sparkling along . . . rejoicing as if escaped
from bondage' (II, pp. 52–3), become an image of her own new freedom
and energies, now harnessed to a bold venture into the wilds of Canada;
Niagara, 'girdle[d]' with greenery and 'breathing perfume' (II, p. 38),
enclosing 'that furious embrace of the waters above and the waters
below' (I, p. 86), symbolises sexual fulfilment which for her has now been
sublimated into physical daring and self-discovery.

The physicality of Kemble's response is equally striking. Made 'half-
crazy' just by the recall of Niagara's 'terrible loveliness',[51] she describes
herself as almost literally carried away by the encounter, her breathing
constrained as if by an iron band across her chest. She too depicts the
water's turbulent progress in powerful metaphors of a creature struggling
for release:

I watched the green, glassy, swollen heaps go plunging down, down, down;
each mountainous mass of water, as it reached the dreadful brink, recoiling,
as in horror, from the abyss; and after rearing backwards in helpless terror,
as it were, hurling itself down to be shattered in the inevitable doom over
which eternal clouds of foam and spray spread an impenetrable curtain. (III,
p. 310)

Overtly sexual, this passage throbs with orgasmic life and enacts
Kemble's desire for the paradoxical release of sensual self-annihilation.

On another occasion, she emphasises the insidious and female allure of the cascade with 'its dazzling brightness, its soothing voice, its gliding motion, its soft, thick, furry beds of foam, its veils and draperies of floating light, and gleaming, wavering diadems of vivid colours' (III, p. 312), images suggestive both of her sexual desire and of her own potential as a seducer. Of all the travellers, Kemble's writing shows most clearly her ready abandonment to the inner turmoil which Niagara aroused in her; her reactions are at the same time indicative of a more general response to a phenomenon which was no mere tourist 'sight' to these women.

The natural wilderness was not the only aspect of 'foreignness' which the New World offered the traveller. The strange or alien was also embodied in the American Indian and the negro. Both represented 'difference', but the former more strikingly signified the exotic and curious, an indigenous but non-European race which seemed to belong to a pre-civilised age. Visits to Indian settlements and encampments were considered an essential feature of the North American tour, especially for those who penetrated beyond the eastern seaboard both westwards and into Canada, though Indians could be viewed throughout most of the continent. Yet in some ways the encounter could prove unsatisfying, certainly in human terms. By the nineteenth century the Indian, driven from his own lands by a rapacious and unscrupulous government, had become mythologised as the Vanishing American, a glamorous but anachronistic figure who was regarded more as a museum piece or a show-ground spectacle than a real human being. (Such was often literally the case: Kemble was deeply pained when she went to see 'the savages' on display in New York, set up like wild animals for people to stare at.[52]) At the same time, many of the travellers interpreted the alien here as both a symbol of a freer, less tramelled existence than theirs and a challenge to their own accepted social values.

All to some extent felt indignant sympathy towards the Indians because of the way the American government had treated them. Trollope, visiting the bureau for Indian affairs in Washington at a time when the President had finally enforced a measure for chasing several remaining Indian tribes from their homelands, regarded such treachery as indicative of the hypocrisy of the whole nation – 'You will see them in one hour lecturing their mob on the indefeasible rights of man, and the next driving from their homes the children of the soil, whom they have bound themselves to protect by the most solemn treaties' (p. 159), she declares hotly. A quarter of a century later, Bird deplored the same outrage:

Year, as it succeeds year, sees them [the Indians] driven farther west, as their hunting grounds are absorbed by the insatiate white races . . . the waters of the lakes over which the red man paddled in his bark canoe are now ploughed by crowded steamers. Where the bark dwellings of his fathers stood, the locomotive darts away on its iron road, and the helpless Indian looks on aghast at the power and resources of the pale-faced invaders of his soil. (*The Englishwoman*, p. 289)

Most of the travellers also recognised that the white man was responsible for corrupting and degrading the Indians by introducing them to spirit-drinking and creating in them the desire for material possessions, thus destroying an organic life-style without replacing it with anything of equal worth.

Inherent here is an ambivalent attitude towards civilisation. To see the Indian as the noble savage, the embodiment of 'what a noble animal man is while unsophisticated' (Grant, p. 50), was to idealise the (supposedly) wholly natural. Houston, travelling in New England in mid-century, regretted the modern farming which had wiped out a more colourful way of life, so that 'in lieu of the *picturesque* idleness of the half-clad savage there is cultivated ugliness everywhere' (*Hesperos*, I, p. 47); she praises the fine eyes, magnificent figures and free and dignified walk of some Indian women she has seen, because they satisfy her taste for 'wild specimens of human nature' (I, p. 140), whereas she summarily dismisses the Tuscorara squaws selling bead-work at Niagara because they fall short of this conception – 'Their dress is very picturesque, but as they speak tolerable English, and are by no means wild or savage looking, I take very little interest in them or their wares' (I, p. 129).

Although such idealisation may be a sign of genuine feeling for the primitive, it hardly 'sees' it, and actually establishes a distance from it. Most of the women, in fact, while recognising how 'progress' was destroying the Indian, believed in the superiority of their own society and reveal this in their writing, albeit often obliquely. Wright is unusual in openly admitting her preference for a more sophisticated way of life. Despite her admiration for the pictorial qualities of the Indians, she considered that in their native condition they were savages holding 'a lower place in creation than men who, to the proud spirit of independence, unite the softer feelings that spring only within the pale of civilized life' (p. 106); for her, the triumph of white over red equalled that of peace over violence. Her Utopian vision of a new America of democratic brotherhood rejected the purely wild: 'how singular, and, for the well-being of man, how glorious the change, which has turned these vast haunts of panthers, wolves, and savages, into the abode of industry and the sure asylum of the oppressed' (p. 135), she exclaims enthusiastically. For Trollope also, 'modernisation' of the Indians was no bad thing: their expulsion from their native lands was especially lamentable because by 'becoming agriculturists' (p. 160), they had begun to show willingness to adapt to the dominant nation's social patterns.

INDIAN WOMAN

from Abbé Dommenech, *Seven Years' Residence in the Great Deserts of North America*

The closer the approximation to Western values, the more attractive the Indians could seem. Finch expresses admiration for a young Indian girl in a camp near Saratoga Springs for her natural refinement and graceful and dignified walk; there is no question of the untamed primitive here. Traill found the same virtues to commend in the Indians with whom she came into contact. She emphasises their amiability, gentleness and simple piety, deciding that the influence of civilisation here has improved on the natural state. She also vindicates the triumph of Christianity over barbarism:

> Certainly in no instance does the Christian religion appear more lovely than when . . . it is displayed in the conduct of the reclaimed Indian, breaking down the strongholds of idolatry and natural evil, and bringing forth the fruits of holiness and morality. (pp. 127–8)

As one who visited Indians in both their winter and summer camps, Traill came to know them better than did many of the travellers and she shows a genuine appreciation of their qualities as human beings, writing carefully and sympathetically about a transient way of life which she found fascinating. But she could not move beyond her own inherited value systems in assessing these qualities; even feminine beauty was subjected to them, as is shown by her description of a young squaw:

> [her] features were positively fine, and though of gipsy darkness, the tint of vermilion on her cheek and lip rendered it, if not beautiful, very attractive. Her hair, which was of jetty blackness, was soft and shining, and was neatly folded over her forehead, not hanging loose and disorderly in shaggy masses, as is generally the case with squaws . . . the black cloth mantle . . . was gracefully wrapped over one shoulder. (p. 160)

The more disturbing elements of primitive femaleness – gipsy blackness, unruly hair, disordered garments – are demystified here, and the girl is safely converted into an image of cultivated refinement.

Many of the travellers, uneasy about this juxtaposition of primitive and progressive, deal less confidently with the 'otherness'. As we shall see with the negro and Eastern races, vindication of the civilised often concealed a deep fear of the barbaric which, like the natural wilderness, threatened the stability of the known. Some observers attempted to maintain a reassuring sense of superiority by stressing the violence and crudity of the primitive. Martineau was both fascinated and horrified by the hatred and evil acted out in indigenous Indian dances, and compares them to the devils' ballet in *Faust*. Duncan deliberately foregrounds the distasteful appearance of an Indian woman near Buffalo:

> Her long yellow teeth, standing like stakes in an ill-fitted up fence, made one think of dried heads of New Zealanders, and other unpleasant specimens

of the human form in savage life, that we have seen in the museums of the civilised.[53]

Bird, showing her customary curious fascination with physical grotesqueness, also implicitly upholds Western standards in her uncompromising depiction of a set of Indians in California ('perfect savages . . . altogether the most degraded of the ill-fated tribes' [*A Lady's Life*, p. 4]):

> They were all very diminutive . . . with flat noses, wide mouths, and black hair, cut straight above the eyes and hanging lank and long at the back and sides. . . . They were all hideous and filthy, and swarming with vermin. (pp. 4–5)

However much it is supposedly dictated by the canons of realism, the description is also controlled by personal prejudice, Bird's disgust clearly revealing her sense of alienation from such sub-species of humanity.

Distance from the strange unknown could also be established by presenting it as an oddity, amusing and hence unthreatening. Houston, for example, portrays 'a fat and unwieldy child' in a papoose in such terms:

> One little red thing amuses me exceedingly . . . its legs being tightly swathed together in red cloth, so that it has all the appearance of a gigantic carrot, with something slightly resembling a human head on the thick end of it. The only part of its person over which it appears to have any control, is its eyes; and those it rolls about in such a comical manner, that I can never look at the little animal without laughing. (I, p. 129)

Hall, watching an Indian 'ball play' near Montgomery, Alabama – a 'sight' she and her husband were determined not to miss – similarly reduces the Indians to curios as she describes them 'throwing themselves into all sorts of fantastic attitudes, like nothing I ever saw except in the plates of Captain Cook's Voyages, and with no more dress on'.[54] Even where there is more sympathy, there may still be some objectification. Moved by the sight of a group of poor overburdened squaws, Stuart-Wortley yet cannot resist pointing to its inherent absurdity – 'They looked bent all manners of ways, and old – no wonder – something like a party of nomadic nutcrackers or itinerant notes of interrogation' (I, p. 247).

Despite these distancing strategies, a female voice of sympathetic identification can be detected in many of the texts. Perhaps unconsciously aligning themselves with an oppressed people, several of the travellers came close to 'seeing' the Indians as real human beings, especially the women, and depict them as such. Grant movingly recalls her youthful memories of the occasion when settlers' children, taken away by the Mohawk Indians, were restored to their rightful parents at the conclusion of peace; she puts herself in the place of the grieving Indian mothers, forced to give up their cherished adopted offspring: 'It was affecting to see the deep and silent sorrow of the Indian women, and of the children, who knew no other mother, and clung fondly to their bosoms, from whence they were not torn without the most piercing shrieks' (p. 231). Wright, too, reflecting on the plight of this race, driven from their homelands and transplanted into a strange culture, finds a parallel in her own feelings of personal disorientation in childhood when, as an orphan, she was brought up in an uncongenial environment:

> I know not if the circumstances of my own early life have tended to make my sympathize peculiarly with such a situation, but the position of the Indian youth, as an alien and an orphan, among his American guardians and playmates, strikes me as singularly affecting. (p. 112)

Perhaps the most sympathetic commentator on American Indian life is Jameson. One of the reasons for her trip into the Canadian outback in the summer of 1837 was to see Indians in their own environment and especially to find out about the position of their women. Before her greater intimacy with Indian society, she could see them only as 'figures', 'a crowd of faces, dusky, painted, wild, grotesque – with flashing eyes and white teeth' (III, p. 42); like other observers, too, she distances herself through ironic representation, as in her portrait of some Pottawattomie warriors:

> [Their] dandyism is inexpressibly amusing and grotesque; I defy all Regent Street and Bond Street to go beyond them in the exhibition of self-decoration and self-complacency. One of these exquisites, whom I distinguished as Beau Brummel, was not indeed much indebted to a tailor, seeing he had neither coat nor anything else that gentlemen are accustomed to wear . . . It is impossible to describe the air of perfect self-complacency with which this youth strutted about. (III, pp. 43–4)

Unlike the others, though, she was not resistant to the excitement which these strangely alien and possibly hostile people aroused in her – an excitement which she specifically links with her reaction to the wild American landscape:

> [I experience] a sort of thrill which enhances the enjoyment I have in these wild scenes – a thrill such as one feels in the presence of danger when most safe from it – such as I felt when bending over the rapids of Niagara. (III, p. 57)

During her trip, Jameson became more intimately acquainted with Indian women than did any of the other tourists. She met and stayed with two half-native sisters, one married to the American Indian agent at Mackinaw, the other to an Anglican missionary, and she also visited their pure-blooded mother. As she grew to know them, while still revering them as symbols of the perfect Natural Woman, released from the restraints and conventions she herself found so irksome, she also learnt to appreciate them as fellow beings. Importantly, too, she came to the

NORTH AMERICA: A NEW WORLD

conclusion that the Indian culture was in many ways superior to the white man's, in particular its attitudes towards the female sex. Describing the Indian marriage ceremony, for instance, she notes the less binding promises, for her an admirable alternative to the system which had trapped her in uncongenial matrimony. She also greatly respected the self-sufficiency of Indian women, especially symbolised by one who had refused to marry and who lived alone and independent in a self-built wigwam. For her, this inner toughness was essential to 'the true importance and real dignity of woman', in contrast with the degradation of being 'idle and useless by privilege of sex, a divinity or an idol, a victim or a toy' (III, p. 312). Her personal circumstances are clearly in part responsible for her observations here and her feminist predilections have preconceptually shaped her responses to a society which she saw as antithetical to, but in some ways more desirable than, her own. But her foreign experience also enlarged her vision of free womanhood, the possibilities thus suggested perhaps helping to console her for her own dissatisfaction.

The women travellers' attitude towards the negroes in the United States was rather more complex than that towards the Indians. Like Indians, negroes represented the alien or 'other', but of a different kind. Lacking a surrounding aura of the exotic or fantastic, they could not be mythologised as the noble primitive; they were part of American society and culture as the Indians were not; and as a people they hardly seemed strange since almost all of the tourists would have seen blacks before. More importantly these women, most of whom went to America before or during the Civil War, took with them pre-conceived notions about the institution of slavery. Bills abolishing the slave trade and making traffic in slaves a felony punishable with transportation were passed in England in the early years of the century, but since this abolition did not lead either to the diminution of the European slave trade or to improved treatment of negroes in the West Indies, anti-slavery campaigns continued in the 1820s and 1830s, championed by Wilberforce and the societies instigated under his influence. Hostility towards the nefarious system was thus inherent in nineteenth-century British social and political thought, and no prospective New World visitor could remain untouched by this. In addition, most would also have felt the impact of one of the most popular books of the time, Harriet Beecher Stowe's *Uncle Tom's Cabin* (1852), with its devastating attack on Southern slavery. Their pre-conceptions variously affected their responses. Not only did what they were actually seeing often blur into what they expected to see, but they had to weigh established arguments about moral culpability *vis-à-vis* supposed economic advantages against personally encountered facts.

Many of the travellers started as, or rapidly became, active supporters

of emancipation programmes. Wright's visionary egalitarianism took her
to the New World in the conviction that slavery was a 'foul blot' (p. 39)
on the country and a fatal barrier to democracy; at first secretly reluctant
to visit the South and see slavery in operation – 'to inhale the impure
breath of its pestilence in the free winds of America is odious beyond all
that imagination can conceive' (p. 267), she declares – she soon
afterwards became an eager pioneering worker for the blacks. Martineau, as a known abolitionist, having already published an anti-slavery
number, 'Demerara', in her series *Illustrations of Political Economy* (1832),
was a 'marked' tourist from the beginning (she was somewhat taken
aback to find that information about her had circulated around the
Americans on board even before landing in the United States). Several of
her American friends in fact advised her against going into the South on
the grounds that she might be in personal danger, but she steadfastly
maintained her determination to see for herself, assured that, since her
principles were common knowledge, at least she could not be regarded as
a spy. In November 1835, she attended an important Abolitionist Meeting
in Boston called by the ladies of the Anti-Slavery Society and, when
requested, delivered a public word of sympathy though, as she had
anticipated, she was subsequently attacked for openly expressing her
views. Other committed abolitionists who deeply regretted America's
'dark shade mingling among its stars and stripes' (Duncan, p. 200) include
Duncan and Bodichon, both visitors in the 1850s; the latter's concern for
the ending of slavery and the rehabilitation of the blacks went hand-in-
hand with her enthusiastic support for women's liberation movements.

As with the Indians, it was often hard for the women to come to terms
with the feelings of alienation or fear produced in them by the negroes.
Those who did not directly encounter the operation of slavery in the
Southern states were most likely to resort to stereotypical representation
as a means of demystifying their unease, a familiar strategy of colonial
discourse. Their depictions, without being as distastefully crude as
popular post-Darwinian cartoons of negroes as apes, frequently reify the
blacks, imaging them as objects which have little or no connection with
the human race. Hall was overtly antipathetic: she considered them
intrusions which disfigured the landscape and smelt obnoxious in hot
weather; the 'nasty black boys' (p. 168) who served her at parties made
her not only irritated but also slightly panicky, as her comments indicate:

> You can't imagine how disagreeable it is to have so many of these creatures
> going about. They are so stupid and so indolent, always in the way when not
> wanted. . . . They are like a species of constant waking nightmare to me.
> (p. 217)

Trotter was similarly repelled by the physical aspects of negritude. She

NORTH AMERICA: A NEW WORLD

recoiled from the sight of the negro waiter's black thumb on her plate at dinner and found the 'real life "Topsy" slave' whom she encountered in Washington 'almost lovable looking' (pp. 114–15) only because the girl had not yet developed the negro cast of countenance; 'the elders', Trotter adds bluntly, 'are hideous to behold, and are only to be tolerated in point of looks, when they wear coloured turbans' (p. 115). Mediating her hostility by converting it into moral propaganda – the blacks' love of sartorial display teaches a salutary 'severe lesson on female vanity' (p. 19) – Trotter here places herself in a position of detached superiority. Maury also resists identification with her own sex in calling attention to the bizarre costumes of New York black women:

> Dress is the prevailing taste of these people, and you often see the most grotesque mixtures . . . a particularly smartly dressed female in Broadway, attired for instance in a white muslin gown, coloured boots, a zephyr scarf, and a bonnet of rose coloured or azure satin. (p. 179)

Even the more inherently sympathetic Kemble reduces the negro women whom she first encountered in New York to 'caricatures'. 'The contrast of a bright blue, or pink crape bonnet, with the black face, white teeth, and glaring blue whites of the eyes, is beyond description grotesque',[55] she mocks, though she was soon to take a very different attitude to the oppressed race.

More overtly humorous representations can indicate equally the desire to impose object status on the observed. Martineau's lively portrayal of the servants at a wayside hotel, for instance, with its use of the present tense and its detached, satirical viewpoint, 'fixes' them in a kind of tableau:

> Little impish blacks peep and grin from behind the stove or shine in the heat of the chimney corner. If any one of them has ever received a compliment on his dexterity, he serves with a most ostentatious bustle, his eyes wide open, his row of white teeth all in sight. . . . An observer may see some fun going on behind the mistress's back; a whisk of a carving knife across a companion's throat; or a flourish of two plates like cymbals over the head. (*Retrospect*, I, pp. 211–12)

Houston dehumanises the black children on a Louisiana plantation as 'irresistibly comic . . . odd little animals' (*Hesperos*, II, p. 157), and Stuart-Wortley types one of these 'little darkies' in the same way – 'it was as black as a little image carved in polished ebony, and as plump as a partridge (in mourning)' (I, p. 219).

Sometimes guilt intervenes to undermine the reductive effect of such discourse. Trotter, for example, having drawn all the comic potential from her visit to a negro chapel in Washington by describing the manic preacher, the hysterical negress who finally collapses in a gibbering fit

NEW ORLEANS BLACK DANDY.

NANCY.

NEGRO CARICATURES

from Matilda Houston, *Texas and the Gulf of Mexico*, 2 vols (London, 1844)

and the extraordinary confessions of an enormous converted sinner who
looks like a London butler, hastily explains that she has not burlesqued the
events in a pure spirit of mockery:

> [Though] I have felt it scarcely possible to describe the scene without a
> certain mixture of the ludicrous, no feeling of irreverence crossed my mind
> at the time. On the contrary, my sympathies were greatly drawn out
> towards these our poor fellow-creatures . . . assembled to enjoy these
> higher blessings. (pp. 129–30)

Trotter's apology indirectly voices a general awareness among these
travellers that women had a special responsibility to respond sympathetically and humanely to an oppressed race. Wright attacks a common
European reaction to the negroes – 'It was with surprise, that I heard this
illiberal disgust expressed, by word and gesture, with peculiar
vehemence, by foreign *women*, and these often *ladies*' (p. 41). Martineau
and Kemble were also appalled by the blunting of the moral sense in
Southern women, who could apparently live contentedly in an environment where they were constant witnesses of brutality and glaring
injustice, Kemble's dismay heightened by her own experiences. Duncan,
too, planning to attend the anniversary meeting of a colonisation society,
was distressed to discover that 'it was so little an object of favour in my
circle, that I could not find a lady inclined to accompany me' (p. 235).

Attempts to implement this recognised need for sympathy, whether
instinctive or conceived as a moral obligation, coexist with the objectify-
ing narrative strategies. Bodichon warms with compassion what would
otherwise be mere 'aesthetic' representation in her depiction of blacks in
New Orleans cathedral:

> Saw a striking picture: two negro women, kneeling, with the red, yellow
> and black handkerchiefs on their heads (which negresses generally wear
> here), their faces full of emotion and expression. (*An American Diary*, p. 69)

Kemble's genuine feeling for the plight of the suffering blacks does not
always prevent her from imaging them through caricature or fantasy, as
we have already seen. So the plantation slaves who came to watch her
writing her journal in the candlelight each evening are depicted as 'a ring
of ebony idols'; and, recalling a particularly filthy and smelly old negress,
she adds dryly, 'I am mightily reminded occasionally in these parts of
Trinculo's soliloquy over Caliban'.[56] Some of her most memorable
descriptions, however, subsume stereotypicality so as to convey a wholly
realistic and moving picture of suffering humanity. The wailings of a
female slave on Butler Island, one of her husband's plantation homes,

> were uttered by a creature which *was* a woman, but looked like a crooked,
> ill-built figure set up in a field to scare crows, with a face infinitely more

like a mere animal's than any human countenance I ever beheld, and with
that peculiar, wild, restless look of indefinite and, at the same time, intense
sadness that is so remarkable in the countenance of some monkeys.
(pp. 127–8)

Here the animal metaphor, rather than being a self-distancing strategy,
conveys a poignant sense of the tragic consequences of slavery.

In dealing with slavery, the travellers centre on two key experiences
common to many tourists in the United States – a visit to a plantation
(which could be merely a brief tour or a sojourn of days, even weeks) and
attendance at a slave auction. Those women who went to America ready
to defend slavery on the grounds of its international economic advantages
as well as its supposed benefits to the slaves themselves tended to take an
essentially optimistic view of the plantation system. It comes as no
surprise to find Hall, for instance, despite her passing admission that
seeing the cowed slaves 'makes one melancholy' (p. 220), eagerly pointing
to the example of a 'good' plantation owner she meets at Darien in
Georgia:

> It does you good to meet such a man, not to reconcile you to slavery on
> principle, but to show how much the evil which appears to be irremediable
> at present may be softened by proper management. (p. 232)

Maury's yet more unequivocal optimism may have been based on
personal ignorance (it is not clear from her book whether or not she
actually visited either a plantation or a slave auction), but it shows the
facile and self-righteous complacency of much pro-slavery opinion:

> I would reside by choice in a Slave State; I like the disposition, I like the
> service, I like the affection of the Slave; I like the bond which exists
> between him and his master . . . such intercourse is equally compatible with
> existing facts, and agreeable to my own views of social and domestic
> arrangements. (p. 193)

Houston is more honest about her rosy view, confessing that on a visit
to one Mississippi plantation the negroes' apparent cheerfulness and the
owner's benevolent paternalism make her feel 'self-reproach at not being
able to commiserate their fate as deeply as I had intended to do' (*Hesperos*,
II, p. 158). A trip into the Louisiana interior to see some more remote
plantations on the Mexican Archipelago, run by crueller Spanish masters,
led her to modify her optimism about slaves' well-being, but her overall
impression remained 'that their bondage is not so irksome, or their
situation half so unhappy as it is represented to be' (II, p. 161). Finch was
also disturbed by the clash between her theories and her observations:
convinced of the utter indefensibility of slavery, she was yet forced to
admit that, on a farm in Richmond which she visited, the blacks' cabins
were clean and well-built, the proprietor seemed humane and none of the
slave mothers or children seemed weak or ill-nourished.

It must, of course, be pointed out that visitors rarely got an opportunity to see below the surface of plantation life, the owners usually taking care to show only the best face of the system. Those who were able to delve deeper, however, found plenty to distress them. Martineau, a more perceptive and thorough investigator as well as a committed opponent of slavery, discovered nothing on her plantation visit to mitigate her feelings of acute unhappiness in the company of slaves – 'No familiarity with them, no mirth and contentment on their part, ever soothed the miserable restlessness caused by the presence of a deeply-injured fellow being' (*Retrospect*, I, p. 141). For her, the experience of seeing the slave quarters, 'something between a haunt of monkeys, and a dwelling place of human beings' (*Society*, I, p. 155), was more painful than visiting a lunatic asylum. Moreover, unlike Hall whose narrative moves smoothly from a brief glance at the conditions of slave life to a detailed account of the social gaieties offered by her southern hosts, Martineau could not ignore the glaring discordance between the hospitality she received and the moral evil underlying this society, which was 'false and hollow, whether their members are aware of it or not' (I, p. 159).

The most perceptive and anguished observer of Southern slavery is Kemble, who was more closely acquainted with its horrors than were any of the other travellers. In June 1834 she had married Pierce Mease Butler, a Philadelphian whom she had met on her acting tour and whose family owned a plantation in Georgia. Though she claimed to have had no prior knowledge of the source of her husband's income, once she discovered it she became increasingly uneasy, and urged Pierce to let her visit the plantation so as to see the situation for herself. After much procrastination, he finally yielded to her pleas and took her and her two small daughters to Georgia in December 1838, for a three-and-a-half-month's stay. Kemble was appalled by what she found, and her distress was exacerbated by her realisation that as the owner's wife she was morally his accomplice, helping to perpetrate a system which she hated yet was powerless to ameliorate. Her experiences on Butler Island and St Simons Island, the plantation's two estates, not only soured her overall attitude to America but also initiated the marital rift which led to the couple's separation in 1845 and culminated in their divorce in 1849. The literary outcome of these experiences, her *Journal of a Residence on a Georgian Plantation*, is one of the most deeply moving contemporary documentations of slavery. Originally a series of daily notes and observations, the manuscript was circulated privately on both sides of the Atlantic but was not then published because of the offence it would have caused to the Butler family. After the outbreak of the Civil War and the British government's apparent disposition to support the Confederate South, Kemble decided to put it into print in order to help understanding of the issues involved and to show the iniquities of slavery, and the book appeared in 1863.[57]

Kemble's portrayal of the slaves' sufferings reaches out towards them in a spirit of compassionate identification. Even though she avowedly went as a biased onlooker – 'for I am an Englishwoman, in whom the absence of such a prejudice would be disgraceful'[58] – her treatment of negro life embodies the disturbing realism of acute personal observation; focusing particularly on the suffering and degradation of the women slaves, it reflects her own sense of helplessness in the face of such tragedy:

> They must learn . . . that there are beings in the world, even with skins of a different colour from their own, who have sympathy for their misfortunes, love for their virtues, and respect for their common nature – but oh! my heart is full almost to bursting as I walk among these poor creatures. (p. 69)

Her description of a visit to the estate hospital on St Simons Island makes painfully clear what caused her so much unhappiness:

> The floor . . . was strewn with wretched women, who, but for their moans of pain, and uneasy, restless motions, might very well each have been taken for a mere heap of filthy rags. . . . One poor woman . . . lay, a mass of filthy tatters, without so much as a blanket under her or over her, on the bare earth in this chilly darkness. (pp. 255, 256)

Kemble's bitter awareness of the parallels between slavery and the constraints of contemporary womanhood increased her distress. Herself a dependant and most restricted where she sought to assist those who were equally powerless, she felt all the impotence of being her husband's property. At last, worn down by his apparent indifference to suffering and by being 'condemned to hear and see so much wretchedness, not only without the means of alleviating it, but without permission even to represent it for alleviation' (p. 211), she was glad to return to Philadelphia. Here she was able to reflect even more closely on the similarities between her own position and that of the slaves, which she had already expressed to her friend and kindred spirit, Jameson:

> In contemplating the condition of women generally . . . it is a pity that you have not an opportunity of seeing the situation of those who are recognized as slaves (all that are such don't wear the collar, you know, nor do all that wear it show it).[59]

If limited observation could mitigate the worst aspects of slavery on the plantations, attendance at a slave auction allowed no escape from its full barbarity. This experience, which shook the travellers out of all complacency, produces some of their most striking and impassioned writing. Even coolly objective commentators like Hall and Trotter confess to feelings of shock and outrage. For Hall the auction is 'a

horrible sight', and she notes with uncharacteristically bitter irony that
'close by were auctions of horses and carriages going on, so near indeed
that it was impossible to distinguish whether the last bid was for the four-
footed or the human animal' (p. 210). On her first visit to a 'slave-pen' in
Louisville, Trotter was temporarily able to retain her determined
optimism by finding 'kindness and benevolence' (p. 242) in the coloured
housekeeper's face and by being assured that 'pains are taken' (p. 243) to
avoid separating families in the sales. But a subsequent visit to a slave-
market in Lexington forced her to admit that 'these pens give one a much
more revolting idea of the institution than seeing the slaves in regular
service' (p. 252).

For the unwavering opponents of slavery, the experience of auctions
was even more painful. Finch describes the disturbing sight of the sale of a
lovely young woman, the most interesting-looking of all the negroes
there; and Bodichon tells how she came away 'very sick with the noise
and sickening moral and physical atmosphere' (p. 105). One of the most
moving pieces of writing in this context is Martineau's depiction of a
mother and her children being sold at a Charleston slave-market, 'a place
which the traveller ought not to avoid to spare his feelings':

> A woman, with two children at the breast, and another holding by her
> apron, composed the next lot. The restless, jocose zeal of the auctioneer
> who counted the bids was the most infernal sight I ever beheld. The woman
> was a mulatto; she was neatly dressed, with a clean apron and a yellow
> head-handkerchief. The elder child clung to her. She hung her head low,
> lower, and still lower on her breast, yet turning her eyes incessantly from
> side to side, with an intensity of expectation which showed that she had not
> reached the last stage of despair. I should have thought that her agony of
> shame and dread would have silenced the tongue of every spectator; but it
> was not so. A lady chose this moment to turn to me and say, with a cheerful
> air of complacency, 'You know my theory, that one race must be
> subservient to the other. I do not care which; and if the blacks should ever
> have the upper hand, I should not mind standing on that table, and being sold
> with two of my children'. Who could help saying within himself, 'Would
> you were! so that that mother were released!' (*Retrospect*, I, pp. 235-6)

There is no attempt at social theorising here, merely the anguish of
personal response, infused with the same kind of impotent rage and
despair which Kemble expresses.

Confrontation with slavery was particularly disturbing for the travellers because it led to disquieting questions about their own positions.
Kemble was not the only one to note the parallels between the situation
of the slaves, as an oppressed race in a hierarchical power-based society,
and the status of women, as 'relative creatures' trapped by patriarchal
values.[60] It is significant that many of them, including Wright, Martineau,
Finch and Bodichon, worked for or supported both anti-slavery and

women's rights movements. Finch and Bodichon directly expound the
analogy between slavery and the female state. Finch, herself much
involved with the women's movement in Boston, is ironic about the
sermons she has heard here positing that both women and slaves must
cultivate virtues of humility and obedience; slavery in every form,
'whether of sex or colour, direct or indirect' (p. 214), must be resisted,
she insists. Bodichon makes the analogy more specifically. Sardonically
quoting her conversations with Southerners – 'There is evidently a
feeling that Abolition and Women's Rights are supported by the same
people and same arguments, and that both are allied to atheism' (p. 61) –
she directly links the two 'causes':

> I feel in England how incapable men and women are of judging rightly on
> any point when they hold false opinions concerning the rights of one half of
> the human race. . . . Slavery is a great injustice, but it is allied to the
> injustice to women so closely that I cannot see one without thinking of the
> other and feeling how soon slavery would be destroyed if right opinions
> were entertained upon the other question. (p. 63)

Her observation of the horrific treatment of slaves in America thus
heightened her awareness of the sufferings of entrapped women at home
for whom, though herself married to an extremely liberal-minded man,
she indefatigably laboured.

Dealing with an issue such as slavery could be somewhat hazardous, as
Kemble and Martineau recognised, and their difficulties foreground
certain problems experienced by the travellers in writing about America.
They were particularly anxious to convey the 'truth' about the country, a
more urgent undertaking than in the case of Italy not only because fewer
of their readers would have visited the New World, but also because
many inaccurate images of it had already become firmly lodged in the
British consciousness through 'the often unfair and unfounded reports of
prejudiced travellers' (Stuart-Wortley, I, p. 26). The existence of
predecessors in the field in some ways made their task more difficult. The
mid-century travellers frequently refer to the American writings of Basil
Hall, Mrs Trollope, Martineau, Marryat and Dickens,[61] and many confess
to reliance on other commentators for their factual or statistical
information. There is a familiar note of apology in Wright's declaration
that 'the ground has been trodden before and . . . in detailing the
appearance and population of towns and districts, I should only write
what others have already written, to whose journals, should you be
curious on these matters, you can refer' (p. 73), and in Jameson's refusal
to encumber her 'little note-book' with too many facts because it is
'information to be obtained in every book of travel and statistics' (*Winter
Studies*, I, p. 145). Another problem was the notorious sensitivity of
Americans to any criticisms of their country, a phenomenon noted by

almost all visitors. Kemble, for instance, describes being challenged by an American lady who defensively predicted that on returning to England the actress would dreadfully abuse the republic (though Kemble smartly put her down by assuring her that 'I was not in the least afraid of staying where I was, and saying what I thought at the same time' [*Journal*, II, p. 142]).

Despite their apparent cautiousness, however, the women offer firm and confident reasons for writing about their American experiences. Some claim to be breaking new ground in writing about ways of life 'so peculiar, so utterly dissimilar to any other that I have heard or read of, that it exhibits human nature in a new aspect' (Grant, p. 16), including pioneering and Indian life. Traill and Moodie relay their experiences to assist prospective emigrants and Martineau, presenting a detailed account of modes of travel in the United States, points to

> the desirableness of recording things precisely in their present state, in order to have materials for some few years hence, when travelling may probably be as unlike what it is now, as a journey from London to Liverpool by the new railroad differs from the same enterprise as undertaken a century and a half ago. (*Retrospect*, I, p. 71)

Information of a more theoretic nature was also intended. We have already seen how Kemble's *Journal of a Residence on a Georgian Plantation* was designed to help understanding of the North/South conflict in the American Civil War. Maury's *An Englishwoman in America* aimed at enlightening its British readers about American politics and at demonstrating the need for better conditions on emigrant ships (her efforts helped to get the Emigrant Surgeons' Bill drawn up and passed).

Many of the women, while not themselves wholly uncritical of America, also saw it as their duty to disabuse their public of gross misjudgements or misconceptions concerning the New World. Wright is perhaps an extreme case – she so deeply deplored the inaccurate and biased reports of previous visitors that she cast herself as a prophet of enlightenment, commissioned to rectify European ignorance about the great principles of American government and social theory. Houston makes a more general point about Anglo–American antagonism: is it any wonder that Americans may seem unfriendly, she asks, when they are submitted to the scrutiny of superficially informed English spies 'whose only object is, as they well know, to *pick up*, and exaggerate their absurdities? . . . [and] *in nine cases out of ten to make a book of them*, and such a book, as, by its ridicule of their entertainers, will ensure to itself popularity in their own country' (*Hesperos*, I, pp. 68–9).

Ironically, the most self-confident purveyor of information about America was also its most notoriously outspoken critic. No writer on

America after 1832 could be unaware of the controversial model set by
Trollope's *Domestic Manners of the Americans*, which far from dispelling
prejudice actually created it. Trollope's very name rapidly became a
byword for arrogant and vituperative diatribe and the Americans
themselves long bristled with indignation about her. Elizabeth Sewell
records a conversation with an American visitor in 1845 about *Domestic
Manners*:

> when I observed what a very vulgar book it was, she said, 'Yes, Mrs
> Trollope had not seen any good society in America, for she had settled
> herself down at Cincinnati, and established a bazaar there, and then, when
> she found people would not take to her shop, she abused the whole
> country'.[62]

Trollope herself was breezily unconcerned, not only acknowledging her
debt to her equally sharp-tongued predeccessor, Basil Hall (he had
encouraged her and helped her to get her book published), but quite
prepared for subsequent abuse since, as she calmly admits, 'I suspect that
what I have written will make it evident that I do not like America' (p.
302).

Most later women writers on America were not anxious to be seen as
infamous successors of hers. Jameson must have been pleased with the
critical opinion which distinguished her from other recently reviewed
lady travellers, including 'the Mrs Trollopes and the Miss Pardoes – the
false and the flippant, – who return from foreign parts yet more self-
complacent in their ignorance than when they left their own firesides'.[63]
At the same time, however, the travellers recognised that Trollope
represented their sex's rights to express personal opinion. Moodie, for
example, counters a Coburg woman's aggressive assertion that 'they did
not want a Mrs Trollope in Canada' by arguing that her 'witty exposure
of American affectation has done more towards producing a reform in
that respect, than would have resulted from a thousand grave animadver-
sions soberly written' (p. 218). Kemble, too, while noting cheekily that 'I
would not advise either Mrs Trollope, Basil Hall, or Captain Hamilton,
ever to set their feet upon this ground again, unless they are ambitious of
being stoned to death' (*Journal*, II, p. 142), defends Trollope, arguing that
she 'must have spoken the truth . . . for lies do not rankle so' (I, p. 67).
Defence of the right to 'say one's say' is pragmatically enacted in these
texts and all the women travellers, to a greater or less extent, show their
readiness to speak with their own voices. In so doing, they often
articulate a distinctively female consciousness.

The significance of the individual feminine viewpoint with regard to
topics such as slavery and the natural environment has already been
stressed. This gendered perception is also evident in areas of more

specifically female concern. The travellers' observations on those aspects
of American social life which attracted the attention of all commentators
– spitting, gross cultural ignorance and absurd prudery[64] are especially
notorious in this respect, though American hospitality receives commen-
dation – are often pertinent and witty. They also take notice of features
such as evidence of poverty, charity schemes and social reforms, having
included on their itineraries female penitentiaries and asylums, girls'
schools, and women's workplaces such as the well-known factory in
Lowell, Massachusetts. But in the social and cultural sphere, their
particularly feminine originality is notable in their treatment of less
widely discussed topics.

First, they always show interest in domestic matters and female
occupations; they comment, for example, on the degree of cleanliness of
private dwellings and hotels, and on methods of household management
such as methods of heating water and the employment and duties of
servants. They were also fascinated by how and what the Americans
ate, and their reactions to New World cuisine is indicative of their
degree of openness to the unfamiliar. Thus pioneering spirits like Stuart-
Wortley and Bird accepted all the oddities with gusto, the former
enjoying wild buffalo, bear, turtle and strange fish, the latter tucking
into hearty breakfasts of johnny-cake, squirrel, buffalo-hump, dampers,
buckwheat, tea and corn-spirit 'with a crowd of emigrants, hunters, and
adventurers' (*The Englishwoman*, p. 144) in the mid-west. Others, however, were less able to cope: gritty corn-bread reminded Houston of a
chopped-up straw bonnet and Finch could really only enjoy squash-pie,
and even then found it hard to get over the name – 'it reminded me so
of killing cockroaches' (p. 16). Many were concerned about the unheal-
thiness of American eating habits – huge piles of ice-cream or hot
buckwheat cakes running in butter, for instance, were regarded with
horror as being absolutely ruinous to the digestive system. Interested
observation did not preclude innate prejudice, of course, and some
travellers were only too ready to point to American vulgarity or
provincialism in such matters. Hall notes the inelegance of dinner
parties where all the courses arrived simultaneously, and Kemble sneers
at the lack of finger-glasses. Houston is heavily ironic about the two-
pronged forks she was forced to use – 'To the stranger, accustomed to
the greater luxury of silver forks, of wider and more useful dimensions,
it is deemed not consistent with feminine grace, to seize a large coarse
knife, and thrust it into the mouth, with, peradventure, a huge oyster at
the end of it' (*Hesperos*, I, p. 220), she pronounces – and, predictably,
Trollope attacks the same 'total want of all the usual courtesies of the
table . . . the frightful manner of feeding with their knives, till the
whole blade seemed to enter into the mouth; and the still more frightful

manner of cleaning the teeth afterwards with a pocket knife' (p. 12).

The behaviour and appearance of their own sex were, not surprisingly, of particular concern to the travellers. Personal viewpoints come prominently into play here. So while North American women in general are seen as lively, attractive and delightfully innocent, many commentators are quick to point to the brevity of their early good looks, considered due to an unhealthy way of life, including poor diet, foolish clothing and not enough exercise. Some, too, found American female taste in dress showy and vulgar. They also almost universally condemned the habit of married couples living in boarding-houses – those 'nests of gossip' (*Texas*, I, p. 148) as Houston calls them – because it exposed bored young wives to bad moral influences and made marital privacy impossible. Sometimes, though, a kind of wistful envy lurks beneath their criticisms. Kemble's depiction of young American women as 'hoydenish', 'laughing, giggling, romping, flirting, screaming at the tops of their voices, running in and out of shops, and spending a very considerable portion of their time lounging about in the streets' (*Journal*, I, p. 257), suggests a subconscious desire for such freedom. Houston, too, while deprecating the want of 'retiring modesty' in independent young New York women, acknowledges the positive side of such self-assertiveness, and in so doing implies the wish to emulate them:

> While descanting on the singular freedom which is allowed to the American ladies, I cannot resist paying tribute to their strength of mind and energy of purpose, in which qualities they stand certainly pre-eminent. (*Hesperos*, I, p. 186)

Though envious of the freedom granted to American women, both in their social relationships and in their ability to travel alone without molestation, the visitors are much more critical of overall female status in the New World. They were quick to recognise the irony that in a land purporting to be founded on democratic or egalitarian principles, women in many ways had less freedom than their British sisters; they also deplored their general woeful ignorance, as well as their exclusion from participation in public affairs. To some of them, in fact, the position of North American women seemed little if any better than that of the indigenous racial minorities. We have already seen how Jameson, by comparing a white woman's situation with that of the apparently degraded and enslaved Indian squaw, shows some of the latter's advantages; going on from this she uses her observations as a springboard for a lengthy and spirited diatribe against the 'civilised' male view of women as 'unresisting and confiding angels' embodying 'the overflowing, the clinging affections of a warm heart, – the household devotion, – the submissive wish to please' (III, pp. 205, 203). Others, as has already been noted, make specific connection between black slavery and female constraint. Like Kemble, Finch and Bodichon, Martineau vigorously attacks the American hypocrisy which, disguised as indulgence, confined woman's intellect, crushed her morals and encouraged her weaknesses as virtues – 'Her case differs from that of the slave, as to the principle, just so far as this; that the indulgence is large and universal, instead of petty and capricious' (*Society*, II, p. 156), she comments acidly. Distance from the enclosing social circumstances of their own country enabled these travellers not only to perceive more astutely the injustices of the female lot, but also to put their own experiences into clearer perspective.

That sharpened perception could still include the unsaid or unacknowledged. If to these women America represented freedom of movement and wider psychic horizons, it could also be suggestive of a more fulfilling female sexuality. The natural environment indirectly awakened them to this awareness, as has been shown; their responses to the more 'unsocialised' of the North Americans similarly reveal subconscious sexual desires. They were especially drawn by backwoodsmen or adventurers, often wildly flamboyant, who represented 'difference', a basic energy and physical potency which at home was carefully excluded from 'woman's sphere'. Moodie's description of Brian, the still-hunter, with his 'strong, coarse, black curling hair' (p. 184), indicates her fascination with his enigmatic physical presence. Stuart-Wortley's and Houston's vivid portrayals of the western men they encountered – pioneers, gold-diggers and bushwhackers, with their rifles, bowie-knives and dogs – obliquely convey the seductive allure of such exotic figures. Of all the travellers Bird, like Kemble in Italy, reacts most directly to this male physicality. On her first trip to America she delighted in the 'dark-browed Mexicans, in *sombreros* and high slashed boots' and the 'rovers and adventurers from California and the Far West, with massive rings in their ears' (*The Englishwoman*, p. 118) whom she saw in Cincinnati; and her description of two 'prairie-men' who sat in front of her on the train to Chicago expresses even more clearly her excitement in the presence of such masculinity:

> Fine specimens of men they were; tall, handsome, broad-chested, and athletic, with acquiline noses, piercing grey eyes, and brown curling hair and beards. . . . Blithe, cheerful souls they were, telling racy stories of Western life, chivalrous in their manners, and free as the winds. (p. 141)

This response anticipates her much more disturbing fascination with Jim Nugent ('Rocky Mountain Jim'), her guide in Estes Park, Colorado, whose combination of physical allure, gentlemanly manner and notoriety she found irresistible. Although in her book she remains silent about her deepest feelings (for publication she edited out of her original letters to

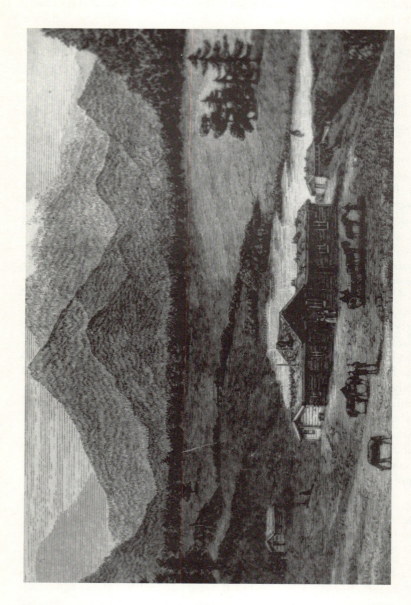

MY HOME IN THE ROCKY MOUNTAINS
from Isabella Bird, *A Lady's Life in the Rocky Mountains* (London, 1879)

her sister any passages which were too revealing), her descriptions of Jim are telling enough. Her admiration of his united handsomeness and repulsiveness (one of his eyes had been clawed out by a bear), coexistent with unease at his wildness (' "Desperado" was written in large letters all over him' [A *Lady's Life*, p. 91]), reveals her highly ambivalent attitude; he represented for her both the seductive freedom of the West and the dangerous attractions of a sexuality which she at once desired and shrank from. Drawn to a man tortured 'with hatred and self-loathing, blood on his hands and murder in his heart', and made desperate by the thought of 'his dark, lost, self-ruined life' (p. 243), Bird found herself compelled to confront her own more unmanageable impulses. Her American experiences had truly opened to her, as to all the women travellers, a New World, whose variety, whether rousing the visitor to anger, mirth or wonderment, was endlessly stimulating.

4

The lure of the East

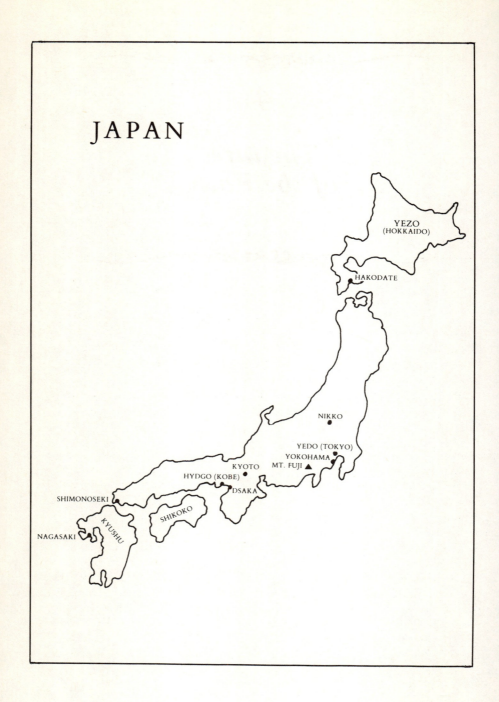

JAPAN

YEZO
(HOKKAIDO)

HAKODATE

NIKKO

YEDO (TOKYO)
YOKOHAMA
MT. FUJI

KYOTO
HYDGO (KOBE)
OSAKA

SHIMONOSEKI

SHIKOKO

KYUSHU

NAGASAKI

Japan

In 1910, after nearly a year and a half of living and travelling in the country, Marie Stopes wrote that 'Japan makes one love her and hate her from day to day, from hour to hour'.[1] Her ambivalence is typical of the response of nineteenth- and early twentieth-century travellers to Japan, who found themselves having to confront a myriad of complexities here. Whereas in Europe and North America expectation and actuality proved largely compatible, Japan's reality was from the start paradoxical. Already mythologised through aesthetic and literary representation, in many ways it seemed to confirm its fantastic and legendary quality. At the same time, as a fast-developing country, rapidly moving towards the West in areas such as education, clothing and sexual roles, it challenged preconception. A land of contradictions, it seemed to the visitor to become increasingly unknowable, refusing to allow easy accommodation to its 'difference'.

Cultural and political conditions added to this sense of impenetrability. Until the treaties concluded with America in 1854 and with Britain in 1858, Japan was virtually unknown to the West and even then, though a few tourists started to arrive at the treaty ports of Nagasaki and Yokohama and missionary activity expanded, foreign presences were hardly encouraged and consular officials were frequently in personal danger.[2] Not until the establishment of the Meiji regime in 1868 and the opening of Tokyo to foreign trade and residence the following year was wider exploration made possible; the Duke of Edinburgh's subsequent visit to the Mikado and the growing numbers of consultative British engineers in the 1870s encouraged more tourists, with the accompanying development of hotels for them. Passports were still needed for travel over twenty-four miles from each treaty port, but these were not hard to obtain and greater penetration of the interior soon ensued. An 1888 *Handy Guide to Japan* divides travel at this time into three categories: trips 'for delicate persons and those who dislike accommodation at Inns kept in pure Japanese style'; tours for 'Lovers of the Curious and Picturesque in robust health'; and the really testing excursions for travellers 'desirous of avoiding the beaten track'.[3] Difficulties still existed, however, not least of which was the linguistic barrier which heightened the sense of separation between 'them' and 'us'.

Women visitors to Japan fall roughly into two categories – those connected with official business, some of whom were residents rather than travellers in the strict sense, and the pleasure-seekers. The first group includes teachers like Ethel Howard, governess of a young Japanese prince and his brothers in 1901; those involved with missionary work, such as Mary Bickersteth, daughter of the Bishop of Exeter and Secretary of the Missionary Guild of St Paul, who went with her father and stepmother in 1891 to stay with her brother, then Bishop of Japan; that rarity of her time, a female scientist, Marie Stopes, better known for her work on birth control, who went to Japan early in the twentieth century to study fossils and coal mines; and diplomats' wives, including Mrs Hodgson whose husband was the first British consul in Nagasaki and Hakodate, Mary D'Anethan, wife of the Belgian Minister in Tokyo, and Mary Fraser, married to the British Minister, Hugh Fraser. The second group can be considered tourists. The earliest, Anna D'A, accompanied her husband to Manila and Japan in 1862; she notes several times how they were much restricted in their movements, only on one occasion daring to venture beyond the permitted bounds. Marianne North's trip to Japan in 1875 was suggested by acquaintances who asked her to join them, rather naïvely assuming that this already much-travelled and independent woman would find her own company irksome. Several travellers stopped in Japan as part of a world tour, usually via North America or China. Sara Duncan, an unattached American, and her young English charge, Orthodocia Love (the latter name is clearly fictitious, but though for the most part the book reads more like a novel than a travel work it is obviously based on Duncan's actual experience), were unashamedly in pursuit of amusement on their tour of 1888–9, not expecting to 'penetrate more deeply into the national life than other travellers have done'.[4] The narrator gleefully records the horror of friends and family at their determination to travel alone – 'Go to Japan without any man whatever – absurd! . . . it was the height of impropriety . . . it was unheard of that two young women should go wandering aimlessly off to the other side of the globe!' (pp. 8, 9, 10). Other world travellers were Mrs Bridges, touring in the 1880s; Lady Brassey, steaming from country to country with her wealthy husband, her children and the family pets, in their yacht 'The Sunbeam', from 1875–6; and Catherine Bond who went with her husband as part of a tour of Japan and Australia in 1896. Some tourists journeyed alone, looking for pleasure, information and, as Isabella Bird, off to Japan in 1878 on her third major 'escape', puts it, the novelty so essential 'to the enjoyment and restoration of a solitary health-seeker'.[5]

A Drag across the Sand in a Jinrikisha.

TRAVEL IN A JINRIKISHA
from Mrs Brassey, *A Voyage in the Sunbeam* (London, 1878)

Many of the travellers sought the 'real' Japan, uneasily aware that they would find only a 'tea-tray' version of the country in cities such as Yokohama and Tokyo, with their well-known sights and tourist shops full of tourists. Even in more distant watering-places and beauty spots, their compatriots were rapidly filling the foreign hotels, and it became more and more difficult to discover the true spirit of the land. North stayed on her own in a purely Japanese hotel in Kyoto for three months, observing and painting,[6] Fraser and D'Anethan were both able to escape the rigours of Tokyo diplomatic life in summer residences in the remote hills and Alice Bacon, an American visitor in the 1890s, plunged into the interior accompanied only by her loyal maid who politely showed no amazement at her odd employer's 'cutting loose from all foreigners and foreign associations . . . stopping only at Japanese hotels, and carrying with me no supplies to eke out the simple Japanese fare'.[7] Stopes also wanted to avoid 'Guide-book' Japan, purchasing a bicycle in order to be more independent and using it to make a trip into the interior, where she stayed at Japanese hotels and ate the local food; in addition, she visited many of Japan's small islands as part of her investigation of mines, often the only European woman to have been there.

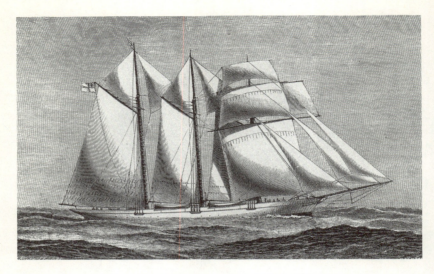

LADY BRASSEY'S YACHT, THE SUNBEAM
from Mrs Brassey, *A Voyage in the Sunbeam* (London, 1878)

Success in discovering the essential Japan depended, for most of the
women, on voluntary secession from home values and associations. This is
why, as we have seen, they so eagerly avoided contact with their fellow
countrymen, and sought 'the greatest fun and novelty'[8] which were to be
found in local inns, 'among the purely Japanese people'.[9] Some of these inns
had their peculiarities – Augusta Davidson, another tourist, chuckles at the
huge carpet slippers offered to the guests, which represent 'the foreign
conception of comfort in footgear',[10] and notes that the towels are always
too small for one of her Western proportions, a common complaint. But
the travellers were convinced that only by fleeing from evidence of Europe
could they begin to attune themselves to the true spirit of the country.

Characteristically it is Bird who takes the furthermost 'unbeaten
tracks' in order to discover Japan's rich variety. With a special passport
and official letters from the consul, Sir Harry Parkes, allowing her to
wander freely and to obtain supplies, she eagerly left 'civilised' Japan and
travelled up to Yezo (now Hokkaido) with only her carefully chosen
guide, Ito. Her ostensible purpose was to visit and study the Ainu race
who lived on the island but, as usual with her, she was also drawn by the
unknown – 'I am once again in the wilds!' (p. 221), she writes from
Hakodate, delighted 'to have got beyond the confines of stereotyped
civilisation and the trammels of Japanese travelling to the solitude of
nature and an atmosphere of freedom' (p. 230). For her 'the wilds' also
meant escape from Western influences. Even before arriving in

Yezo, she sought out local Japanese inns, and avoided places visited by other foreigners:

> I no longer care to meet Europeans – indeed I should go far out of my way to avoid them. I have become quite used to Japanese life, and think that I learn more about it in travelling in this solitary way than I should otherwise. (p. 165)

Bird suffered considerable hardship on this expedition, partly perhaps because she refused to make compromises. Her tribulations included voracious mosquitoes, perpetual dampness (for most of the journey it seems never to have stopped raining), inadequate sustenance and bad mounts, all exacerbated by chronic back pain which was sometimes so severe that she could barely stay in the saddle. In Yezo tracks were often almost impassable, and she was quite seriously injured when she fell off her horse. Other women encountered fewer discomforts, either because of their greater cautiousness or because even by the next decade conditions had vastly improved. Fraser and D'Anethan experienced terrible floods at their summer residences and the latter had to struggle back to Nikko on foot, the main route having been washed away after eight days of rain, but most of their expeditions culminated in comfortable hotels offering the blessings of a hot bath and a good – usually European – meal. With jinrickishas or chairs to take them over the roughest terrain, most female tourists had little to complain of, though some preferred walking to the jolting and swaying of porterage. Earthquakes were a constant source of potential danger, but the visitors, like the Japanese, soon learned to accept them, and none was seriously injured in one.

Importantly, one benefit guaranteed the woman traveller in Japan was personal safety. This was a feature of travel also much noted in the United States, and perhaps says as much about the woman's self-protective obliviousness to possible danger as about the conditions themselves. But the conviction certainly gave them the assurance to strike out where they wished. North felt perfectly secure alone in Kyoto; and though Bird confesses to some initial anxiety about 'being frightened . . . being rudely mobbed' (p. 36), her subsequent experience proved it to have been groundless:

> My fears, though quite natural for a lady alone, had really no justification. I have since travelled 1200 miles in the interior, and in Yezo, with perfect safety and freedom from alarm, and I believe that there is no country in the world in which a lady can travel with such absolute security from danger and rudeness as in Japan. (p. 45)

Davidson, journeying nearly thirty years later, confirms this absence of danger: at native inns, 'you are as safe as you would be in Grosvenor

Square' (p. 74), she observes, with admirable British confidence. She herself, equally anxious to see the real Japan, explored many areas on her own by bicycle and always travelled second-class on the railways to avoid encountering any other foreign tourists. Soon after her arrival she went alone to Yezo, relying on strong-mindedness and a few phrase-book sentences to carry her through – 'I have come to Japan . . . determined from the first to have nothing to do with guides, but to buy my own experience' (p. 17), she states firmly.

Though most travel in late nineteenth-century Japan could scarcely be called pioneering, experience taught that proper preparation for journey-ing into the interior was essential. Many of the women offer advice for prospective female visitors, stressing that if they are unwilling to 'go native' they should carry their own supplies, including bed-linen, oiled paper against fleas, pillows or air-cushions, and familiar food – as Davidson, herself quite happy with Japanese cuisine, says darkly, 'I should not recommend anybody to go very far without some [European-type food] unless they are quite sure they know what is in store for them' (p. 49). Bird also details the equipment she carried – a collapsible canvas stretcher, an air-pillow and a few emergency edible goods – 'as a help to future travellers, especially ladies, who desire to travel long distances in the interior of Japan' (p. 36).

Finding the real Japan was not however merely a question of physically going off the beaten track. As the more sensitive visitors realised, in order to know – or to try to know – the country they had somehow to reach beneath the surface of etiquette, formal politeness and constant smiling with which they were everywhere greeted. One of the most thoughtful observers is Fraser, who quickly fell in love with Japan's external charms but who also recognised that these were not all. For her, Japan offers restoration of a more spiritual kind than that noted by Bird:

> I cannot imagine a better cure for weariness of spirit than a first visit to Japan. The country is absolutely fresh. All that one has read or heard fails to give any true impression of this vivid youngness of an atmosphere where things seem to sort themselves out in their real, and, to me, new values.[11]

But she also sees that only through openness to Japan's complexities can the visitor hope to tear away the veil of colourless conventionalities in which the Japanese wrap themselves, and find the reality beneath. Fraser herself managed to escape the narrowing confines of diplomatic superior-ity and, as we shall see, of all the travellers comes closest to understand-ing the 'other'.

For most of the women, for whom the opportunity of communication with other women – a 'closed' area barred to their male counterparts – particularly alerted them to the possibilities of empathising or identifying with the foreign, Japan's apparent impenetrability was particularly problematic. They tend to show unease, conscious of a 'difference' which excludes them. When writing about Japan, they move between holding to this difference as a source of stability and seeking to transcend it. On the one hand, their responses reveal certain aspects of what Edward Said has termed 'orientalism', an attempt to 'fix' the foreign country and its inhabitants according not to a verifiable, referential reality, but to a set of created assumptions which have attained the status of accurate represen-tation.[12] On the other hand, they frequently display an attempt to undermine this authoritative stance and to substitute a more impressio-nistic, flexible viewpoint. Here, as in Tibet, their assessments of the alien 'other', reflecting their often complex responses to eastern culture, demonstrate their negotiations between their society's values and their own more individual attitudes, notably towards gender and race. As a recent critic has argued with reference to women travellers in South-East Asia,[13] examination of such accounts shows that though partly depending on contemporary ideology they may also express positions different from dominant white, male or western ones – that while revealing some traits of 'orientalism', female observers may seek to establish familiarity and mutuality, qualities of cultural or moral relativity which permit new insights and understanding.

The simplest and most comforting strategy for dealing with the inaccessibility was to reify the country and its inhabitants according to current preconceived images. As a recent study has demonstrated,[14] the Victorians viewed Japan as a strange, remote place of romance and mystery, an idea reinforced by periodical literature of the time which portrayed it as unreal, magical, something out of the Arabian Nights, the abode of an unchanging, amiable people. Displays of Japanese art in London and Paris in the 1850s, followed by a major showing of artefacts at the London International Exhibition of 1862, increased cultural familiarity with the country and inspired a flood of reproductions and the promotion of 'things Japanesy', culminating in the mock-orientalism of Gilbert and Sullivan's The Mikado (1885). Many visitors, armed with these pre-established images, set off in search of scenes which would confirm them, in an attempt to come to terms with a world which seemed to have no connection with existence back at home and which often seemed to embody pure fantasy. If Italy was magical for women travellers because its sensuality awakened feelings suppressed by the normality of domestic life, Japan was a legendary fairyland, bewitching the observer with a remote enchantment. Thus to confirm its fantasy was both to render it accessible and to open the individual consciousness to a new imaginative freedom.

Throughout the accounts, Japan is imaged as dreamlike, on the one

hand symbolised by the perfectly manicured gardens, with their exquisite
floral representations, their dwarf plants and their miniature bridges and
temples, and on the other hand by the pervasive sense of timelessness.
Even the most pragmatic travellers allow themselves to be seduced by
this illusory world. Abandoning her normal brisk realism, Bird, for
instance, turns to a highly poetic style to express her sense of enchantment when she describes the visionary experience of a beach-scene at Usu
Bay on Yezo:

> Wooded, rocky knolls, with Aino huts, the vermilion peaks of the volcano
> of Usu-taki redder than ever in the sinking sun . . . a single canoe breaking
> the golden mirror of the cove by its noiseless motion, a few Aino loungers,
> with their 'mild-eyed, melancholy' faces and quiet ways suiting the quiet
> evening scenes, the unearthly sweetness of a temple bell – this was all, and
> yet it was the loveliest picture I have seen in Japan. (p. 307)

Bird responds here to the static and timeless beauty in an almost trancelike
state during which her normal personality is momentarily suspended.

D'Anethan has a similar feeling of magical transcendence on a
nocturnal boat-trip to see a temple ceremony at Miyajima. The scene
before her, with its 'distant and weird strains' 'of ghostly' music and the
priests and priestesses dancing on the shore, seems like a hallucination:

> These spectral figures, attired in flowing robes of the richest white silk, and
> dancing slowly with strange but graceful gestures in the magic moonlight
> . . . accompanied . . . by the strains of that unearthly music . . . enthralled
> my imagination . . . The white figures, till now so calm and dignified,
> flitted round and round, backward and forward, faster and faster, till, with
> one long wail of the music, one final rapid yet floating movement of the
> elfish dancers, musicians and performers vanished into the night shadows as
> if by enchantment, and were seen and heard no more.[15]

Unsure whether or not she is dreaming, D'Anethan here re-enacts a
visionary encounter in which she is hypnotised into self-forgetfulness.

Imaging the 'otherness' of Japan as mystery or magic could also have a
therapeutic effect for these travellers, released from the mundane
realities of their own worlds. Many of them discovered an inner
peacefulness in the dreamlike environment, signalling a more profound
response than merely accommodation to its strangeness. The subdued
charm of Nikko, for instance, with its sombre colours and famous Shogun
temples amidst avenues of dark cryptomeria pines – a very different
fairyland from the one of bustling tea-houses and dazzling cherry
blossoms – taught their 'strained Western senses' a new spiritual
awareness,[16] and provided them with memories for recall later. Elsewhere, too, the magical combination of colours made, as Stopes expresses
it, 'a harmony that thrills one's very soul' (p. 183).

MOUNT FUJISAN
from Isabella Bird, *Unbeaten Tracks in Japan* (London, 1911)

For almost all visitors the most potent symbol of Japan's magic was
Mount Fujiyama, a mirage of beauty suspended in the sky. Already
familiar through countless reproductions, it nevertheless transcended pre-
knowledge and spoke directly to them. Like Vesuvius or the Niagara
Falls, it encapsulated the aspirations and meaning of their travels, the
allure of the romantic and the exotic; unlike them, however, it also
represented the unattainable – physically, because none of them seems to
have attempted its ascent (though some women climbers had done so),[17]
and spiritually because, as Bird observes, its 'lonely majesty, with nothing
near or far to detract from its height and grandeur' (p. 6) distanced it
from the observer and compelled a kind of religious awe. The unforget-
table sight of the mountain silhouetted against the sky is a leitmotif in
Stopes's text, a symbol of eternal reassurance throughout her visit; when,
on saying farewell to Japan, she is finally blessed with her first view of its
summit clear of cloud, the vision becomes emblematic of her whole

Japanese experience and a fitting conclusion to her book:

> Round the mountain top light clouds collected and dispersed like flying
> veils; one rose from the crater and dissolved like a puff of smoke, some
> circled the base and shut off the crown from the black fringing trees below.
>   So, as I left Japan, her greatest beauty showed herself to me. (p. 264)

For Fraser, observing it from their summer residence at Karuizawa, it
functioned as a spiritual comforter, embodying harmony and peace –
'sorrow is hushed, longing quieted, strife forgotten in its presence', she
muses (II, p. 140) – and Howard, just landed in Yokohama and
apprehensive about her new life as a governess in an alien country, found
it a symbol of assurance, its snowy slopes gleaming in the sun.

If preconception played only a part in the women's response to Japan as
an enchanted land, it had a larger role in their attempts to reduce the
country's alienness to manageable proportions. One way of confronting
the inaccessible is to recreate it in familiar terms and here the 'known'
images of Japan – its miniature scale, its quaintness, its childlike people –
become the key to interpretation. This strategy, with its roots in the
desire to separate the self from the foreign, is one which many of the
travellers sought to resist, conscious of the barriers between themselves
and the 'other', and of the difficulties 'of touching the living reality in the
Japanese'.[18] It was, however, often easier for them to cling to their pre-
established notions, especially at the beginning of their visits. North is a
good example of this. Far from insensitive to the strange new world
around her, she converts it into meaningfulness through a mixture of
condescending humour and aesthetic distancing. Houses are 'quaint', the
Japanese people look 'as if they had walked out of a fairy tale' (I, p. 216),
and Yokohama is full of

> tiny men in the oddest dresses, some looking like the straw umbrellas they
> put over beehives, some in strange stripes and checks . . . with their funny
> tufts of back-hair turned over their bald crowns, like clowns in pantomimes,
> and all their ways of doing things so unlike the ways of the rest of the world.
> (I, p. 213)

She also derives much entertainment from all the 'funny little people' (I,
p. 214) with their childlike habits, an unconscious assertion of her own
white, middle-class superiority. This is the same kind of distancing
strategy employed by travellers to the United States with regard to the
Negroes and the Indians.

Other women similarly negotiate their sense of alienation which may
be underpinned by unease as much as by purely racist superiority. Bond
comments on the 'quaintness' of all she sees, including the dolls' house
dwellings, the 'funny little shops' and the 'nice little girls' who wait so
deferentially on her at the tea-houses.[19] D'Anethan depicts the native-

clad Japanese women as 'dainty personages in their brighly-coloured and graceful raiment . . . appearing like butterflies from the seclusion of feathery bamboos', and, as they trip across the ancient stone bridges in the old-world gardens, looking 'for all the world just like a willow-pattern plate' (p. 38). Bridges's first amused impressions of Japan are of the 'funny little men with quaint paddles' who propel the boats in Yokohama harbour, and of the peculiarities of the 'funny little people' at their hotel:

> Japanese housemaids, little men in black tights and straw sandals, their hair done up in door-knockers at the top of their head, bowed politely, skipped about, got all our luggage together, and instructed us in the art of ringing the electric bells, much in use in this 'go-ahead' land.[20]

The deliberate sexual confusion – housemaids are men – contributes to the caricature register here. It is also convenient for Bridges to see the Japanese as children, delightfully amused at everything but rather stupid – 'like clever monkeys, they can copy anything, but are "impervious to reason" ' (p. 330). Altogether, she concludes, 'one never gets over the impression of being amongst dolls and living in a toy-house' (p. 298).

Many of the women, though, even while drawing on such preconceived images, are aware of their falsity. The novelist Norma Lorimer, an early twentieth-century visitor (the title of whose book encapsulates a European attitude to Japan),[21] details the dolls' house items used in this 'queer' (p. 27) and 'topsy-turvey' (p. 56) country with its 'funny little families' (p. 99), but rejects the stereotyped English picture of Japan as 'a land of pleasure, and of toy women and pigmy men':

> if I shut my eyes and let my thoughts go back to my life in Japan, what I see is not a land of tea-houses and gaily-dressed *geisha* girls, but a quiet, gentle land, with grave hard-working people, a land where very little laughter is heard. (p. 84)

Davidson's first exposure to the more sombre aspects of Japan, in Yokohama harbour, alerted her too to the realisation that 'in spite of youthful conceptions derived from "The Mikado", perhaps this land we were approaching never had been quite all tea and ceremonies and Fujiyama' (p. 2). She also acknowledges that the Japanese in their national costume, albeit picturesque, are not the idealised figures portrayed on screens and fans, nor 'my old friends the quaintly gorgeous folk of the tea-cups' (p. 4), though her occasional patronising tone – she enjoys chatting to the maids at local inns, for example, because 'it amuses me to hear them talk, and to try to find out what sort of minds lie beneath their marvellous coiffure' (p. 66) – gives away her uneasy sense that even with a mind cleared of preconceptions she will be unable to reach the 'living' Japan.

Fraser points to the same discrepancy between fictionality and
actuality here. Now, she argues in her introduction to her book (1899),
the time has passed when 'every foreigner saw the same sights in the
Island Empire, obtained the same stereotyped glimpses of the people's
life, and was contented with the half-comprehended information given
by his guide', a time when 'it was easy, and alas! fashionable, to describe
the "toy country" and its "fairy-like" inhabitants with glib security in
large print' (I, p. vii). Though she herself was always delighted and
amused by what she saw – the cake-sellers carrying fairy temples of wood
and paper full of goodies, for instance – she never seems condescending
and indeed shows regret about being an outsider, observing the scenes of
which she could never fully become part. Drawn to the window of her
room at the British Legation, she wistfully details 'the many-sided,
brightly coloured life' (I, p. 153) going on in the courtyard below, her
physical separation from it emblematising the foreigner's sense of Japan's
eternal remoteness. Like Stopes, who realised that 'In my deep desire to
understand, and come in close touch with the Japanese, I was handi-
capped, as every European must be, by our national traditions' (p. xiii),
Fraser saw that even willing sympathy was inadequate wholly to close the
gap.

Bird's more rigorous rejection of falsifying images of Japan is indicated
in the opening pages of her *Unbeaten Tracks* (the title itself is a signifier)
where she defends its original, if unpalatable, realism:

> Some of the Letters give a less pleasing picture of the condition of the
> peasantry than the one popularly presented, and it is possible that some
> readers may wish that it had been less realistically painted; but as the scenes
> are strictly representative, and I neither made them nor went in search of
> them, I offer them in the interests of truth. (p. 2)

As always, Bird balances interpretative observation and directness of
response. Although the people of Tokyo initially appeared familiar, 'so
like are they to their pictures on trays, fans, and tea-pots' (p. 16), on later
acquaintance they came to seem far less attractive and she found little to
admire in 'the yellow skins, the stiff horse hair, the feeble eye-lids, the
elongated eyes, the sloping eyebrows, the flat noses, the sunken chests,
the Mongolian features, the puny physique, the shaky walk of the men,
the restricted totter of the women, and the general impression of
degeneracy conveyed by the appearance of the Japanese' (p. 260). If this is
honesty, it also, it must be admitted, smacks strongly of the discourse of
white supremacy, as well as indicating personal distaste for non-Western
racial characteristics, a prejudice already noted in Bird's writings.

Bird's ambition of encountering 'real Japan' (p. 11) was achieved on

ATTENDANT AT TEA-HOUSE
from Isabella Bird, *Unbeaten Tracks in Japan* (London, 1911)

her expedition to Yezo to see the native Ainu. As her biographer notes, her descriptions of them 'so differed from the customary globe-trotter's glowing pictures of quaint, cherry-blossom-pretty Japan that her publisher suggested she tone them down',[22] but Bird refused to comply with his request. She intends her readers to be shaken out of their illusions, as she is, by the primitivism, dirt, poverty, and disease of this region:

> truly this is a new Japan to me, of which no books have given me any idea, and it is not fairyland. (pp. 87–8)

> I looked at the dirt and barbarism, and asked if this were the Japan of which
> I had read. (p. 130)

Bird, of course, always demanded the challenge of the unorthodox, and in
some ways is begging the question by focusing on a very particular and
restricted element of the Japanese environment. It would have been hard
for anyone to have found quaintness here. But she is as honest in her
depiction of the Ainus' greed, drunkenness and childishness as of their
generosity, their soft eyes and their sweet smiles. She is also careful to
acknowledge her own failures to separate the true from the idealised.
One of her first impressions of the tribe, during an evening visit, is in
particular visually memorable:

> I never saw such a strangely picturesque sight as that group of magnificent
> savages with the fitful firelight on their faces, and for adjuncts the flare of
> the torches, the strong lights, the blackness of the recesses of the room and
> of the roof, at one end of which the stars looked in, and the row of savage
> women in the background. (p. 247)

Thinking over her impressions a little later, however, she takes a
somewhat different view:

> The glamour which at first disguises the inherent barrenness of savage life
> has had time to pass away, and I see it in all its nakedness as a life not much
> raised above the necessities of animal existence, timid, monotonous, barren
> of good, dark, dull, 'without hope, and without God in the world'. (p. 259)

In contrast, when Howard, temporarily released from her pupils, went
to Yezo (by then called Hokkaido) to see the Ainu nearly thirty years
later, she regarded them more as museum pieces, an 'indeed original',
fine, gipsy race, belonging to a legendary world:

> they had gentle faces, and some of them had quite beautiful eyes, which
> were not only of a wonderful brown colour, but were dreamy looking and
> full of soul. The men wore their hair long and parted down the middle, and
> had wavy beards, calling to mind 'Old Father Christmas'.[23]

Unlike Bird, Howard remained literally and metaphorically separated
from the Ainu, not actually entering any of their houses but merely
observing them from outside and content to retain her idealising vision.

Dealing with the 'other' also demands some degree of self-assessment,
the need to view oneself through the alien's eyes. For women, accustomed to being objectified or marginalised, this process is perhaps less
disorienting than for men, but the travellers still found it problematic.
The more insensitive of them merely welcomed confirmation of the gap
between 'them' and 'us'. Bond, for instance, discovering that their
physical stature was the cause of the constant staring to which she and her
husband were subjected, takes pleasure in this acknowledgement of

BIRD'S WET-WEATHER GEAR IN
JAPAN
from Isabella Bird, *Unbeaten Tracks in Japan*
(London, 1911)

differences – 'This idea would never have occurred to us, as at home we are considered short, and we feel we like Japan more than ever', she says brightly (p. 131). Bridges, however, equally unable to cope with the decentring of response required of her, felt distinctly uncomfortable at being an object of curiosity to the natives. Surrounded by fascinated crowds wherever she went, she suffered 'a sort of hunted-animal feeling', and found the perpetual scrutiny of her movements 'insupportable' (p. 323). North is much more wry about how she appeared to the Japanese – that is, 'gigantic and clumsy . . . I felt quite Brobdingnagian in Japan' (I, p. 215), and her observation is echoed by Fraser who muses, 'I fancy in their [the Japanese women's] hearts they put us down as big clumsy creatures with loud voices and no manners' (I, p. 35). Fraser actually unflatteringly

AINOS OF YEZO
from Isabella Bird, *Unbeaten Tracks in Japan* (London, 1911)

recasts herself in Japanese eyes as 'a blue-eyed creature in strange
garments, [a] foreign barbarian woman' (II, p. 118), showing a real
attempt to identify with the Japanese viewpoint. Bird, too, can laugh at
how she appears to the local people; she notes amusedly how in her
American 'mountain dress', Wellington boots, and light straw or waxed
paper cloak she is often taken for a man (p. 93).

   Attempts to understand the foreignness of Japan involved not only
revaluation of the visitor's own self-image but also of her values,
assumptions and customs. Understandably, in approaching the unfamiliar,
the travellers paid particular attention to matters of inherent interest to

their own sex. Some of these, such as food, clothing, cultural activities and domestic arrangements, permitted an essentially objective response; others, including sexual mores, marriage customs and the position of women, demanded the potentially more disturbing application of moral and religious principles, both institutional and personal. As in earlier instances, we find here much ambivalence, reactions ranging from rejection of the alien to eagerness to embrace the new and different, as national and individual prejudices came into play. The degree of openness further illuminates the significance of the foreign experience for these women, faced with the choice of adjustment or resistance.

Reactions to Japanese food and living conditions depended as much as anything on physical adaptability. The universal cleanliness (in great contrast to China, as is often remarked) met with approval, but the food often proved literally hard to swallow, particularly for the less intrepid travellers. Some, resolutely sticking to tourist hotels serving European fare, demonstrate their gastronomic insularity by refusing the dishes of 'queer looking things'[24] offered them to be consumed with an unmanage-able pair of wooden sticks. Querulous references to ubiquitous meals of 'rice and seaweed and biological problems'[25] abound, coupled with the general complaint about the inadequacy of Japanese food to satisfy Western appetites – as Davidson puts it, there are 'all sorts of mysteries interesting to the inquiring mind, but not very satisfying to the hungry body' (p. 40). Domestic discomforts, such as the lack of tables and chairs, opaque paper windows and sliding screens which excluded air but let in all the noise of a Japanese household, are also frequently noted, though surprisingly even the most conservative travellers took pleasure in sleeping on a futon.

Japanese music and drama presented the same difficulties of apprecia-tion, though being less essential items in the traveller's foreign experience they could be more cursorily dealt with. The music often seemed discordant to Western ears, and the drama a bewildering and meaningless set of gestures. But, again, only the most insensitive of the women dismissed or ridiculed these, in their reluctance to open themselves to the unfamiliar. D'A categorises Japanese theatre as gaudy and aurally unbearable, while Bridges comments on the grotesquerie of a dinner entertainment:

> Between the courses the maidens danced, or, rather, went through a series of pantomime postures . . . while some of them played curious instruments, and made a noise exactly like cats screaming. (p. 289)

Bond uses the same tasteless metaphor to describe Japanese music – 'loud octaves played, all out of tune and out of time – a veritable cat's concert' (p. 154) – though she does have the grace to admit that her own lack of

education prevents enjoyment here. And D'Anethan displays crass and
inexcusable ignorance in her reaction to the traditional and solemn Noh
drama:[26] 'an extremely amusing spectacle. . . . It is long since I laughed
so much' (p. 43). Other women reveal a genuine desire to appreciate these
aspects of Japanese culture. Fraser and Howard were moved to melancholy, not horror, by the music, which to the former seemed 'the saddest
in the world' (II, p. 206). She was also so engrossed by Noh dancing that it
induced in her painful feelings of anxiety and restlessness. Davidson
confesses to having to revise her notions of native drama: finding it
neither comic nor barbaric, she acknowledges its profound effect on her –
'the impression made even on my uncomprehending mind was somehow
one of a curious solemnity, so serious and dignified was the whole' (p.
321).

Japanese dress introduced more disquieting questions about the significance of Western influence on Oriental life. The abandonment of obvious
'barbarisms' such as a woman's shaving her eyebrows and blackening her
teeth after marriage was unequivocally seen as progressive, but the
replacement of national costume by European styles seemed aesthetically
and culturally more dubious. It also, by extension, challenged the validity
of Western assumptions of superiority. Those unable to deal with the
questions raised take refuge in the reductive facetiousness which we have
already seen. Bridges, for example, seizes on the absurdity of the
headgear worn by the Kioto town dignitaries in religious processions:

> The citizens of this ancient capital of the land of the Rising Sun seem to
> imagine that an old English hat, very tall and wide brimmed, gives a certain
> dignity to their appearance, and is altogether a suitable head-dress for
> solemn occasions. (p. 315)

Japanese women in Western dress generally elicit less mockery and
more regret. For the travellers, their own sex in particular had to remain
an inviolable part of the dream world they came to find, and thus they
could not bear the shattering of the illusion. Bird, enchanted by the
Minister of Education's wife in her 'exquisite Japanese dress of dove-
coloured silk *crêpe*', argues that 'she looked as graceful and dignified in her
Japanese costume as she would have looked exactly the reverse in ours'
(p. 35). Fraser and D'Anethan, too, hated to see Japanese women at
diplomatic receptions trying to emulate European styles. Stopes even
more emphatically deplored the gradual disappearance of national dress,
considering it a diminution of Japan's innate loveliness:

> the beautiful and dignified robes, the silken skirts and kimonos of both men
> and women . . . are giving place to a hybrid mixture of all the vulgar and
> hideous garments of 'civilisation'. (p. 46)

The same feeling of regret, fuelled by the desire to maintain Japan's other-worldliness, underlies criticism of the introduction of European furnishings and architecture here, replacing with clumsy ugliness the simple beauty of Japanese artistry. And yet, as the more perceptive observers realised, might not such 'progress' be part of the 'real' Japan? And might not their own desire to keep the country as a timeless fairyland be mere solipsistic escapism? The dilemma became even more pressing for the women when they confronted more profound moral and social phenomena.

Religion in Japan was one such matter. As with the music and drama, inability to comprehend concealed itself behind mockery. Curious devotional practices and odd ceremonies were laughed at or dismissed as absurd. On the other hand, despite their allegiance to an overtly Christian homeland, nearly all the travellers admitted some good in Buddhism, though they found Shintoism cold and meaningless, too remote from the idea of a comforting faith. Thus the dilemma recurred – how to reconcile inherited beliefs and a growing sense that the propagation of these beliefs elsewhere might not always be desirable. Unlike in Italy or North America, here they had to confront the notion that Christianity might not have a monopoly on the truth. Bird, later to be connected with missionary activity in the East, is representative of the committed Christian who was also a sensitive receiver of alien ideologies. She takes Christian standards as her measure of Japanese behaviour but at the same time recognises the inappropriateness, even hypocrisy, of this:

> one comes to forget that one is doing them a gross injustice in comparing their manners and ways with those of a people moulded by many centuries of Christianity. Would to God that we were so Christianised that the comparison might always be favourable to us, which it is not! (p. 191)

Bird remained the clergyman's daughter, but she was honest enough not only to see the shortcomings of her own faith but also to question its applicability to all societies.

Many of the women, while not doctrinally convinced by Buddhism (if they took the trouble to investigate its complexities), were emotionally seduced by it as part of Japan's magic. Responses to the huge Buddha at Kamakura, a famous monument to the national faith which deeply moved even the most sceptical who saw it, symbolise this great impact. Viewing it was a kind of mystical experience for the beholder: everything was 'consoled, fulfilled, harmonised in that vibrating silence',[27] proving 'the eternity of goodness'[28] in that immense calm. Stopes sums up its power as an emblem of spirituality beyond doctrinal differences or aesthetic limitations:

> Most Japanese Buddhas are travesties of nature and abominations of art – but this one compels reverence and attracts devotion. Its stillness (a stillness

far greater than that of a house, a statue, or any ordinary inanimate thing), its great size and the wonderful calm on the face, the beautiful human lips and broad-based nose, all make one dream. (pp. 86–7)

This, again, is the Japan of desire, transcending the physical reality.

Sexual mores – including marriage customs, attitudes towards chastity, and female roles – were a particularly testing area for the women visitors, caught between a desire to express a 'feminine' tolerance, and an inability or unwillingness to reject the values on which their own lives were predicated. Moreover, even for the most iconoclastic observers, some 'regressive' Japanese sexual customs could call into question the very radicalisms which as 'New' women they upheld.

To many women, the most overtly startling aspect of Japanese behaviour was its element of apparent immodesty. There are many complaints about the lack of privacy in hotels, including being expected to share rooms with strangers and the difficulties of taking a bath, the Japanese mind apparently finding it quite acceptable to share both water and receptacle. Bodily exposure, of such traumatic significance to the Victorians, also caused the travellers some difficulties. D'A retreats into self-righteous indignation on first viewing the natives in Nagasaki Bay:

> The boatmen are almost naked, and look most disgusting, for, unlike the Hindoo, they are by no means of a very dark complexion, their skin being almost as fair as that of the European; so that the exhibition of their forms appeared to us all the more glaring, lending no charm to the surrounding scene, but rather forming an eyesore one would gladly dispense with. (p. 185)

Significantly, it is the men's disturbing similarity to 'civilised' races which makes her so uneasy; the indecency literally comes too close to home. As in other cases, irony often functions to relieve embarrassment. Bridges, for instance, notes dryly that 'on the whole – and we have opportunities of judging here – the costume of Eden is not becoming to fat, middle-aged ladies' (p. 328). The costume of Eden as seen at community bath-houses (the custom of public bathing was gradually dying out, but still prevailed when many of the women were in Japan) also offended some sensibilities. D'A, of course, found it all 'absurdly indecent' (p. 208), but Fraser merely chuckles on remembering the three ladies bathing at Ikao who jumped up out of their tub to look at her passing, while Fisher was only momentarily disconcerted when at a small local inn a naked man came to join her at her ablutions.

The important point here is not the nudity as such, but the fact that it challenged one of the taboo areas of women's lives. References to bodily functions are notably absent from their travel accounts, except in the most oblique forms, and it was clearly hard for them to fit this overt acknowledgement of 'unaccommodated man' into the context of their idealised, romantic land. Those who rose to the challenge had to rethink their own values. Bacon, considering the general half-nakedness in rural areas, comes to the conclusion that 'there is certainly a high type of civilization in Japan, though differing in many important particulars from our own' (p. 258). And she succinctly reminds her readers that what to the Japanese is healthful exposure of the body becomes to them highly indelicate if carried out merely for show, a point which Western women, anxious to display their bodily charms at social occasions, would do well to contemplate. Fraser went even further in accepting the spirit of the country in this respect. Though she found it necessary to banish from the Legation an old woman who persisted in coming stark naked into the kitchen, in another context female nudity came to signify for her the legendary magic of Japan. The sight of a young girl bathing in the hills near the Legation summer residence was a visionary experience, which she recalls tenderly and poetically:

> there she stood, naked and unashamed, her arms stretched high above her head, laughing out the joy of her heart to the rising sun and breathing in all the freshness of the new day. I never saw a more beautiful picture of innocence and happiness. (I, p. 181)

Fantasy and actuality have become one in such a scene.

Japanese marriage customs – especially the position of wives – and attitudes towards sexual promiscuity were matters of even more pro-blematic concern. If, as Said claims, the East lured male travellers by its seductiveness, actualised in the opportunities for sexual encounter, for women the existence of systems such as legalised concubinage and openly accepted prostitution, still in operation in turn-of-the-century Japan, could only be deeply disturbing. They were seen as evidence of moral corruption by committed Christians like Bird, who regretted the 'very sad fact' (p. 50) that so many of the pretty tea-houses (at which of course she could not stay) were brothels, or Bacon, who stoutly supported the efforts of the Woman's Christian Temperance Union of Japan to effect change. Attitudes towards the prostitutes themselves were more ambivalent. As at home, the women felt both moral indignation and sisterly sympathy, though none was able to move beyond viewing the fallen woman as victim, since this would have rocked the ethical foundations of their lives. So Gertrude Fisher, while refusing to blame the prostitutes' apparent lack of shame, ponders what pain may lie beneath the merry exteriors 'of a sisterhood that knew not its own needs'; though her heart is 'wrung . . . with pity',[29] it is easier for her to see these women as unconscious sufferers than as complicit in their own fate, a notion reinforced for her by the sad eyes of the glossy, puppet-like girls in a famous procession of courtesans.

Concubinage, by which a man's mistresses were fully accepted in his household, also moved many of the women not to self-righteous disgust but to sympathy for these unfortunates who had no rights and who were denied natural maternal relationships with their children. Fraser, moreover, again comes closest to challenging the hypocrisy of Western values in her suggestion that such a system, deplorable though it is, may be preferable to the hole-and-corner attitude of so-called Christian Europe to these matters. She also recognised that reforms might in fact be merely 'the thin edge of the wedge of external respectability according to Western ideas' (II, p. 233).

The position of Japanese wives touched the travellers more personally, since more than vicarious sympathy was involved here. Whether married or not, by their very undertakings abroad they were enacting some degree of independence and could not fail to be struck by the restrictively patriarchal, even misogynistic, nature of Japanese society, in which the general lot of women seemed drearily unfulfilling. To almost all the visitors, the Japanese wife, betrothed by arrangement (unmarried women were almost unknown here), the slave of her husband and of her domineering mother-in-law, allowed no feelings, and liable to instant divorce, was a pitiable creature. Western notions of matrimony are of course in operation here: Howard, for instance, sentimentalises over the Japanese wife's lack of 'the joy of her own little home, where she can wisely influence her husband and prove what a helpmate she can be' (p. 262). More radical thinkers implicitly condemn their own society's values in interpreting the foreign customs: Lorimer considers that 'wifehood in Japan is mere slavery and child-bearing' (p. 22), and Fraser sees how Japanese husbands' tyranny is encouraged by their wives' 'unnatural heroic unselfishness' (II, p. 221). A more overtly feminist observer like Bacon looks to the development of women's rights to remedy what she sees as the most blatant evil in Japan:

> until the position of wife and mother in Japan is improved and made secure, little permanence can be expected in the progress of the nation toward what is best and highest in Western civilization. Better laws, broader education for the women, a change in public opinion . . . these are the forces which alone can bring the women of Japan up to that place in the home which their intellectual and moral qualities fit them to fill. (p. 115)

Genuine concern for members of their own sex and respect for foreign values were, however, in conflict here. While wishing Japanese women to enjoy the same privileges as they did, many of the travellers felt compelled to admit that what was progress in their own culture might not be so for a very different one. Fraser argues that though the notion of arranged and apparently loveless marriages seems quite dismal – 'the best European woman, educated in the full consciousness of her own value, would feel that she lost her integrity by entering such bondage' (II, p. 223) – so-called love matches at home are often a mockery of the romantic ideal. Even on the matter of mistresses, 'steeped as we are in the laws and prejudices of the West, it is not easy for us to judge of these questions' (II, p. 225), she wisely concludes. Some of the women were further prepared to admit that the sacrifice of female virtue for a husband, considered by Westerners the highest degree of female immorality, might have to be seen as dutiful and self-forgetful wifely devotion. As Bacon posits:

> Just at this point is the difference of moral perspective that foreigners visiting Japan find so hard to understand. . . . Let us take this difference into our thought in forming our judgment, and let us rather seek the causes that underlie the actions than pass judgment upon the actions themselves. (pp. 216, 218–9)

In the same way, their enthusiasm for developments in female education in Japan (many of them visited the Peeress's School in Tokyo, a model of 'new' Japanese education on Western principles) was tempered by the recognition that, together with the intellectual and social advantages, some of the worst aspects of 'fast' Western womanhood could be passed on to the girls.

As these travellers were finding out, beneath the reassuring image of Japan which they had brought with them lay a country of complexity and paradox which resisted simple interpretation. Even their readiness to respond to the indigenous women in terms of their own 'otherness' could result not in understanding and increased self-knowledge but in greater disorientation. In this sense, the trip to Japan became more than merely an exploration of the geographical unknown. Though its magic was so soothing, it also demanded of its visitors re-assessment not only of their own society but also of their own self-perception. Few can have left it wholly unchanged.

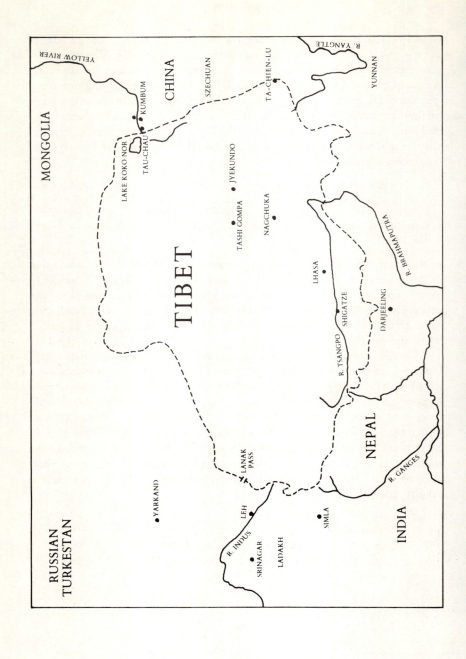

Tibet

In 1904, Jane Duncan, a traveller in north-western (Little) Tibet, laughingly notes the sudden access of lady visitors to the region – ten recorded at Leh that year and, as her guide remarks on seeing an English couple, 'he had been eight times in Baltistan without seeing a single mem sahib, and this was the sixth this summer. The country is overrun with us!'.[30] The exceptions only prove the rule, however, and Duncan herself indicates that she was the first European woman in many of the villages she visited. Her observation is confirmed by others; in the late nineteenth and early twentieth centuries any travellers, but especially women, were a rare species in Tibet.[31] Although Tibet had been fairly accessible, politically at least, to European visitors in the eighteenth century – the period of greatest infiltration by Catholic missionaries – by the beginning of the nineteenth century it was closed to all foreigners except the Chinese, who maintained an effective if somewhat loosely defined political and commercial control over it, though leaving it autonomous in its religious and cultural affairs. Various explorers, including Rockhill, Hedin, Prjevalski and British army officers such as Deasy, Welby and Malcolm, tried to discover more about this tantalisingly unknown land, but not until the Younghusband Expedition of 1904 was entry gained right to its centre, Lhasa.[32] Even this opening was merely temporary: once the expedition had left, the country resealed its borders and Lhasa was again closed to outsiders.

The political hazards of travel in Tibet – interlopers were liable to arrest – were in themselves a strong deterrent to extensive exploration. Of the women travellers to be treated here, most stayed within Little Tibet, a region encompassing the states of Kashmir and Ladakh (whose capital was Leh) which had always been easier to enter because penetrable from British territories to the south and west. In addition, the physical perils of such a venture exceeded almost anything experienced by the other travellers in this study. The combination of inadequate topographical information, the highest mountain passes and greatest extremes of temperature in the world, and huge expanses of wilderness made travel here an undertaking for only the most courageous – or most foolhardy. Even the less intrepid women, cushioned by extensive support from a retinue of servants, at times suffered serious discomforts and difficulties. Yet the fact that they aspired to the undertaking and, having started, were often unwilling to turn back, shows an extraordinary spirit of determination. When the Littledales, a wealthy English couple who tried to cross the Tibetan plateau in 1895, were forced to retreat in appalling conditions because Mrs Littledale, a semi-invalid, became too ill to continue, it was reputedly against her wishes.[33] As we shall see, the frequent discrepancy between apparent female frailty and almost super-human endurance is particularly notable here. Apparently the lure of this mysterious and forbidden land was irresistible to those female travellers who, as true pioneers, represent the most far-reaching, both physically and psychologically, of their class.

An examination of the accounts of their journeys shows that in many ways their responses to Tibet were far less conditioned than those of travellers in more familiar areas. Not only were they often unprepared for the degree of hardship involved, but fewer preconceived images were available to them. In his *Tibet the Mysterious* (1906), Thomas Holdich claims that the Younghusband expedition finally lifted the veil of mystery overhanging Tibet, revealing, among other things, that Lhasa contains very little 'to justify that mystic fascination which has somehow or other exercised so powerful an influence on European minds', and made it 'almost as familiar to the public as any continental town'. Quite apart from the factual dubiousness of this statement, most of the women travellers discussed here were pre-Younghusband and would therefore have had slender knowledge of what lay behind the veil.[34] It is also clear that for them there was plenty of mystery in Tibet. They were in fact genuine 'explorers' in all senses, striking out into an unknown sphere where the possibilities for unrestricted self-development and self-testing were boundless, and able to recreate their experiences without the established models of literary tradition behind them. This is not to deny the possibility of writing about Tibet in a 'colonial' mode. Holdich's work – avowedly a study of the exploration of the country from the viewpoint of possible British expansion, rather than a travel book – demonstrates this. For him, the hostile border tribes are 'but half-clothed aborigines of those jungles which they infest' (p. 336), Tibetan government officials are 'functionaries with unpronounceable names' (p. 49) and 'quaint' religious ceremonies come 'perilously close to the realm of pantomime' (p. 300); he even looks forward to 'those good times when the last relics of savage barbarism' (p. 219) will disappear, and there will be a Tibetan branch of the Assam railway and spacious hotels for sightseers and sportsmen. In contrast, the women travellers, while not wholly free from an aura of national superiority, reveal an openness to the new experience, seeking to

LEH
from Isabella L. Bishop, *Among the Tibetans* (London, 1904)

apprehend it in ways that will break down the barriers of prejudice.

Because of its remoteness, few late-nineteenth-century women visitors went to Tibet as tourists. One exception is Mrs F. D. Bridges, in Kashmir as part of a two-and-a-half-year world tour which, as we have seen, included Japan. She travelled from Srinagar to Leh in 1883, staying several weeks in Ladakh's capital and attending a religious festival at the great monastery at Hemyss. She seems to have had less sense of adventure than most of the others: though she suggested to a tea-merchant from Lhasa that she should accompany him and his wife back to the forbidden city, she did so 'just to see how they would take it',[35] with no intention of actually implementing her proposal. Twenty years later, another 'tourist' displayed a far more enterprising spirit. Jane Duncan, in Kashmir in 1904, planned a trip to Leh in order to escape the summer heat of Srinagar, one of her goals being to watch the famous Devil Dance of masked lamas at Hemyss. But she was attracted as much by the possibilities of freedom and novelty which this region offered. Exploiting her 'femaleness' with deliberate irony, she explains the delights of such travel for one of her sex: formal plans can be dispensed with – 'The feeling of being able to turn back naturally did away with the wish for it – naturally so in the case of a woman at least' (pp. 1–2); another blessing is the escape from sartorial proprieties, impossible at home – 'many a time after returning to civilisation I longed to be in the desert again, where the crows and the goats did not care what I wore' (p.

LABUL VALLEY
from Isabella L. Bishop, *Among the Tibetans* (London, 1904)

11), she sighs. It was not just the relaxation, the refuge from 'the
interruptions which make modern life a series of hurries' and the peace,
'whose healing influence lasted for years afterwards' (p. 16), however,
which appealed to her. She was driven on eastwards, beyond Leh (though
not attempting to cross into Great Tibet) by the beautiful isolation of this
'earthly paradise' which 'has laid its spell on me' (p. 228). Though she might
have been less enthusiastic had she experienced the terrible conditions
encountered by those who crossed the Himalayan ranges, she nevertheless
represents the female urge to flee the oppressive constraints of 'civilisation', and her text sparkles with her joyous sense of release.

The other women travellers discussed here had ostensibly more 'serious'
or specific purposes. Annie Taylor and Susie Rijnhart were missionaries,
Isabella Bird had a committed interest in the country because of the work
of the Church Missionary society there, and Alexandra David-Neel
wanted to open up Lhasa's mysteries to the outside world as well as to
further her Bhuddist studies (although her claim to have actually got into
Lhasa was disputed at the time, and has been since, this study assumes the
veracity of her text). Yet beneath these avowed aims lay deeper, more
personal desires, dreams of freedom and solitude, an urge to test the self to
the limits of physical and psychological endurance and a longing to
penetrate the unknown.

The missionaries consistently foreground their overt goals. Taylor, who had dedicated herself to Christ's service at the age of thirteen and had waged an ongoing battle with her father, first over her taking medical training, then over her going to China with the China Inland Mission, first went to Tibet in July 1887 for the great religious fair at Kumbum monastery; when she returned to Central Asia in 1890, she settled at Tau-chau on the Chinese border for a year, then in September 1892 set off to take the Gospel into the interior, accompanied by Pontso, the young Tibetan she had befriended. Her evangelical purpose clearly predominated – in fact to William Carey, who edited and published her diary, it was inconceivable that any motive other than religious zeal could have inspired her to such an extraordinary undertaking.[36] But though her diary is full of pious references to God's guidance and protection (after the death of one of her servants, she comments, 'The Master has called to account the strong, and left the weak to go and claim Tibet in his name'),[37] some love of exploration for its own sake, perhaps inherited from her much-travelled father, probably also impelled her. According to Carey, too, she may have felt drawn towards the faraway mysterious land in childhood, though she herself does not mention this.

The Rijnharts, medical missionaries (she was Canadian, he Dutch), may have been inspired by Taylor's example to try to reach Lhasa and take Christianity to the benighted Tibetans. After living at Kumbum for a year, they opened a mission at Tankar in 1896; two years later, they decided to make their mammoth trip, hoping for the downfall of 'the barriers that too long have kept a people in darkness, and bid defiance to the march of Christian civilization'. As Rijnhart explains, they 'had thought, read, and dreamed much about Lhasa even before we reached the border', but their dream was oriented wholly towards one end:

> Let it be clearly understood that the purpose of our journey was purely missionary; it was not a mere adventure or expedition prompted by curiosity or desire for discovery, but our desire to approach our fellow men with the uplifting message of Truth and to share with them blessings that God had ordained for all mankind.[38]

She voices a terrible single-mindedness here which, ignoring all obstacles, impelled them to plunge into the unknown, taking along an eleven-month-old baby, through terrain and in conditions which even the most intrepid explorers feared. Even at the end of her dreadful return journey, having lost both child and husband, Rijnhart still maintained that the undertaking was worth it, as a direct response to a Divine command.

Having so definitively committed herself to God's service, Rijnhart seems to have experienced no powerful underlying urge to seek a new selfhood in the wilderness. Though she enthuses about the beautiful solitude of Lake Koko-nor, a landmark on the eastern route into Tibet, 'far away from the turmoil of civilization, nor within sight or sound of the rudest encampment or settlement of any kind' (p. 44), she was never comfortable in the uncompromising desolation of the Tibetan hinterland. If the blue hazy mountains drew her on it was not, as with Bird and David-Neel, because they represented the challenge of the unknown but because they held out bright hopes of new fields of labour. Their barren isolation chilled her, and when she was left alone with her child and dog, while her husband tried to find their two runaway servants, she transferred her fears and anxieties onto them – 'There is no solitude like that of the mountains, perhaps because their majesty impresses one so, and makes nature too far away to be friendly' (p. 238).

Bird, on the other hand, despite the missionary interests which ostensibly took her to Kashmir, had too much of the born traveller's restlessness in her ever to be led to an area by 'purpose' alone. Although she seems to have had no longings to reach Lhasa itself, clearly the wildness and 'uncivilised' environment of this remote region was of long-standing appeal. Her biographer, Anna Stoddart, records that Bird's husband, Dr John Bishop, 'used to say, "I have only one formidable rival in Isabella's heart, and that is the high tableland of Central Asia" '.[39] Visiting Srinagar in 1889, after his death, Bird decided to move on from there not, like Duncan, because it was too hot, but because it was flooded with tourists socialising and playing tennis; at the end of her trip, only with great regret did she return to the 'amenities and restraints of the civilisation of Simla'.[40] In addition, her wish really to get 'among the Tibetans' (p. 39) encouraged her to make an expedition from Leh into the Lahul valley to see the nomadic tribe of Chang-pas encamped there.

An early awakened desire to penetrate the magic and mystery of Tibet was one of the major impulses which took David-Neel to Tibet. Her account of her childhood longings to find solitude, albeit coloured by retrospective interpretation, indicates her innate restlessness:

> I wished to move out of the narrow limits in which, like all children of my age, I was then kept. I craved to go beyond the garden gate, to follow the road that passed it by, and to set out for the Unknown. . . . I dreamed of wild hills, immense deserted steppes and impassable landscapes of glaciers![41]

Later interest in Oriental philosophy and Buddhism, furthered by a meeting with the exiled Dalai Lama at Kalimpong during her researches in India and Burma for the French Ministry of Education, aroused the wish to go to Tibet to extend her knowledge. Tibet thus had for her a sociological, cultural and visionary appeal. On one level, her journey embodies clear political purpose. She explains that though at first she had no overriding desire to go to Lhasa, what really decided her 'was, above

all, the absurd prohibition which closes Thibet [*sic passim*]' (p. xx). Entry
into the forbidden land, she argues, would enable intimate acquaintance
with a virtually undiscovered society, a privilege which she, disguised as
a poor Tibetan lama woman, could uniquely enjoy:

> I knew . . . that under cover of my inconspicuous garb of a poor pilgrim I
> should gather a quantity of observations which would never have come
> within reach of a foreigner, or even, perhaps, of a Thibetan of the upper
> classes. (p. 76)

Her challenge to authority also has a powerful feminist motivation:

> I took an oath that in spite of all obstacles I would reach Lhasa and show
> what the will of a woman could achieve! (p. xxv) . . . Not for one minute
> did I consider the idea of giving up the game. I had sworn that a woman
> should pass, and I *would*. (p. 66)

On a deeper level, David-Neel was drawn to Tibet by its isolation and
other-worldliness which offered the chance to abandon her old self and
find a new psychic identity. Finally in 'the calm solitudes of which I had
dreamed since my infancy' (p. xix), she was 'bewitched' by the country's
'severe charm' (p. 25). Part of its charm lay in the total absence of the
restraints and trappings of civilised existence – unlike Holdich, she was
appalled at the thought of a 'Transasiatic Express' carrying parties of
tourists from India to Mongolia. Here too, she could enjoy 'the delights of
my solitude in the absolute silence, the perfect stillness of that strange
white land, sunk in rest, in utter peace' (p. 160). In such a state, David-
Neel delighted in that loss of self which so many women travellers
experienced. Her disguise literally enacted this – she and her young lama
companion, Yongden (whom she later adopted), planned to
' "disappear", as we used to say, and assume other personalities' (p. 8).
Sometimes this disguise was so effective that she was half-convinced by it
herself – 'my enthusiasm for my so-styled mother country was so
genuinely sincere that no one could have guessed my lie. . . . After all,
was it entirely a lie?', she asks (p. 61). So disguised, she could enjoy new
and iconoclastic freedoms; deconstructing traditional Christian mytho-
logy, she images herself as a post-lapsarian Eve, released into a boundless,
unconstrained being:

> Even if Eve's mind were of a similar cast to mine, she might have found
> interest in the adventure which opened to her the wide unknown world
> beyond the inclosure of Paradise. But I, her little grand-daughter, although
> I had wandered for years in my fairyland, I was far from having exhausted
> its interests. Had I been compelled to turn back now, I would never have
> known the new landscape hidden behind the woody hill that shut off my
> horizon, nor penetrated beyond that other rosy-coloured one which stood
> behind it. (p. 40)

As has been indicated, extreme physical hardship awaited the female traveller who dared to enter this magical but awesome land. Yet even the frailest proved to possess almost endless resilience. Bird, a constant sufferer from bodily ailments since childhood, displayed her usual indifference to discomfort once away from the confines of civilised life. She claims renewed health and strength in the exhilarating air of Ladakh, sceptical about 'the supposed severities of the journey to lesser Tibet' (p. 20). On several occasions, she glories in her own sense of well-being, in contrast to her feebler native servants who complain about the damp and are prostrated by mountain sickness. Camping in Nubra at an altitude equivalent to the summit of Mont Blanc, which causes her attendants considerable distress, she notes with brisk superiority, '[I] felt no inconvenience' (p. 62). At another wet and uncomfortable campsite, she even admits to amusement at their wretchedness – 'Their misery had a comic side to it, and as the temperature made me feel specially well, I enjoyed bestirring myself' (p. 137) (to such effect that, after reviving them with ginger and hot water and mocking their poor-spiritedness, 'as we had no more bad weather, there was no more trouble' [p. 139]). As usual with her, too, she refused to allow bodily weakness to interfere with her progress. Having disregarded the local opinion that 'the "European woman" and her "spider-legged horse" ' (p. 72) would never be able to cross the great fords of Shayok at the most dangerous time of the year, she actually had a close brush with death there when she was thrown under her horse into the raging current. But her version of the accident minimalises its seriousness:

> I escaped with a broken rib and some severe bruises, but the horse was drowned. Mr Redslob [her fellow traveller], who had thought that my life could not be saved, and the Tibetans were so distressed by the accident that I made light of it, and only took one day of rest. (pp. 76–7)

Self-projection is clearly important to Bird here, but in itself the incident displays her amazing fortitude.

Taylor, another who enjoyed poor health, also shows extraordinary powers of endurance. Delicate since childhood, she coped with conditions far worse than Bird experienced. She slept in caves and open holes in the ground for many nights in sub-zero temperatures, was blinded by violent snowstorms and often had no hot food or no food at all. At one point, affected by recurrent palpitations, she was so weak that she had to be held on to her horse. Though admitting that by now, she was 'not strong enough to walk' because 'I have got so thin and am so exhausted',[42] she, like Bird, is often extremely laconic about her sufferings. In her *National Review* article she is even more prosaic about these – 'The cold was so intense that one of the horses was found frozen in the morning. It had

snowed nearly every night'. Beneath this understatement, though, lies
pride at her ability to withstand the horrors: 'That I should have survived
the exposure of this journey, to which two strong men had succumbed,
was indeed marvellous',[43] she remarks coolly. For her, as for the others,
the extremes of travel released an inner spirit of toughness.

The two 'tourists', Bridges and Duncan, supported by attendants and
extensive supplies, experienced fewer discomforts on their easier routes.
They were still, however, prepared for hardship. Bridges made no
complaint about having to stagger up the steep pass into Little Tibet, even
though her feet were frozen and she was soaked through; fortified with
brandy diluted with snow, she declared herself quite ready to continue.
Duncan – who wryly defines herself 'a hopeless sybarite' (p. 12) since, as
well as having a large furnished tent and several servants, including a
cook to prepare her European food, she took table-cloths and napkins,
and even some paper doylies – was well-cushioned against disaster. But
though she did undoubtedly suffer some discomfort, she is refreshingly
honest in her refusal to aggrandise her misfortunes. Undeterred by
reports of adverse conditions and glorying in her spendid health even at
high altitudes, she minimises her fears and anxieties by means of self-
mockery – as for instance when she laughs at her momentary reluctance
to eat, while on a particularly hazardous mountain path (p. 135). She also
deliberately scales down her re-enactment of her experiences. Here she
describes traversing a high-altitude pass, over which, according to her
guide, a lady has never been before:

> I was in the saddle for seven and a half hours continuously that day without
> feeling tired. . . . I gave this account of crossing the Chang La to a literary
> friend to read, and his criticism was that I did not harp sufficiently on the
> agonies of the journey; but as I did not suffer any agonies, I do not quite see
> how the harping is to be done. At the time it seemed throughout an easy,
> commonplace affair which anybody could have accomplished, and I have no
> gift of fine writing to cast a glamour over it and make it appear the
> tremendous achievement it was not. (pp. 82–3)

Some of the worst conditions were experienced by David-Neel, who
fortunately seems to have been blessed with an astonishingly stout
constitution. Accomplishing almost all of her journey on foot, she was
able to endure going for six days without solid food, being nearly buried
in snow, and for several nights having no shelter from the intense cold.
She also achieved the extraordinary act of *thumo-reskiang* or self-warming
(the veracity of her account here was later much challenged); this enabled
her to generate heat in herself and create a spark to ignite their fuel, their
flint and steel being soaked and they themselves freezing to death.
Clearly largely oblivious to physical pain, she is complacent about her
own fortitude – 'People whose hearts are not strong and who cannot

sufficiently master their nerves are wiser to avoid journeys of this kind.
Such things might easily bring on heart failure or madness', she remarks
patronisingly (p. 32).

In such extreme circumstances, the women travellers not only reveal
extraordinary innermost resources but they also recreate themselves in
new heroic moulds. If they, like others of their kind, needed to guarantee
their femininity through 'appropriate' interests and apparel, they were
also directly challenging traditional notions of womanhood by taking on
qualities which often ran counter to current ideology. So as well as
glorying in their powers of endurance, they cast themselves as authoritative figures capable of triumphing over all obstacles. One of their
greatest problems was troublesome servants. Bridges could rely on her
personal attendant, Kamala, who, after a particularly tough day would
take off her shoes, wrap up her feet in his shawl and get her a hot meal;
and Duncan was loyally served by hers, Aziz Khan, whose invaluable
assistance she fulsomely acknowledges. But others had to impose a firmer
hand. Bird discovered that her fantastic 'swashbuckler' (p. 35) Afghan
escort, Usman Shah, who threatened the other servants and the locals,
was a mutineer and a murderer (which actually made him more attractive
to her – she was always drawn to glamorous ruffians, it seems). Taylor, as
well as having most of her supplies stolen by robbers soon after starting,
lost two of her five servants on the way (one by death, one by defection),
and had continual *contretemps* with the irascible and treacherous wife-
beating Noga, who not only tried to cheat her but on two occasions
threatened her life. Rijnhart, left completely on her own after her
husband's disappearance, suffered a succession of untrustworthy guides,
the worst of whom tried to molest her sexually, something to which no
other lone woman traveller in Tibet was exposed; she vividly describes
the horror of the experience:

> I rode astride, as all Tibetan women do, and as he rode along beside me his
> knee brushed against mine, and taking his sword from its scabbard, he held
> the naked blade over me, bidding me dismount and give him my horse. I
> looked into his face, that was very near to me, saw his eyes glassy from
> alcohol, realized that he was scarcely responsible for his actions, and my
> heart was convulsed. (p. 375)

Protected from such experiences by her old woman's disguise, even
David-Neel had occasional difficulties with her faithful Yongden, for
which she had to reprimand him; it is clear though that she was always in
command during their journey, however much she relied on him as the
negotiator between herself and the Tibetan people.

In each case, however, these women foreground the successful exercise
of their authority. Bird (whose pleasure at being the centre of male
attention is demonstrated by her vivacious account of the swirling mass of

horsemen who swooped down and escorted her to the Chang-pas'
camping-ground) relished starting her journey 'with but a slender stock
of Hindustani, and two men who spoke not a word of English' (p. 28),
priding herself on being able to manage recalcitrant servants; not only did
she deal sternly with Usman Shah, but she organised a difficult ford-
crossing which the local muleteers were too scared to contemplate –
'Much experience of Orientals and of travel has taught me to surmount
difficulties in my own way' (p. 121), she comments briskly. Less
enthusiastically, but equally resolutely, Taylor found ways of dealing
with Noga and of enlisting local help against him. Rijnhart, too, at the
point of her greatest unprotectedness, still managed to keep the upper
hand, largely by means of the revolver left her by her husband, showing
the treacherous guides 'that I was to be treated with respect, and that I
would not tolerate either familiar language or gesture' (p. 333). Self-
depiction here depends on essentially 'non-feminine' qualities, and in
parading these the women are deliberately overthrowing current
ideologies of womanhood.

The greatest need for self-assertion – and, subsequently, the greatest
opportunity for self-dramatisation – occurred during confrontation with
the Tibetan authorities, a constant risk taken by those who penetrated
Greater Tibet. The laconic brevity of much of Taylor's diary gives way
to much greater expansiveness when she describes how she was stopped
by guards and taken to the officials to be interrogated. Uncowed by the
formality and possible dangerous consequences of the encounter, she can
even find humour in the situation – one of the chiefs is 'quite a dandy in
his way, does his hair with a fringe in front and a fantastic plait at the
back. This makes him look like a woman' (pp. 250–1). A strong sense of a
capable and self-assured personality, less evident elsewhere in her text,
comes across as she records her demands and details the exchanges
between herself and her accusers. Insisting that Noga be brought to
justice and that she be treated courteously, she stresses her refusal to
capitulate weakly, stating composedly, 'I had to be very firm, as our lives
seemed to rest on my taking a firm stand . . . [since] I have no intention of
being a regular prisoner . . . I act just as usual' (pp. 252, 253). She even
relays verbatim her indignant reactions to the manner in which she is
being treated: 'Is this Tibetan justice? . . . [you] seek to get rid of me, not
killing me yourself, but getting me killed by others' (p. 269).

Taylor's final success in obtaining the horses, food and guides for her
forced retreat is remarkable, but equally noteworthy is her self-creation as
heroine in her own drama; from being a pious and somewhat self-effacing
narrator, she becomes a fully centralised figure, re-enacting her moment of
triumph.[44] Similarly, Rijnhart dramatises her show of strength on the
crucial occasion when she had to insist on an interview with the

local chief in order to obtain an escort back to Jyekundo; the 'I' which was relatively dormant in the narrative before her husband's disappearance now becomes prominent as she takes on her new role of self-responsibility.

The traveller who most consciously manipulates her text in order to dramatise herself and her actions, especially at tricky moments, is David-Neel. In many ways, as a recent study has pointed out,[45] she deliberately exploits her narrator-figure (the 'I' who is the actor as well as the writer) as a means of authentification, establishing herself in a superior position and validating her transcendance of the difficulties of her journey. She frequently 'scripts' key situations, highlighting her skill at talking herself out of a potentially dangerous circumstance as when, while sheltering for the night in a village farmhouse, she has to find her 'strategem' (p. 145) for dealing with threatened discovery by the host; she describes how, on this occasion, she pretended to be in a state of senile dependence on her 'son', the lama (Yongden) (pp. 144–5). At another time, she relates her cunning manner of preventing a group of robbers from seeing the contents of their bags, which 'would have awakened suspicion as to our identity' (p. 221). She lists her tactics (screaming about her poverty and uttering dreadful imprecations) in a consciously constructed 'scene' which she controls – 'I found the plot of the drama to be played on that rustic stage and began my part . . . at that moment I felt myself rising to the height of a powerful tragedienne' (p. 222). It is perhaps significant that before undertaking her extensive travels in the East, David-Neel was an opera singer, highly praised for her interpretation of tragic roles.

The travellers' self-positioning as figures of power within their texts, which is both a conscious literary strategy and a triumphant personal response to challenge, does not necessarily represent an assertion of national or racial superiority. Bird can admit the attractiveness of her villainous attendant, while Rijnhart points out that the chiefs who arrest her and her husband are merely doing their duty and are, as far as they are allowed, fair and kind. At the same time, their writing reveals their uneasy attempts to accommodate the 'otherness' of this land, so much stranger and more remote than any of the other countries visited.

As in Japan, the strange appearance and customs of the natives are familiarised through ridicule or condescension. Bridges is amused by the 'funny little babies' (p. 85) (again the ubiquitous 'funny little'), and finds the women in their odd outfits so ugly that 'their existence would be a crime anywhere out of Tartary' (p. 93). The observation is echoed, somewhat surprisingly, by Bird, who not only comments on the 'pre-eminent' (p. 45) unattractiveness of the Tibetan female costume, but, using the same implicit Western yardstick she applied to the Japanese, gives a mercilessly factual description of the 'irredeemable ugliness' of the Tibetans:

They have high cheekbones, broad flat noses without visible bridges, small, dark, oblique eyes, with heavy lids and imperceptible eyebrows, wide mouths, full lips, thick, big, projecting ears, deformed by great hoops, straight black hair nearly as coarse as horse-hair, and short, square, ungainly figures, (p. 43)

David-Neel slips into uncharacteristic mockery in portraying a primitive Tibetan home:

In one of these we found an idyllic pair of lovers. Youth had long since passed for both, though they were not yet old. The man had a wen on his neck, and his spouse herself was no beauty. (p. 202)

Another, less offensive, method of distancing the alien is to recast it in aesthetic terms, however inappropriate these may seem. Bridges frequently resorts to this. Seeing a 'red-clothed, red-capped, shaven-headed Lama, mounted on a fat white pony, rosary in hand, quite startling in his likeness to a jolly friar of mediaeval days', she immediately names him 'Cardinal Wolsey' (p. 89), and later, at Hemyss, the magnificent lamas remind her of figures on old playing cards. Similarly, a merchant's wife looks 'as if she just walked off a Chinese teapot' (p. 98), and three nuns in a cornfield, 'their red dresses amongst the green barley under the apricot blossoms, lit up by the setting sun, had quite a pre-Raphaelite effect' (p. 93). Both Taylor and Duncan also use artistic metaphors as a means of representation. Taylor comments that the inhabitants of Gala bear a strong resemblance to portraits of the time of Charles the First, and also notes that the lamas at the Tashi Gumpa monastery 'look quite academical in their red gowns' (p. 235). Duncan reflects that there is 'a very picturesquely mediaeval air to the proceedings' (p. 62) at Hemyss, and reconstructs the groups of gaily attired men and women treading out the golden barley at Khapalla as 'a scene in an opera or pastoral play' (p. 206):

The whole scene, the grey-green foliage, the silvery haze, the soft blue sky, the dancing figures, were like a picture of Corot's. I was in Arcadia here in this beautiful bagh with its vista of trees, the shadows flickering on the grass . . . the flower bedecked people sitting about, with the little children in their quaint caps playing round them. . . . It was perfect staging for Shakespeare's comedies. (p. 214)

For David-Neel, too, reality and fantasy interweave in her imaging of Tibet's mysterious magic. Beautifully dressed Tibetan horsemen look 'like those knights of yore one sees in old paintings', riding through the 'mystic landscape' (p. 179). The Potola, the Dalai Lama's palace in Lhasa, is 'a fairy setting' (p. 296) for its religious pageant. In the snow, she and Yongden are ghosts or wizard's attendants. In such an environment, reality itself can be questioned; sheltering in a farm for the night and watching three women preparing for bed, David-Neel meditates:

> But are we really awake? the picturesque spectacle which we perceive between our half-closed eyelids makes us almost doubt it. . . . The flames which first gleam and dance and then darken to mere glowing embers, surround them with a weird light. They look like three young witches preparing for their Sabbath. (p. 103)

This kind of idealising negotiation is not always possible and other aspects of the Tibetan environment and culture confronted the travellers more uncompromisingly. Dress was not really a problem as far as the travellers themselves were concerned: for David-Neel and Taylor native costume was essential for their disguises, but most of the others donned it for its practicality, since nothing else could have protected them from the elements. Adaptation in this respect was fairly painless, though some are a little wry about their strange appearances, and Rijnhart explains that it was not easy to get the clothes made for them. They found most of the food extremely unpalatable and monotonous since it consisted mainly of tsampa (a barley-flour dish), curds, sometimes a little dubious meat and occasional fruit in more fertile areas. The least appetising item to Western tastes was Tibetan tea made from rancid butter, block Chinese tea and hot water (several of the women seem to take a perverse pleasure in describing in detail how it is prepared), and much diplomacy had to be exercised in order to refuse it without giving offence. When in the direst straits, of course, they were only too glad to eat anything available, though on one memorable occasion even the ever-hungry David-Neel rejected a soup made of animal's stomach stuffed with rotting entrails.

Lamaism, the Tibetan branch of Buddhism and the central focus of Tibetan life, was, like Buddhism in Japan, an alien feature to most of the travellers. Although they could respond to its external exoticism, most of its beliefs and ceremonies seemed bizarre and incomprehensible. Not surprisingly, the committed Christians found it hardest to accept. Bird admits that the musical ceremony at a nearby monastery is tremendously thrilling, but has no hesitation in dismissing most lamas as idle, irreligious and superstitious. Rijnhart, though acknowledging its aesthetic attractiveness and arguing that it must not be ridiculed because it does represent a kind of godliness, naturally enough regards Buddhism as an evil to be eradicated; it is 'a whited sepulchre, having a beautiful exterior, but full of rottenness and dead men's bones within' (p. 66), whose teachers are generally childish, ignorant, superstitious and intellectually atrophied, 'like all priesthoods that have never come into contact with the enlightening and uplifting influence of Christian education' (p. 125). She also punctures any illusions about the holiness of lamaseries: it is only an 'uninformed and rose-coloured imagination' (p. 132) which creates such a picture, she posits. As a less committed observer, Duncan calls many aspects of Buddhist ceremonial extremely childish and its monastery treasures mere trumpery, but having no evangelising purpose does not insist on the need for conversion to Christianity. In contrast to these largely hostile or indifferent attitudes, David-Neel's discipleship (she had herself studied to be a lama) made her loyal to its tenets and receptive to some of its most mystical doctrines. But she separates herself in this respect from the uneducated, naïve Tibetans, and is ironic about their wholehearted trust in lamaistic wisdom, especially when embodied in Yongden and herself, impostors trying to ingratiate themselves with the local people and prevent detection.

Despite their unease, it is noteworthy that the women travellers to Tibet are, as has already been suggested, more open to the foreignness, and their responses less coloured by pre-established prejudice, than is the case in other countries. All stress the unexpected friendliness, cheerfulness and hospitality of the Tibetans, while in varying degrees they sought contact and integration. Old values were abandoned as new ones came into play, and as the conditions of travel grew more primitive, more refined or 'civilised' standards seemed increasingly irrelevant. The Tibetans, for example, never washed, and their dirtiness, commented on by all observers, is acknowledged as an acceptable, if unappealing characteristic, though Rijnhart does admit that when she was medically treating some of the women their smell was almost unbearable. For the sake of creating intimacy between themselves and the locals, the travellers were prepared to overcome their inhibitions and to accept the latter on their terms. Bird, with her usual enthusiasm, having found throughout her tour the 'intensely human interest' (p. 40) which she sought, stresses that despite appearances to the contrary the Tibetans are not savages but warm and generous people. For her, part of the joy of journeying in this remote region was to be able to join them round the campfire at night and listen to their gossip, in an act of intimacy and fellowship. (It is worth remembering that nearly all the travellers took the trouble to try to learn the language here, partly because without it they would have had little chance of establishing any contact with the people.) Always interested in domestic and family affairs – she is, for instance, wryly amused by, but not convinced of, the benefits of polyandry[46] – Bird shared the life of the Nubra tribes for several weeks. By the end of this time, she was able to assert positively that 'Many of their ideas and feelings are akin to ours, and a mutual understanding is not only possible, but inevitable' (p. 96).

Taylor expresses an interest in the Tibetans' appearance and is

TIBETAN GIRL
from Isabella L. Bishop, *Among the Tibetans* (London, 1904)

particularly fascinated, like the others, by the women's hairstyles with their myriad of greased and decorated plaits. Though the nature of her record does not allow for extensive social commentary, she too confirms their kindness, jollity and generosity, recognising that their occasional hostility to foreigners is not inherent but fuelled by the lamas and the Chinese. As she explains in a later account:

> I have nothing but praise to give the Tibetans for their chivalry and kindness. Setting aside their raiding proclivities (of which, after all, in earlier times, we have had lively examples on our own borders), they are hospitable, friendly, trustworthy, and by no means averse to intercourse with Europeans.[47]

If this is still rather a generalising view, it is nevertheless a direct response to personal experience.

A CHANG-PA WOMAN
from Isabella L. Bishop, *Among the Tibetans*
(London, 1904)

As is true of all the women discussed in this study, their approach towards members of their own sex most reveals their feminine openness to the alien. Even a 'separated' observer like Bridges momentarily displays sympathetic fellow-feeling for a poor old blind lama woman, 'as she stood trying to feel her way with a long staff through the stream, lifting up her sightless eyes, and shaven head crowned with the high peaked yellow lama cap' (p. 143). Rijnhart's attitude changed markedly as her misfortunes multiplied. At first, though revealing some – partly professional – interest in the women and their affairs, she dissociated herself from their questionable morality and dubious domestic relationships which, she argues, needed much purifying. But while temporarily left alone in the mission at Tankar, she began to acknowledge a growing intimacy between herself and the local women who had invited her into their homes and brought her gifts: 'during those memorable weeks I learned to understand and sympathize with the heathen women as never before' (p. 155). This sympathy made it even harder for her to leave Tankar on their journey into the interior. Moreover, though she still regarded the women as spiritually misguided, her evangelism was now not so much ideological as humanitarian:

> My heart sometimes overflows as I think of the love and tenderness of these dark-faced women, and wish it were within my power to do more for them, to bring them out of the condition in which they live into the liberty which the gospel brings to women wherever it is known. (p. 203)

Hierarchies of any kind were forgotten on her dreadful solitary return, when, frightened by her guides and her utter isolation, 'the little children and the women shed some pleasure into my lonely heart' (p. 366) in the homes which provided the occasional oases of shelter. Significantly, too, at her moment of greatest helplessness she recognises that the women are the ones who can act as mediators between herself and the hostile men.

David-Neel's narrative, controlled though it is by an overriding sense of self, is also punctuated with an identifying pity for the less fortunate of her own sex – for the old grandmother who knows that her daughter-in-law desires her death; for the wives 'whose tears have reddened their eyes' (p. 121) because of their husbands' sufferings; for the dying pilgrim by the roadside whose plight reminds the narrator of her powerlessness 'to relieve the countless sorrows which lie along all the roads of the world' (p. 253). In responses such as these, forming some of the most moving parts of the texts, national and racial differences are passed over in a desire for integration and relationship.

In their re-telling of their Tibetan ventures, the women travellers are especially anxious to convey the sense of remarkable experience, in both personal and environmental terms. As usual, they 'cover' their urge towards self-expression by justification and apologia. Bird says she has described Leh in detail because it is so remote from most people's thoughts. Duncan explains that she hopes to add to the recent political and military studies of Tibet 'an account of what may be called the domestic details of the western portion of the country', and trusts that this 'will be of interest to the general reader' (p. vi) as well as encouraging others to travel there. David-Neel gives similar, though more radically propagandist, reasons for writing:

> Now that success has been mine, I can calmly expose the obscure situation of Thibet today. Perhaps some of those who read of it, will remember that if 'heaven is the Lord's,' the earth is the inheritance of man, and that consequently any honest traveller has the right to walk as he chooses, all over that globe which is his. (p. xxv)

Introduction to Taylor's diary is left to its editor, Carey – who applauds its value as the document of a journey 'which stands apart as one of the great deeds of the time' (p. 4) – but in her subsequent addresses to meetings of the Scottish Geographical Society, she herself offers some self-justification, modestly claiming that despite her deficiencies as a scientific observer, so little is known about Tibet that 'a short relation of my experiences, and a statement of facts . . . will not be uninteresting'.[48] Rijnhart, though apologetic about the lack of literary finish to her work, is more affirmative about its worth as a source of original information:

> My close contact with the people during four years has enabled me to speak with confidence on these points, even when I have found myself differing from great travelers [sic] who, because of their brief sojourn and rapid progress, necessarily received some false impressions. (pp. 1–2)

Beneath these explanations and justifications lies the unconfessed desire to record more personal, often deeply emotional, responses. More profoundly than Japan – because its magic was on a grander, less human scale – Tibet was felt as a land of mystery and romance. It was a place where, despite the travellers' ostensible concern with 'facts', the imagination came most freely into play. Bird calls the view from an idyllic campsite 'the poetry' of travel (p. 114), and later describes another beautiful camping-ground near the Lachalang Pass in a manner which may itself be termed poetic:

> Long after the twilight settled down on us, the pinnacles above glowed in warm sunshine, and the following morning, when it was only dawn below, and the still river pools were frozen and the grass was white with hoar-frost, the morning sun reddened the snow peaks and kindled into vermilion the red needles of Lachalang. That camping-ground under such conditions is the grandest and most romantic spot of the whole journey. (p. 145)

It is a measure of the scene's powerful effect on her that she should treat it so richly in this, one of the most generally prosaic of her travel works.

Rijnhart, caught by the intense beauty of Lake Koko-nor, before successive tragedies diminished the magic of the scenery for her, turns to religious address to express her wonder – 'Thou inland sea, in silence lifting thy unsullied waters to the pure heavens' (p. 189). Elsewhere, too, the Christian missionary is replaced by the ecstatic nature-worshipper contemplating the exquisite landscape:

> [the mountains] ranged against the horizon in glittering masses, rugged, fantastic and multiform in outline, and of varied tints, the brilliant green of their sloping pasture land mounting gradually and fading into the delicate purple and grey of the rocky summits . . . the hillocks . . . with their side-garments of deep verdure tapering off into rocky, sun-gilded crests, like

monarchs of a lower rank reflecting the splendour of the kingly giant-like elevations whose heads, towering far above, were crowned with azure and gold. (p. 291)

Self-conscious though this writing is, it strives to articulate feelings which can be indulged only in such a setting.

Both Duncan and David-Neel are inspired by an other-worldly quality in the Tibetan landscape. For Duncan, there is 'almost unearthly beauty' (p. 201) in the mountains at dawn, and her last view of the Indus valley seems more like a mirage than material reality:

Up above there was a vision in the sky of a calm silver sea, rocky islands rising out of it with bays and headlands, a stretch of wide sandy beach curving along the foot of the hills, round whose heads filmy vapours floated, and in front a range of peaks powdered with snow. Were those real mountains climbing towards the heavens? (p. 315)

David-Neel also images the natural environment as magical, unreal, a place where one might come upon 'some elfs seated on sun rays, or . . . the Enchanted Palace of the Sleeping Beauty' (p. 79). This is a visionary world, remote from normal terms of reference:

an unexpected clearing suddenly revealed, behind the dark line of tall fir trees, extraordinary landscapes of shining snow-clad mountains, towering high in the blue sky, frozen torrents and glittering waterfalls hanging like gigantic and immaculate curtains from the rugged rocks. We looked at them, speechless and enraptured, wondering if we had not reached the confines of the human world and were confronted with the abode of some genii. But as we continued on our way the forest again surrounded us, and the vision disappeared. Yet tomorrow or the day after a new fantastic apparition would rise before us in the same instantaneous way! (p. 194)

It is interesting that here, as elsewhere, it is mountain scenery (splendid to Rijnhart when seen from a distance) which releases the observers from the confines of 'factual' prose and permits unrestrained expression of heightened response. In an environment wholly remote from the every-day, these travellers articulate their eagerness to embrace the fantasy and self-forgetfulness it offers.

The other main way in which the women highlight the extraordinary nature of their undertakings is to impose a dramatic structure on their narratives at certain key moments. We have already seen how they centralise themselves as heroines in their texts when they wish to foreground their positions of authority; in addition, they employ narrative strategies such as creating suspense, building up to a climax and directly addressing an 'audience', in order to remind readers that the writer is the actor and teller of her own story. This technique is most noticeable in the works of Rijnhart and David-Neel. Rijnhart increases the impact of her tragic misfortunes and their consequences in this way, especially in connection with the disappearance of her husband. Her account of her anxious time alone in the mountains while her husband leaves her to find the runaways, to be replaced by her false sense of security on returning to the 'sunshine, green grass and bright crystal streams below' (p. 241), ironically foreshadows the second occasion when she is left and he does not come back. This too is treated dramatically, and she exploits her narrative in order to build up to the final shocking realisation of his permanent loss. She describes their relief, after their expulsion from the country and painful retreat, on seeing at last an encampment, and their confident hopes that 'our difficulties were all ended' (p. 307). When the full force of this illusion hits her, as she waits in vain for him to return from his exploratory forages, she effectively focuses on her own despair, contextualising it within the appropriate environment:

> Dusk settled into darkness, and a desolate solitude reigned over hill and valley, almost chilling me to the heart as I sat alone in the stillness of that oriental night, broken by no sound of human voice, with no sympathy of friends to fall back on. (pp. 314–15)

David-Neel's narrative is most evidently and effectively manipulated in this respect. She writes to give the impression of her own direct involvement in the experiences described, concentrating on specific events as they occur and enhancing the illusion of immediacy by using the present tense – 'The moon, screened by a high peak, sheds but a dim light upon the valley. The wind blows hard. I feel exceedingly cold and my fingers freeze' (p. 151). At the same time her text is consciously retrospective and 'shaped'. She anticipates ('The morrow was to be the first of a series of eventful days. . .' [p. 54]), foreshadows ('I was to experience various things which until then I had only observed from afar' [p. 75]), and creates suspense ('I was far from suspecting that this bit of rough scouting, such as I had so often done in Thibet, was to lead me into a short but rather exciting adventure' [p. 156]). She reminds us that she has a public in view (readers are directly addressed as 'you'), and draws attention to her own quasi-fictional techniques ('What followed was first-rate material for a novelist' [p. 172]). Her journey is formulated as a quest, with Lhasa as the goal towards which all the happenings lead. For instance, the old bonnet she picked up early on, which Yongden wanted her to throw away but which later proved so useful as a disguise, becomes a kind of leitmotif, structuring the narrative. We have seen something of this technique in other women travellers' works – the sense of overriding purpose, such as the desire to see Mount Fuji or to visit Rome, and the build-up of expectation articulated by those confronting Niagara for the first time – but none achieves an equally self-conscious and dramatic work of art, in a text whose 'sincerity' is conveyed as much by artistic as by experiential detail. David-Neel was an exceptional woman and in many respects her work stands on its own, but her responses voice the extraordinary influence of Tibet on all those women who visited it.

Afterword

'No foreign nation possesses that same class of women from which the great body of our female tourists are drafted', declares Elizabeth Rigby, with admirable loyalty to her country and her sex, enthusiastically itemising the characteristics of the species – 'well-read, solid thinking, – early rising – sketch-loving – light-footed – trim-waisted – straw-hatted specimen of women'.[1] A more critical historical awareness has taught us to distrust generalisations, and certainly today any conclusions to be drawn about female travel and travel literature in the nineteenth and early twentieth centuries can only be tentative. But having followed this wide-ranging group of figures through a variety of regions, contrasting socially and topographically, we can see certain common features. As the numbers of texts attest, the extent of this activity in itself belies the pervasive image of restricted and thwarted Victorian womanhood; these travellers were privileged members of their society, it is true, but there were many of them and their ranks swelled over the period. Moreover, their determination to fulfil their aspirations, and the vigour with which they sought to overcome all obstacles, reveal a considerable degree of control over their own lives and indicate resistance to the ideology of female subordination and passivity current in their age.

A particularly noteworthy aspect of this phenomenon is the similarity of reaction to the foreign environment, despite variations in time and place. The almost universal enthusiasm with which the women ventured into strange territories, and the eagerness with which they sought to move beyond the 'known' and commonplace, indicate how important it was to them to widen their horizons, spiritually and physically. Seeking the different, the new and the exotic, they found novelty in the smallest details as well as in the grand sights and regarded nothing as beneath their notice. Even well-trodden ground such as Italy, familiarised by preconception, elicited individualistic, fresh responses, signified as much by the vitality of their writings as by the energy of their explorations. The travellers' emotions were heightened by awareness of the precarious nature of this freedom, often so long desired; beneath their wonder and excitement lies the sense that escape from the confines of domestic and social duty to solipsistic pleasure-seeking was at best transient and often unrepeatable. The moments of intensest urgency in their accounts are foregrounded by the implicit realisation that only through memory and literary expression may such rich experience be relived.

Another significant feature of their response is the way in which their deepest feelings were called up by particular aspects of the foreign. These feelings, often sexual in origin and psychically disturbing, could not surface at home where women were taught to distrust excessive self-concern, as well as to repress the more passionate or libidinal elements of their natures. In the context of the wild, the 'uncivilised' or the strange, however, they reveal subconscious desires, their emotions channelled into the 'acceptable' enthusiasm drawn forth by the notable environment. Moreover, if such encounters offered an indirect means of self-discovery this could be articulated only with equal indirectness. For nineteenth-century women, travel writing, poised between the private sphere of the diary or journal, from which the texts often derived, and the public sphere of the objectified and informative account, could be particularly problematic. Hence there is often a dichotomy in their works between the conscious narrator, analysing what she has seen, and the woman who is most personally and profoundly engaged in the experience, expressing her feeling obliquely through highly charged, metaphoric writing.

Though these shared characteristics suggest a common ground of apprehension and approach, it is less easy to argue from this the existence of a distinctively female tradition of travel writing. It would be very questionable, for example, to assert that interest in foreign social customs or concern for less privileged peoples are peculiarly womanly traits, any more than white, middle-class racism should be seen as exclusively masculine. But because, as women, the travellers both had and knew the value of access to areas of the foreign from which men were excluded, their accounts highlight certain aspects of their encounters. They focus intimately on the familial and domestic angles of foreign life, for example, especially as these concerned members of their own sex. Many of them, too, were uncomfortable with the stance of racial and national superiority bred into them, and attempted to take a more open position vis-à-vis the 'other'. So, while to some extent reliant on the comfortable self-assurance of the colonial spirit, they also acknowledged the need for wider sympathy, and sought points of contact with the alien. Even where direct contact was impossible because of social or linguistic barriers, they often convey a wistful sense of regret at being unable to share fully the spirit of the country and its people. Though for these women, conscious of their own marginalisation, travel abroad could exacerbate their sense of unease about their equivocal gender and social roles, it also inspired a willingness to embrace 'difference'. It is this openness, combined with so much evident enjoyment of the treasured 'spaces' of foreign travel, which makes them so fascinating as adventurers and writers and which gives them value today as interpreters of a significant area of Victorian female experience.

Notes

Preface

1. Marianne North, *Recollections of a Happy Life, Being the Autobiography of Marianne North edited by her sister Mrs J. Addington Symonds*, 2 vols (London, 1892), II, pp. 212–13.

Chapter 1

1. Lillias Campbell Davidson, *Hints to Lady Travellers at Home and Abroad* (London, 1889), p. 255.
2. [Elizabeth Rigby], 'Lady Travellers', *Quarterly Review*, LXXVI, no. CLI, (1845), p. 120.
3. Frances Power Cobbe, 'Celibacy v. Marriage', *Fraser's Magazine*, LXV (February, 1862), p. 233.
4. *Lady Morgan's Memoirs: Autobiography, Diaries and Correspondence*, ed. W. Hepworth Dixon, 2nd edn, 2 vols (London, 1863), II, pp. 99–100.
5. Mary Shelley, *Rambles in Germany and Italy in 1840, 1842, and 1843*, 2 vols (London, 1844), I, p. 160.
6. 'Lady Travellers', pp. 102–3.
7. Frances Anne Kemble, *Record of a Girlhood*, 3 vols (London, 1878), I, p. 108.
8. Frances Anne Kemble, *A Year of Consolation*, 2 vols (London, 1847), I, p. 100.
9. George Nathanial Curzon, Letter to *The Times*, 31 May 1893.
10. William Carey, *Travel and Adventure in Tibet, Including the Diary of Miss Annie R. Taylor's Remarkable Journey from Tau-Chau to Ta-Chien-Lu* (London, 1902), pp. 14, 13, 15, 135.
11. *Ibid.*, pp. 15–16.
12. W. H. Davenport Adams, *Celebrated Women Travellers of the Nineteenth Century* (1883), 8th edn (London, 1903), p. 253.
13. Quoted in Barbara Leigh Smith Bodichon, *An American Diary 1857–8*, ed. Joseph W. Reed (London, 1972), p. 30.
14. Letter to William Allingham, p. 49.
15. Sarah Mytton Maury, *An Englishwoman in America* (London and Liverpool 1848), p. cv.
16. *The Letters of Mary Wollstonecraft Shelley*, ed. Betty T. Bennett, 3 vols (Baltimore and London, 1980–1988), II, 4.

17. Cicely Havely, *This Grand Beyond: The Travels of Isabella Bird Bishop* (London, 1984), p. 29.

18. *Journals and Correspondence of Lady Eastlake*, ed. Charles Eastlake Smith, 2 vols (London, 1895), II, p. 197.

19. Elizabeth Missing Sewell, *Journal of a Summer Tour from Ostend through Germany, Switzerland, and part of the Tyrol to Genoa* (London, 1852), Part II, p. 108.

20. Marianne North, *Some Further Recollections of A Happy Life Selected from the Journals of Marianne North Chiefly between the years 1859 and 1869; edited by her sister Mrs J. Addington Symonds* (London, 1893), pp. 315–16.

21. Frances Trollope, *Travels and Travellers: A Series of Sketches*, 2 vols (London, 1846), II, p. 155.

22. Mrs F. D. Bridges, *Journal of a Lady's Travels round the World* (London, 1883), p. 412.

23. 'Mrs Bishop', *Edinburgh Medical Journal*, n.s. XVI (1904), p. 383.

24. She was careful to point out how very respectably feminine this attire was, after being accused of wearing 'masculine habiliments'. See Pat Barr, *A Curious Life for a Lady* (Harmondsworth, 1985), pp. 184–5.

25. Mrs Dalkeith Holmes, *A Ride on Horseback to Florence through France and Switzerland*, 2 vols (London, 1842), II, p. 400.

26. Anna Brownell Jameson, *Winter Studies and Summer Rambles in Canada*, 3 vols (London, 1838), III, p. 144.

27. *Ibid.*, II, p. 208.

28. Frances Anne Kemble, *Records of Later Life*, 3 vols (London, 1882), III, p. 119.

29. Shelley, *Letters*, I, p. 363.

30. *Anna Jameson: Letters and Friendships (1812–1860)*, ed. Mrs Steuart Erskine (London, 1915), p. 60.

31. North, *Some Further Recollections*, I, p. 179.

32. *Ibid.*, I, p. 180.

33. Frances Trollope, *A Visit to Italy*, 2 vols (London, 1842), II, pp. 230–1.

34. Shelley, *Rambles*, II, p. 280.

35. Mary G. L. Duncan, *America as I found it* (London, 1852), p. 242.

36. Matilda Charlotte Houston, *Texas and the Gulf of Mexico: or Yachting in the New World*, 2 vols (London, 1844), I, p. 163.

37. Harriet Martineau, *Society in America*, 2 vols (Paris, 1837), I, p. xiv.

38. Alice Mabel Bacon, *Japanese Girls and Women* (London, 1905), p. viii.

39. *Anna Jameson: Letters and Friendships*, p. 38.

40. Elizabeth Missing Sewell, *Extracts from a Private Journal Kept from 1845 to 1891*, printed for private circulation (Edinburgh, [1891]), p. 135.

41. North, *Some Further Recollections*, p. 233.

42. *Ibid.*, p. 261; *Recollections of A Happy Life, being the Autobiography of Marianne North edited by her sister Mrs J. Addington Symonds*, 2 vols (London, 1892), II, p. 88.

43. Sewell, *Private Journal*, p. 124.

44. Matilda Charlotte Houston, *Hesperos: or, Travels in the West*, 2 vols (London, 1850), I, p. 1.

45. Mary, Baroness d'Anethan, *Fourteen years of diplomatic life in Japan* (London, 1912), p. 3.

46. Harriet Martineau, *Retrospect of Western Travel*, 2 vols (London, 1838), I, p. 8.

47. Emmeline, Lady Stuart-Wortley, *Travels in the United States etc During 1849 and*

1850, 3 vols (London, 1851), p. v.

48. Isabella Trotter, *First Impressions of the New World* (London, 1859), p. v.
49. Isabella Bird, *The Englishwoman in America* (1856), reprint (Milwaukee, 1966), p. 4; p. 1.
50. Isabella Bird, *A Lady's Life in the Rocky Mountains* (1879), Virago reprint (London, 1983), p. vii.
51. Jameson, *Winter Studies*, I, p. v.
52. *Anna Jameson: Letters and Friendships*, p. 157.
53. Anna Brownell Jameson, *Visits and Sketches at Home and Abroad*, 4 vols (London, 1834), III, pp. 195–6.
54. Selina Martin, *Narrative of a Three Years' Residence in Italy 1819–1822* (London, 1828), p. v.
55. Maria Graham, *Three Months Passed in the Mountains East of Rome During the Year 1819*, 2nd edn (London, 1821), p. iii.
56. Anna D'A, *A Lady's Visit to Manilla and Japan* (London, 1863), pp. vii–viii. The identity of this writer has not been definitively ascertained. Some bibliographical sources give her surname as D'Aguilar; others suggest D'Almedia.
57. Mrs Hugh Fraser, *A Diplomatist's Wife in Japan*, 2 vols (London, 1899), I, p. x.
58. Bacon, p. vii.
59. Marie C. Stopes, *A Journal from Japan: A Daily Record of Life as seen by a Scientist* (London, 1910), p. vii.
60. *Ibid.*, p. xi.
61. Jameson, *Winter Studies*, I, p. vii.
62. Frances Anne Kemble, *Journal*, 2 vols (London, 1835) I, p. viii; *Records of Later Life*, I, p. 18.
63. Susanna Moodie, *Life in the Clearings* (1853), reprint (Toronto, 1976), p. 208.
64. Sydney, Lady Morgan, *Italy*, new edn, 3 vols (London, 1821), I, p. 117.
65. Trollope, *A Visit to Italy*, II, p. 65.
66. Frances Trollope, *Domestic Manners of the Americans* (1832), reprint (Gloucester, 1984), p. 32.
67. Trollope, as we have seen, needed the money after the failure of her bazaar in Cincinnati; Blessington, settled in London after the death of her wealthy and indulgent husband, and comparatively badly off because of legal complications over his will, had to write in order to maintain the life-style to which she had become accustomed.
68. 'Lady Travellers', p. 98.
69. Margaret Fuller Ossoli, *Woman in the Nineteenth Century and Kindred Papers Relating to the Sphere, Condition, and Duties of Woman* (Boston, 1855), pp. 286–7. Fuller does not actually refer to Rigby's article by name, but it seems most likely that this is what she is referring to.

Chapter 2: Italy

1. Frances Trollope *A Visit to Italy*, 2 vols (London, 1842), I, p. 7.
2. Mary Shelley, *Rambles in Germany and Italy in 1840, 1842, and 1843*, 2 vols (London, 1844), II, p. 225; I, p. 2; II, p. 214. Despite the fact that Italy had

such tragic associations for Shelley, she still always longed to return there; her letters in the years following Percy's death in 1823, when she was back in grey and dreary England, are full of fervid desire for Italian sunshine and blue skies.

3. Elizabeth Missing Sewell, *Impressions of Rome, Florence, and Turin* (London, 1862), p. 380.

4. Elizabeth Missing Sewell, *Ivors*, 2 vols (London, 1856), II, p. 240. This is one of Sewell's later novels, in which she re-enacts many of her experiences of Italian travel, including the powerful effect of Venice on her. Parts of the description here are taken almost verbatim from her *Journal of a Summer Tour* (1852).

5. Trollope, I, p. 126.

6. Hon. Mrs Alfred Montgomery, *On the Wing: a Southern Flight* (London, 1875), p. 54.

7. Catherine Taylor, *Letters From Italy to a Younger Sister*, 2 vols (London, 1840), I, pp. 7, 94.

8. Sidney, Lady Morgan, *Italy*, new edn, 3 vols (London, 1821), I, p. 52; II, pp. 170, 329, 66.

9. Marguerite, Countess of Blessington, *The Idler in Italy*, 2nd edn, 3 vols (London, Vols I and II, 1839; Vol III, 1840), III, p. 331.

10. Frances Anne Kemble, *A Year of Consolation*, 2 vols (London, 1847), I, p. 95.

11. When Kemble first met Jameson in 1828, she was initially taken aback not only to find her very much alive and well, but also 'in a very becoming state of plumpitude'. (Quoted in *Anna Jameson: Letters and Friendships*, ed. Mrs Steuart Erskine (London, 1915, p. 75).

12. Frances Anne Kemble, *Record of a Girlhood*, 3 vols (London, 1878), I, pp. 202–3.

13. Frances Anne Kemble, *Journal*, 2 vols (London, 1835), II, p. 207.

14. Kemble, *Year of Consolation*, I, pp. 115–16.

15. *Ibid.*, II, pp. 11–12.

16. Anna Brownell Jameson, *Visits and Sketches at Home and Abroad*, including new edn of *Diary of an Ennuyée*, 4 vols (London, 1834), IV, p. 69. The *Diary*, first published in 1826, is contained in volumes III and IV of this work.

17. Sewell, *Ivors*, II, p. 240.

18. Elizabeth Missing Sewell, *Extracts from a Private Journal Kept From 1845 to 1891*, printed for private circulation (Edinburgh, [1891]), p. 71.

19. [Elizabeth Rigby], 'Lady Travellers', *Quarterly Review*, LXXVI, no. CLI (1845), p. 119.

20. Selina Martin, *Narrative of a Three Years' Residence in Italy 1819–1822* (London, 1828), p. 164.

21. Frances Power Cobbe, *Italics: brief notes on politics, people, and places in Italy in 1864* (London, 1864), p. 428.

22. Among other things, these included cheaper food and rents, and the enjoyment of luxuries such as a carriage and a thrice-weekly box at the opera.

23. She dwells on her loneliness in several places in *Diary of an Ennuyée*.

24. See *Lady Morgan's Memoirs: Autobiography, Diaries and Correspondence* ed. W. Hepworth Dixon, 2nd edn, 2 vols (London, 1863) Volume II, for details of Colburn's proposal.

25. *Ibid.*, II, p. 80.

26. Kemble, *Year of Consolation*, I, p. 29.
27. Quoted in Dorothy Hewlett, *Elizabeth Barrett Browning* (London, 1953) p. 222.
28. Elizabeth Missing Sewell, *Journal of a Summer Tour From Ostend through Germany, Switzerland, and part of the Tyrol to Genoa* (London, 1852), Part III, p. 7.
29. Kemble, *Year of Consolation*, I, pp. 126–7; 151–2; 127.
30. *Journals and Correspondence of Lady Eastlake*, ed. Charles Eastlake Smith, 2 vols (London, 1895), II, p. 88.
31. Frances Anne Kemble, *Records of Later Life*, 3 vols (London, 1882), III, p. 262.
32. Sewell, *Extracts from a Private Journal*, p. 158.
33. Sewell, *Summer Tour*, Part III, pp. 101, 114. *Ivors*, II, pp. 312, 345.
34. Sewell, *Summer Tour*, Part III, p. 115.
35. Mrs Dalkeith Holmes, *A Ride on Horseback to Florence through France and Switzerland*, 2 vols (London, 1842), I, p. 123; II, p. 153.
36. *Memoirs*, II, p. 139.
37. Emily Birchall, *Wedding Tour, January–June 1873*, ed. David Verey (Gloucester, 1985), pp. 77, 78, 79.
38. *Anna Jameson: Letters and Friendships*, p. 62.
39. Sewell, *Impressions*, pp. 237, 245, 246–7.
40. Sewell, *Summer Tour*, Part III, p. 196.
41. *Memoirs*, II, p. 90.
42. Mrs G. Gretton, *The Englishwoman in Italy: Impressions of Life in the Roman States and Sardinia, During a Ten Years' Residence*, 2 vols (London, 1860), I, p. 1.
43. The liveliness of Morgan's writing cheered up even the lugubrious Jameson of the *Diary*, though she was not entirely happy about her 'peculiar and rather unfeminine habits of thinking' (*Visits and Sketches*, IV, p. 48).
44. Percy Bysshe Shelley, *Essays, Letters from Abroad, Translations and Fragments*, ed. Mrs Shelley, 2 vols (London, 1852), p. 4. This quotation is from her *Journal of a Six Weeks Tour* which she included in Volume II of the work.
45. See *Athenaeum*, nos 781, 782 (15 and 22 October 1842), and *Tait's Edinburgh Magazine*, IX (November 1842), for comments of this nature.
46. Mariana Starke, *Travels in Italy between the Years 1792 and 1798*, 2 vols (London, 1802), I, pp. 4, 246.
47. Michael Sadleir, *Blessington D'Orsay: A Masquerade* (London, 1933), p. 61.
48. *Ibid.*, p. 277.
49. *Memoirs*, II, p. 94.
50. *The Letters of Mary Wollstonecraft Shelley*, ed. Betty T. Bennett, 3 vols (Baltimore and London, 1980–1988), I, p. 78.
51. Kemble, *Year of Consolation*, I, p. 175; II, p. 64.
52. Sewell, *Impressions*, pp. 55, 229.

Chapter 3: North America

1. Isabella Bird, *The Englishwoman in America* (1856), reprint of first edition (Milwaukee, 1966), p. 89.
2. Mrs Trollope's comment about America's unfamiliarity to her sons, who visited her there, validates this: 'Had they visited Greece or Rome, they

would have encountered objects with whose images their minds had been long acquainted; or had they travelled to France or Italy they would have seen only what daily convention had already rendered familiar; but at our public schools America . . . is hardly better known than fairy land'. (*Domestic Manners of the Americans*, 1832; reprint Gloucester, 1984, p. 70).

3. Frances Anne Kemble, *Record of a Girlhood*, 3 vols (London, 1878), III, pp. 229–30.

4. Harriet Martineau, *Autobiography* (1887), Virago reprint, 2 vols (London, 1983), II, p. 4.

5. *Ibid.*, II, p. 2.

6. Frances Wright, *Views of Society and Manners in America*, ed. Paul R. Baker (Cambridge, Mass., 1963), pp. ix–x, 250, 96.

7. Harriet Martineau, *Society in America*, 2 vols (Paris, 1837), I, p. ix.

8. Captain Basil Hall's *Travels in North America in the Years 1827 and 1828,* 3 vols (Edinburgh, 1829) criticised, among other things, the general shoddiness of American manufacture, the nation's obsession with its victory in the Revolution and its endless insistence that it be acknowledged the best country in the world. Despite his prefatory claim that he had found much to admire during his visit, his book aroused almost universal resentment.

9. Matilda Charlotte Houston, *Hesperos: or, Travels in the West*, 2 vols (London, 1850), I, p. 149.

10. Matilda Charlotte Houston, *Texas and the Gulf of Mexico: or, Yachting in the New World,* 2 vols (London, 1844), I, p. 2.

11. Marianne North, *Recollections of a Happy Life, being the Autobiography of Marianne North edited by her sister Mrs J. Addington Symonds*, 2 vols (London, 1892), I, p. 39.

12. Frances Anne Kemble, *Records of Later Life*, 3 vols (London, 1882), II, p. 38; I, p. 64.

13. Kemble, *Record of a Girlhood*, III, p. 229.

14. Emmeline, Lady Stuart-Wortley, *Travels in the United States etc. During 1849 and 1850*, 3 vols (London, 1851), I, p. 58.

15. *Letters of Anna Jameson to Ottilie von Goethe*, ed. G. H. Needler (London, 1939), p. 56.

16. *Anna Jameson: Letters and Friendships (1812–1860)*, ed. Mrs Steuart Erskine (London, 1915), pp. 129, 132.

17. Harriet Martineau, *Retrospect of Western Travel*, 2 vols (London, 1838), I, p. 18.

18. Sarah Mytton Maury, *An Englishwoman in America* (London and Liverpool, 1848), p. 45.

19. Kemble, *Records of Later Life*, I, p. 72.

20. Anna Jameson, *Winter Studies and Summer Rambles in Canada*, 3 vols (London, 1838), I, pp. 231–2.

21. North, *Recollections,* II, p. 199.

22. Stuart-Wortley, I, p. 214.

23. Bird, p. 168.

24. Victoria Stuart-Wortley, *A Young Traveller's Journal of a Tour in North and South America During the Year 1850* (London, 1852), p. 95.

25. Frances Anne Kemble, *Journal*, 2 vols (London, 1835), II, pp. 97–8.

26. This fact is confirmed by the geologist Charles Lyell, who went to America in the 1840s. He notes that women 'may travel alone here in stage-coaches, steam-boats, and railways, with less risk of encountering disagreeable

behaviour, and of hearing coarse and unpleasant conversation than in any country I have ever visited'. (Charles Lyell, *Travels in North America*, 2 vols, London, 1845, I, p. 71).

27. From a reminiscence of Jameson by Henry Scadding, an immigrant clergyman in Ontario. Quoted in Clara Thomas, *Love and Work Enough: The Life of Anna Jameson* (London, 1967), p. 120.
28. Isabella Bird, *A Lady's Life in the Rocky Mountains* (1879), Virago reprint (London, 1983), p. 6.
29. Frances Anne Kemble, *A Year of Consolation*, 2 vols (London, 1847), I, pp. 65–6.
30. Kemble, *Journal*, I, p. 66.
31. Catherine Parr Traill, *The Backwoods of Canada: being Letters from the Wife of an Emigrant Officer, Illustrative of the Domestic Economy of British America* (1836), new edn (London, 1846), pp. 23, 39, 48, 87.
32. Susanna Moodie, *Life in the Clearings* (1853), reprint (Toronto, 1976), p. 247.
33. Susanna Moodie, *Roughing it in the Bush, or Life in Canada* (1852), Virago reprint (London, 1986), p. 172.
34. Isabella Trotter, *First Impressions of the New World* (London, 1859), p. 217.
35. Houston, *Texas*, I, p. 117.
36. Kemble, *Records of Later Life,* III, p. 128.
37. *Ibid.,* I, p. 238.
38. Mrs A. Grant, *Memoirs of an American Lady* (1808), reprint (New York, 1846), pp. 193, 196.
39. Letter to Ellen Nussey, 7 August 1841 (*The Brontës: their Lives, Friendships and Correspondence*, eds T. J. Wise and J. A. Symington, 4 vols Oxford, 1980, I, p. 240).
40. *Anna Jameson: Letters and Friendships*, p. 157.
41. Frances Anne Kemble, *Journal of a Residence on a Georgian Plantation in 1838–9*, ed. John A. Scott (London, 1961), p. 96.
42. Kemble, *Record of a Girlhood*, III, p. 314.
43. Trollope, p. 273.
44. The Clifton House Hotel, at which most tourists stayed, was situated right beside the Falls. It was able to accommodate about four hundred guests and was an abode of much gaiety in the summer months.
45. Kemble, *Journal*, II, pp. 285–7. In this account she does not mention Trelawney by name, but in the later version she explains how she met this much-travelled and colourful figure, a friend of the Shelleys, in June 1833 on the boat taking them to Niagara. He became one of their party and acted as their guide; according to Kemble, he prevented her from hurling herself into the cataract in her enthusiasm.
46. Marianne Finch, *An Englishwoman's Experience in America* (1853), reprint (New York, 1969), p. 366.
47. Kemble, *Record of a Girlhood*, III, pp. 308, 304–5. In her *Journal*, she comments that 'most describers launch forth into vague and intangible rhapsodies which, after all, convey no express idea of any thing but water in the abstract' (II, p. 205).
48. Trollope, p. 286; Bird, p. 223; Stuart-Wortley, I, pp. 22, 20; Houston, *Hesperos* I, p. 129; Trollope, p. 286; Wright, p. 126; Finch, p. 367.
49. *Hesperos*, I, p. 136; Trollope, p. 282.
50. *Anna Jameson: Letters and Friendships*, p. 152.

51. Kemble, *Record of a Girlhood,* III, p. 305.
52. Kemble, *Journal,* II, p. 211.
53. Mary G. L. Duncan, *America as I found it* (London, 1852), p. 321.
54. [Margaret Hunter Hall], *The Aristocratic Journey, Being the Outspoken Letters of Mrs Basil Hall written during a Fourteen Months' Sojourn in America 1827–1828,* ed. Una Pope-Hennessy (New York and London, 1931), pp. 241, 243.
55. Kemble, *Journal,* I, pp. 74–5.
56. Kemble, *Journal of a Residence,* pp. 216, 302.
57. She gives the history of its publication in *Records of Later Life,* I, pp. 260–2.
58. Kemble, *Journal of a Residence,* p. 11.
59. Kemble, *Records of Later Life,* I, pp. 227–8.
60. For readers of *Jane Eyre* the parallels between servitude in slavery and female submission to patriarchy, albeit disguised as adulation, would have been plain enough. See especially Chapter 24.
61. Such references are not always complimentary. Several of the travellers were not wholly happy with Trollope's acerbic treatment of America, and others express unease about previous commentators. Bodichon, for example, is highly critical of the mellow representation of slavery given by writers such as Amelia Murray, Frederika Bremer and Dickens, and Kemble points to the dangerous lack of veracity in Basil Hall's contentious book.
62. Elizabeth Missing Sewell, *Extracts from a Private Journal Kept from 1845 to 1891,* printed for private circulation (Edinburgh, [1891]), p. 3. Sewell herself never went to America, but always longed to; one of her pupils at her small school in the Isle of Wight was the sister of the American novelist, F. Marion Crawford (and of Mrs Hugh Fraser, discussed here in the chapter on Japan), and a Bostonian lady was her valued friend and correspondent for nearly thirty years.
63. 'Mrs Jameson's *Winter Studies and Summer Rambles',* *British and Foreign Review,* VIII (January, 1839), p. 148.
64. Both Finch and Kemble tell funny stories about the American terror of acknowledging the fact that women have legs, and Finch speculates that one particularly prudish lady she encounters may be 'one of those *refined females,* who covered the legs of her piano, and could not take her tea, if she saw a man's figure painted in the saucer' (p. 355).

Chapter 4

1. Marie C. Stopes, *A Journal from Japan: a Daily Record of Life as seen by a Scientist* (London, 1910), p. xiv.
2. One of the worst instances of this occurred in the early hours of 6 July 1861, when the British Legation in Edo (Tokyo) was attacked by hostile Japanese. Several of the diplomatic staff were badly wounded, including Laurence Oliphant, a member of the Elgin Mission, whose reminiscences are a valuable source of information for life in the pre-Meiji regime. (*Narrative of the Earl of Elgin's Mission to China and Japan in the years 1857, '58, '59,* 2 vols Edinburgh, 1859).

NOTES 185

3. Quoted in Pat Barr, *The Deer Cry Pavilion: A Story of Westerners in Japan 1868–1905* (London, 1969), p. 161.
4. Sara Jeannette Duncan, *A Social Departure: How Orthodocia and I went round the world by ourselves* (London, 1890), pp. 59–60.
5. Isabella Bird, *Unbeaten Tracks in Japan* (1880), Virago reprint (London, 1984), p. 1.
6. At this time (1875), it was still necessary for the foreign tourist to get a special passport in order to visit the former capital.
7. Alice Mabel Bacon, *Japanese Girls and Women* (London, 1904), p. 325.
8. Douglas Sladen and Norma Lorimer, *More Queer Things about Japan*, p. 7. Part I of this work, 'Japan from a Woman's Point of View' is by Lorimer.
9. Marianne North, *Recollections of A Happy Life. Being the Autobiography of Marianne North edited by her sister Mrs J. Addington Symonds*, 2 vols (London, 1892), I, p. 222.
10. Augusta M. Campbell Davidson, *Present Day Japan* (London, 1904), p. 58.
11. Mrs Hugh Fraser, *A Diplomatist's Wife in Japan. Letters from Home to Home*, 2 vols (London, 1899), I, p. 7.
12. Said develops at some length his theories of the Orient as an image in the Western mind, constructed by literary and political attitudes and represented by a discourse particular to it, in his *Orientalism* (London, 1978).
13. Susan Morgan, 'An Introduction to Women's Travel Writings about Southeast Asia', *Genre*, XX (Summer, 1987), pp. 189–208.
14. Toshio Yokoyama, *Japan in the Victorian Mind: A Study of Stereotyped Images of a Nation 1850–80* (London, 1987).
15. Mary, Baroness D'Anethan, *Fourteen Years of Diplomatic Life in Japan: Leaves from the Diary of Baroness Albert D'Anethan* (London, 1912), p. 435.
16. Fraser, *A Diplomatist's Wife*, II, p. 169.
17. Until the end of the nineteenth century, women were not allowed to climb to the summit of Fujiyama, being considered too lowly to tread the sacred ground at its crest. Fraser records a conversation with one young Japanese woman who had made the ascent, but who 'told me that nothing would induce her to go through such hardship again' (II, p. 137). For a short account of how late-nineteenth-century tourists conquered Fuji, see Pat Barr, *The Deer Cry Pavilion*, pp. 168–71.
18. Stopes, *A Journal from Japan*, p. xii. She may have found this especially difficult since she became emotionally involved with a Japanese professor while in Tokyo, a relationship whose failure may have contributed to the break-up of her first marriage to a Canadian botanist, Reginald Gates.
19. Catherine Bond, *Goldfields and Chrysanthemums: Notes of Travel in Australia and Japan* (London, 1898), pp. 122, 123. 'Quaint' is not only Bond's favourite adjective, but also that of several others of the travellers.
20. Mrs F. D. Bridges, *Journal of a Lady's Travels Round the World* (London, 1883), pp. 272, 273.
21. See note 10.
22. Introduction to *Unbeaten Tracks* by Pat Barr, Virago 1984 reprint, pp. xix–xx.
23. Ethel Howard, *Japanese Memories* (London, 1918), p. 151.
24. Bond, *Goldfields and Chrysanthemums*, p. 142.
25. Davidson, *Present-Day Japan*, p. 124.
26. Noh theatre, which flowered in Japan in the fourteenth and fifteenth

centuries, has its roots in Zen-based spiritual and aesthetic ideals. It is a masked musical dance drama, usually revolving around a dramatic encounter between a troubled spirit and a priest or bystander. The actors' masks, often denoting states of mind or spiritual conditions, distort the voice to an unearthly quality, and the varying dance movements heighten the intensity. It may seem bizarre to Western eyes, but it is of the highest seriousness, and certainly contains no intentionally humorous elements.

27. Fraser, *A Diplomatist's Wife*, I, p. 425.
28. Howard, *Japanese Memories*, p. 107.
29. Gertrude Adams Fisher, *A Woman Alone in the Heart of Japan* (London, n.d.), p. 24.
30. Jane E. Duncan, *A Summer Ride Through Western Tibet* (London, 1906), p. 280.
31. The fact that only six travellers are discussed here – though one or two others, such as Fanny Bullock Workman, the American climber, could have been included – points to this paucity in contrast to the other geographical regions discussed.
32. For details of the history of Tibetan exploration, see the studies by Holdich and Hopkirk, listed in the Bibliography.
33. See Peter Hopkirk's account of them in his *Trespassers on the Roof of the World* (London, 1982).
34. Sir Thomas Holdich, *Tibet the Mysterious* (London, 1906), pp. 300, 294. Of the few accounts which would have been available to the nineteenth-century traveller to Tibet, the best known was probably that of the Abbé Huc, a Jesuit missionary (*Recollections of a Journey through Tartary, Tibet and China*, 1852).
35. Mrs F. D. Bridges, *Journal of a Lady's Travels Round the World* (London, 1883), p. 139.
36. William Carey, *Travel and Adventure in Tibet, Including the Diary of Miss Annie R. Taylor's Remarkable Journey from Tau-Chau to Ta-Chien-Lu through the heart of the Forbidden Land* (London, 1902), p. 16.
37. *Ibid.,* p. 207.
38. Susie Carson Rijnhart, *With the Tibetans in Tent and Temple* (Edinburgh and London, 1901), pp. 192, 193, 195.
39. Anna M. Stoddart, *The Life of Isabella Bird*, 3rd edn (London, 1908), p. 149.
40. Isabella Bird Bishop, *Among the Tibetans* (1894), reprinted (London, 1904), p. 159.
41. Alexandra David-Neel, *My Journey to Lhasa* (1927), Virago reprint (London, 1988), p. xvii. This text, unlike most of David-Neel's other works, was originally written in English, not in her native French, thus suggesting that the tradition of female travel writing cuts across barriers of culture and language.
42. Carey, *Travel and Adventure*, pp. 225–6.
43. Annie R. Taylor, 'An Englishwoman in Thibet', *National Review*, XXII (September, 1893), p. 34.
44. It must of course be pointed out that since Carey carefully edited her diary, the picture we get of Taylor is to some extent the result of his control over her narrative.
45. L. Sara Mills, 'A Foucauldian Perspective on Literariness and Fictionality in Travel Writing' (unpublished PhD thesis, University of Birmingham, 1988).

46. The custom by which only the eldest son in the family marries, and his wife accepts his brothers as additional husbands, all ensuing children being legally his.
47. Annie R. Taylor, 'My Experiences in Tibet', *Scottish Geographical Magazine*, X (January, 1894), pp. 7–8.
48. *Ibid.,* p. 1.

Afterword

1. [Elizabeth Rigby], 'Lady Travellers', *Quarterly Review*, LXXVI, no. CLI, (1845) p. 102.

Bibliography

Primary sources

These items are grouped according to the country of visitation. There is occasional repetition where the writer went to more than one of the places listed. The dates given are those of the editions consulted, which, unless otherwise stated, are the first.

Italy

Birchall, Emily, *Wedding Tour, January-June 1873*, ed. David Verey (Gloucester, 1980).

Blessington, Marguerite, Countess of, *The Idler in Italy*, 2nd edn, 3 vols (London; vols I and II, 1839, vol III, 1840).

Campbell, Harriet Charlotte Beaujolois, *A Journey to Florence in 1817*, ed. G. R. de Beer (London, 1951).

Cobbe, Frances Power, *Italics: brief notes on politics, people and places in Italy in 1864* (London, 1864).

Cobbe, Frances Power, *Life of Frances Power Cobbe, by Herself*, 3rd edn, 2 vols (London, 1894).

Cobbe, Frances Power, The *Cities of the Past* (London, 1864).

[Eastlake, Elizabeth], *Journals and Correspondence of Lady Eastlake*, ed. Charles Eastlake Smith, 2 vols (London, 1895).

Graham, Maria, *Three Months Passed in the Mountains East of Rome During the Year 1819*, 2nd edn (London, 1821).

Gretton, Mrs G., *The Englishwoman in Italy: Impressions of Life in the Roman States and Sardinina, During a Ten Years' Residence*, 2 vols (London, 1860).

Hall, Mrs Newman, *Through the Tyrol to Venice* (London, 1860).

Holmes, Mrs Dalkeith, *A Ride on Horseback to Florence through France and Switzerland. Described in a Series of Letters*, 2 vols (London, 1842).

[Jameson, Anna Brownell], *Anna Jameson: Letters and Friendships (1812–1860)*, ed. Mrs Steuart Erskine (London, 1915).

Jameson, Anna Brownell, *Visits and Sketches at Home and Abroad,* 4 vols (London, 1834).

Kavanagh, Julia, *A Summer and Winter in the Two Sicilies,* 2 vols (London, 1858).

Kemble, Frances Anne, *A Year of Consolation,* 2 vols (London, 1847).

Kemble, Frances Anne, *Record of a Girlhood,* 3 vols (London, 1878).

Kemble, Frances Anne, *Records of Later Life,* 3 vols (London, 1882).

Martin, Selina, *Narrative of a Three Years' Residence in Italy 1819–1822 with illustrations of the present state of religion in that country* (London, 1828).

Montgomery, the Hon. Mrs Alfred, *On the Wing: a Southern Flight* (London, 1875).

Morgan, Lady Sidney, *Italy,* new edn, 3 vols (London, 1821).

[Morgan, Lady Sidney], *Lady Morgan's Memoirs: Autobiography, Diaries and Correspondence,* ed. W. Hepworth Dixon, 2nd edn, 2 vols (London, 1863).

Sewell, Elizabeth Missing, *Journal of a Summer Tour from Ostend through Germany, Switzerland, and part of the Tyrol to Genoa, kept for the Children of a Village School* (London, 1852).

Sewell, Elizabeth Missing, *Ivors,* 2 vols (London, 1856).

Sewell, Elizabeth Missing, *Impressions of Rome, Florence, and Turin* (London, 1862).

Sewell, Elizabeth Missing, *Extracts from a Private Journal kept from 1845 to 1891,* printed for private circulation (Edinburgh, 1891).

Shelley, Mary, *Rambles in Germany and Italy in 1840, 1842, and 1843,* 2 vols (London, 1844).

Shelley, Mary, *The Letters of Mary Wollstonecraft Shelley,* ed. Betty T. Bennett, 3 vols (Baltimore and London, 1980–1988).

Starke, Mariana, *Travels in Italy between the Years 1792 and 1798,* 2 vols (London, 1802).

Taylor, Catherine, *Letters from Italy to a Younger Sister,* 2 vols (London, 1840).

Trollope, Frances, *A Visit to Italy,* 2 vols (London, 1842).

North America

Bird, Isabella, *The Englishwoman in America* (1856), reprint (Milwaukee, 1966).

Bird, Isabella, *A Lady's Life in the Rocky Mountains* (1879), Virago reprint (London, 1983).

Bodichon, Barbara Leigh Smith, *An American Diary 1857–8,* ed. Joseph W. Reed (London, 1972).

Duncan, Mary G. L., *America as I found it* (London, 1852).

Finch, Marianne, *An Englishwoman's Experience in America* (1853), reprint (New York, 1969).

Grant, Mrs A., *Memoirs of an American lady, with Sketches of Manners and Scenery in America as they existed previous to the Revolution* (1808), reprint (New York, 1846).

[Hall, Margaret], *The Aristocratic Journey, Being the Outspoken Letters of Mrs Basil Hall written during a Fourteen Months' Sojourn in America 1827–1828* ed. Una Pope-Hennessy (New York and London, 1931).

Houston, Matilda Charlotte, *Texas and the Gulf of Mexico: or, Yachting in the New World,* 2 vols (London, 1844).

Houston, Matilda Charlotte, *Hesperos: or, Travels in the West,* 2 vols (London, 1850).

Jameson, Anna Brownell, *Winter Studies and Summer Rambles in Canada*, 3 vols (London, 1838).

[Jameson, Anna Brownell], *Anna Jameson: Letters and Friendships (1812–1860)*, ed. Mrs Steuart Erskine (London, 1915).

[Jameson, Anna Brownell] *Letters of Anna Jameson to Ottilie von Goethe*, ed. G. H. Needler (London, 1939).

Kemble, Frances Anne, *Journal*, 2 vols (London, 1835).

Kemble, Frances Anne, *Journal of a Residence on a Georgian Plantation in 1838–9*, ed. John A. Scott (London, 1961).

Kemble, Frances Anne, *Record of a Girlhood*, 3 vols (London, 1878).

Kemble, Frances Anne, *Records of Later Life*, 3 vols (London, 1882).

Martineau, Harriet, *Society in America*, 2 vols (Paris, 1837).

Martineau, Harriet, *Restrospect of Western Travel*, 2 vols (London, 1838).

Martineau, Harriet, *Autobiography* (1887), Virago reprint, 2 vols (London, 1983).

Maury, Sarah Mytton, *An Englishwoman in America* (London and Liverpool, 1848).

Moodie, Susanna, *Roughing it in the Bush, or, Life in Canada* (1852), Virago reprint (London, 1986).

Moodie, Susanna, *Life in the Clearings* (1853), reprint (Toronto, 1976).

Murray, Hon. Amelia M., *Letters from the United States, Cuba and Canada* (1856), reprint (New York, 1969).

North, Marianne, *Recollections of a Happy Life, being the autobiography of Marianne North edited by her sister Mrs J. Addington Symonds*, 2 vols (London, 1892).

North, Marianne, *Some Further Recollections of a Happy Life selected from the journals of Marianne North chiefly between the years 1859 and 1869: edited by her sister Mrs J. Addington Symonds* (London, 1893).

Pfeiffer, Ida, *A Lady's Second Journey Round the World*, 2 vols (London, 1855).

Stuart-Wortley, Lady Emmeline, *Travels in the United States etc. During 1849 and 1850*, 3 vols (London, 1851).

Stuart-Wortley, Victoria, *A Young Traveller's Journal of a Tour in North and South America During the Year 1850* (London, 1852).

Traill, Catherine Parr, *The Backwoods of Canada: being Letters from the Wife of an Emigrant Officer, Illustrative of the Domestic Economy of British America*, new edn (London, 1846).

Trollope, Frances, *Domestic Manners of the Americans* (1832), reprint (Gloucester, 1984).

Trotter, Isabella, *First Impressions of the New World* (London, 1859), p. v.

Wright, Frances, *Views of Society and Manners in America*, ed. Paul R. Baker (Cambridge, Mass., 1963).

Japan

Bacon, Alice Mabel, *Japanese Girls and Women* (London, 1904).

Bennett, Ella M. Hart, *An English Girl in Japan* (London, 1904).

Bickersteth, Mary, *Japan as we saw it* (London, 1893).

Bird, Isabella, *Unbeaten Tracks in Japan* (1880), Virago reprint (London, 1984).

Bond, Catherine, *Goldfields and Chrysanthemums: Notes of Travel in Australia and Japan* (London, 1898).

Brassey, Lady Annie, *A Voyage in the Sunbeam, our Home on the Ocean for Eleven Months* (London, 1878).

Bridges, Mrs F. D., *Journal of a Lady's Travels Round the World* (London, 1883).

D'A, *A Lady's Visit to Manila and Japan* (London, 1863).

D'Anethan, Eleanora Mary, *Fourteen Years of Diplomatic Life in Japan: Leaves from the Diary of Baroness Albert D'Anethan* (London, 1912).

Davidson, Augusta M. Campbell, *Present-Day Japan* (London, 1904).

Duncan, Sara Jeannette, *A Social Departure: How Orthodocia and I went round the world by ourselves* (London, 1890).

Fisher, Gertrude Adams, *A Woman Alone in the Heart of Japan* (London, n.d.)

Fraser, Mrs Hugh, *A Diplomatist's Wife in Japan. Letters from Home to Home*, 2 vols (London, 1899).

Hodgson, C. Pemberton, *A Residence at Nagasaki and Hakodate in 1859–60 with an account of Japan generally* (London, 1861) (includes one chapter of Mrs Hodgson's narrative).

Howard, Ethel, *Japanese Memories* (London, 1918).

North, Marianne, *Recollections of a Happy Life, being the autobiography of Marianne North edited by her sister Mrs J. Addington Symonds*, 2 vols (London, 1892).

Sladen, Douglas and Norma Lorimer, *More Queer Things about Japan* (London, 1904).

Stopes, Marie C., *A Journal from Japan: a Daily Record of Life as seen by a Scientist* (London, 1910).

Tibet

Bishop, Isabella Bird, *Among the Tibetans* (1894), reprint (London, 1904).

Bridges, Mrs F. D., *Journal of a Lady's Travels Round the World* (London, 1883).

Carey, William, *Travel and Adventure in Tibet, including the Diary of Miss Annie R. Taylor's Remarkable Journey from Tau-Chau to Ta-Chien-Lu through the heart of the Forbidden Land* (London, 1902).

David-Neel, Alexandra, *My Journey to Lhasa* (1927), Virago reprint (London, 1988).

Duncan, Jane E., *A Summer Ride Through Western Tibet* (London, 1906).

Rijnhart, Susie Carson, *With the Tibetans in Tent and Temple* (Edinburgh and London, 1901).

Taylor, Annie R., 'An Englishwoman in Thibet', *National Review*, XXII (September 1893), pp. 25–35.

Taylor, Annie R., 'My Experiences in Tibet', *Scottish Geographical Magazine*, X (January 1894), pp. 1–8.

Secondary material

These items include general and more specific studies on travel and travel literature, and also biographical works about some of the women discussed.

Adams, Percy G., *Travel Literature and the Evolution of the Novel* (Lexington, 1983).

Adams, W. H. Davenport, *Celebrated Women Travellers of the Nineteenth Century*, 8th edn (London, 1903).

Aitken, Maria, *A Girdle Round the Earth* (London, 1987).

Allen, Alexandra, *Travelling Ladies: Victorian Adventuresses* (London, 1980).

Athenaeum, nos 781, 782 (15 and 22 October 1842).

Barr, Pat, *The Coming of the Barbarians: A Story of Western Settlement of Japan 1853–1870* (London, 1967).

Barr, Pat, *The Deer Cry Pavilion: A Story of Westerners in Japan 1868–1905* (London, 1968).

Barr, Pat, *A Curious Life for a Lady: The Story of Isabella Bird, Traveller Extraordinary* (Harmondsworth, 1985).

Birkett, Dea, *Spinsters Abroad: Victorian Lady Explorers* (Oxford, 1989).

Black, Jeremy, *The British and the Grand Tour* (London, 1985).

Blanch Lesley, *The Wilder Shores of Love* (London, 1954).

Blanch, Lesley, *Under a Lilac-Bleeding Star: Travel and Travellers* (London, 1963).

Bobbë, Dorothy de B., *Fanny Kemble* (London, 1932).

Borghi, Liana, Nicoletta Livi Bacci and Uta Treder, eds, *Viaggio e Scrittura: Le Straniere nell'Italia dell'Ottocento* (Firenze, 1988).

Cameron, Ian, *To the Farthest Ends of the Earth: the History of the Royal Geographical Society* (London, 1980).

Churchill, Kenneth, *Italy and English Literature 1764–1930* (Totowa, New Jersey, 1980).

Cobbe, Frances Power, 'Celibacy v. Marriage', *Fraser's Magazine* LXV (February 1862), p. 233.

Collcutt, Martin, Marius Jensen and Isao Kumakura, eds, *Cultural Atlas of Japan* (Oxford, 1988).

Conrad, Peter, *Imagining America* (London, 1980).

Cortazzi, Hugh, *Victorians in Japan, in and around the Treaty Ports* (London, 1987).

Cumming, C. F. Gordon, *Wanderings in China*, 2 vols (London, 1886).

Curzon, George Nathanial, Letter to *The Times*, 31 May (1893).

Cust, Mrs Henry, *Wanderers: Episodes from the Travels of Lady Emmeline Stuart-Wortley and her daughter Victoria 1849–1855* (London, 1928).

Davidson, Lillias Campbell, *Hints to Lady Travellers at Home and Abroad* (London, 1889).

Dodd, Philip, ed., *The Art of Travel: Essays on Travel Writing* (London, 1982).

Fowler, Marion, *The Embroidered Tent: Five Gentlewomen in Early Canada* (Toronto, 1982).

Frank, Katherine, *A Voyager Out: The Life of Mary Kingsley* (London, 1987).

Furnas, J. C., *Fanny Kemble: Leading Lady of the Nineteenth-Century Stage* (New York, 1982).

Fussell, Paul, *Abroad: Literary Traveling Between the Wars* (New York and Oxford, 1982).

Grylls, R. Glynn, *Mary Shelley: A Biography* (London, 1938).

Hall, Basil, *Travels in North America in the Years 1827–1828*, 3 vols (Edinburgh, 1829).

Hamalian, Leo, *Ladies on the Loose: Women Travellers of the Eighteenth and Nineteenth Centuries* (New York, 1981).

[Hamilton, Thomas], *Men and Manners in America*, 3 vols (Edinburgh, 1833).

Havely, Cicely, *This Grand Beyond: The Travels of Isabella Bird Bishop* (London, 1984).

Hearn, Lafcadio, *Writings from Japan*, ed. Frances King (Harmondsworth, 1984).

Hewlett, Dorothy, *Elizabeth Barrett Browning* (London, 1953).

Hibbert, Christopher, *The Grand Tour* (London, 1969).

Holdich, Sir Thomas, *Tibet the Mysterious* (London, 1906).

Hopkirk, Peter, *Trespassers on the Roof of the World: The Race for Lhasa* (London, 1982).

Kenyon, Frederick, G., ed., *Letters of Elizabeth Barrett Browning*, 2 vols (London, 1897).

Lochhead, Marion, *Elizabeth Rigby, Lady Eastlake* (London, 1961).

Lyell, Charles, *Travels in North America: with Geological Observations on the United States, Canada, and Novia Scotia*, 2 vols (London, 1845).

Marshall, Dorothy, *Fanny Kemble* (London, 1977).

Middleton, Dorothy, *Victorian Lady Travellers* (London, 1965).

Miller, Luree, *On Top of the World: Five Women Explorers in Tibet* (London, 1976).

Mills, L. Sara, 'A Foucauldian Perspective on Literariness and Fictionality in Travel Writing' (unpublished PhD thesis, University of Birmingham, 1988).

Moers, Ellen, *Literary Women* (London, 1977).

Morgan, Susan, 'An Introduction to Victorian Women's Travel Writings about Southeast Asia', *Genre*, XX (Summer, 1987), pp. 189–208.

'Mrs Bishop', *Edinburgh Medical Journal*, n.s. XVI, (1904), p. 383.

Mulvey, Christopher, *Anglo-American Landscapes: a study of nineteenth-century Anglo-American travel literature* (Cambridge, 1983).

Oliphant, Laurence, *Narrative of the Earl of Elgin's Mission to China and Japan in the years 1857, '58, '59*, 2 vols (Edinburgh, 1859).

Ossoli, Margaret Fuller, *Woman in the Nineteenth Century and Kindred Papers Relating to the Sphere, Condition, and Duties of Woman* (Boston, 1855).

Pemble, John, *The Mediterranean Passion: Victorians and Edwardians in the South* (Oxford and New York, 1987).

Pine-Coffin, R. S., *Bibliography of British and American Travel in Italy to 1860*, (Firenze, 1974).

Pope-Hennessy, Una, *Three English Women in America* (London, 1929).

Rigby, Elizabeth [Lady Eastlake], 'Lady Travellers', *Quarterly Review*, LXXVI, No CLI (1845), pp. 98–137.

Russell, Mary, *The Blessings of a Good Thick Skirt: Women Travellers and their World* (London, 1986).

Sadleir, Michael, *Blessington D'Orsay, A Masquerade* (London, 1933).

Said, Edward, *Orientalism* (London, 1978).

Shelley, Percy Bysshe, *Essays, Letters from Abroad, Translations and Fragments*, ed. Mrs Shelley (London, 1852).

Stevenson, Catherine Barnes, *Victorian Women Travel Writers in Africa* (Boston, 1982).

Stoddart, Anna M., *The Life of Isabella Bird (Mrs Bishop)*, 3rd edn (London, 1908).

Tait's Edinburgh Magazine, no. IX (November, 1842).

Thomas, Clara, *Love and Work Enough. The Life of Anna Jameson* (London, 1967).

Trollope, Frances, *Travel and Travellers: A Series of Sketches*, 2 vols (London, 1846).

van Thal, Herbert, *Victoria's Subjects Travelled* (London, 1951).

Vaughan, John, *The English Guide Book c.1780–1870* (Newton Abbot, 1974).

Wise, T. J. and J. A. Symington, eds, *The Brontës: their Lives, Friendships and Correspondence*, 4 vols (Oxford, 1980).
Yokoyama, Toshio, *Japan in the Victorian Mind: A Study of Sterotyped Images of a Nation 1850–80* (London, 1987).

Index

197